A WILLIAMSBURG GALAXY

Williamsburg in America Series
VI
*The sixth in a series of popular histories
of Williamsburg and Tidewater Virginia in
the eighteenth century.*

☆ ☆ ☆ ☆ ☆ ☆ ☆ ☆ ☆ ☆

A
WILLIAMSBURG
GALAXY

Burke Davis

COLONIAL WILLIAMSBURG
Williamsburg, Virginia

DISTRIBUTED BY
HOLT, RINEHART AND WINSTON, INC.
New York

☆ ☆ ☆ ☆ ☆ ☆ ☆ ☆ ☆ ☆

Library of Congress Catalogue Card No. 68–12135

PRINTED IN THE UNITED STATES OF AMERICA

Distributed simultaneously in Canada by
Holt, Rinehart and Winston of Canada, Limited

To Charles R. Sanders, Jr.

CONTENTS

ILLUSTRATIONS

PROLOGUE

IN his old age Thomas Jefferson looked back with fond memories to the colonial capital of his boyhood, where he had come of age as a student, lawyer, politician, and man of the world. "Williamsburg," he said, "was the finest school of manners and morals in America."

It was much more. Its eighty-one years as Virginia's capital spanned five British reigns and the terms of almost a dozen resident governors, two of them elected to head the new commonwealth. In these formative years the miniature metropolis of a vast dominion was the center of educational, religious, political, military, economic, and social life for most Virginians. The merchants and craftsmen of Williamsburg competed with those of towns which grew larger, in their more favorable locations; its financiers, public office holders, and professional men influenced the lives of families scattered from the Atlantic shore to the Mississippi.

The town's first householders faced the restrictions of a city plan drawn before the end of the seventeenth century, in a time when Indian tribesmen were familiar visitors in the capital. Its first legislators, proud and stubborn heirs of men who had pioneered in representative government at Jamestown, did not hesitate to challenge their governors and to assume new powers of their own. In these early clashes, as more than one governor saw, were omens of defiance and republicanism, a long-range forecast of revolution.

Because it was a government town from the start, Williamsburg was the logical forum for Virginians to express themselves in—and they responded incessantly, keeping legislative halls, courtrooms, college buildings, newspapers, jail, taverns, and streets (and sometimes the church) abuzz when they thronged in for public occasions. The capital was thus by no means a typical Virginia town, but in its daily life it inevitably reflected the society that was being built as the colonists won the land, settled and developed it, and left it to succeeding generations.

Such a center inevitably drew men of affairs and ambition. The executive training of the day began with plantation management, but experience in government administration in most of its forms was to be had only in Williamsburg. Professional men also came out of necessity. Patrick Henry, after six weeks of intensive study, came for his law license, just as did scores of men of more conventional training. George Washington had to apply to the College of William and Mary for his surveyor's license, and only in the capital could he obtain militia commissions, or be assigned the dangerous missions on the frontier which helped to make him famous. Even such men of influence as William Byrd I and his son, Council members and landlords on an imperial scale, had to lobby for favorable regulations concerning their enterprises—tobacco laws, land grants, regulations concerning the Indian trade into the interior, or approval for the settlement of immigrants in their new cities.

Though Williamsburg was a tiny city, with a population of one thousand to two thousand, it was the capital of a vast empire. Land-hungry Virginians, like Thomas Lee in his report to the Board of Trade in London, claimed that the western boundary of the colony was the Pacific Ocean. But even east of the Mississippi, there was a domain of almost 360,000 square miles, an area about three times as large as the British Isles. At the end of the Revolution, Virginia was still larger than all of New England.

It was also the most populous colony, and was long regarded as the chief link with the mother country in the new world. Hugh Jones, a shrewd commentator, noted in 1724:

> If New England be called a receptacle of dissenters, and an Amsterdam of religion, Pensylvania the nursery of Quakers, Maryland the retirement of Roman Catholicks, North Carolina the refuge of run-aways, and South Carolina the delight of buccaneers and pyrates, Virginia may be justly esteemed the happy retreat of true Britons and true churchmen for the most part; neither soaring too high nor drooping too low, consequently should merit the greater esteem and encouragement.

In 1763 the Virginia population was estimated at about 120,000; it was then growing at the rate of about 5,000 each year. The people were also moving rapidly westward, leaving behind the British-inspired life of country squires on Tidewater plantations to face pioneer conditions.

Unlike some colonies, Virginia developed stable political habits early in the eighteenth century; after Bacon's Rebellion in 1676 the domestic peace was not disturbed, except for Indian fighting on the western borders. There were no foreign invaders, and the ruling class, secure in its plantation holdings, heard nothing to disturb it until after 1750, when the first protests of coming revolution began to sound. The plantation society existed with little influence from the outside world—beyond the fluctuating price of tobacco. It was a society in which it was possible for a landlord like Lord Fairfax to control his five million acres in northern Virginia as an independent potentate. The pattern was repeated in miniature throughout eastern Virginia.

It was a rich land in which the fortunate lived well. Mrs. Robert Carter, of Nomini Hall, listed the supplies consumed on that plantation in one year, enough for a small town: "27000 Lb of Pork, & twenty Beeves. 550 Bushels of Wheat. besides corn—4 Hogsheads of Rum, & 150 Gallons of Brandy." Management of such enterprises gave wealthy Virginians matchless training in affairs of government and politics.

Travelers who came much later, like J. F. D. Smyth on the eve of the Revolution, found Tidewater Virginians a tightly organized aristocracy: "There is a greater distinction supported between the different classes of life here, than perhaps in any of the rest of the colonies; nor does the spirit of equality, and levelling principle, which pervades the greatest part of America, prevail to such an extent in Virginia." The French Marquis de Chastellux, who saw Virginia during the Revolution, wrote: "The government may become democratic . . . but the national character, the spirit of the government itself, will be always aristocratic." The marquis did not see what was happening on Virginia's rapidly expanding frontier.

The great changes in Virginia society, economy, and politics came with the movement westward, toward the highlands where tobacco was not king and where smaller, but still self-sufficient, farms were developed. A new breed of Virginian developed in the hills and along the great Shenandoah Valley. The colony's spirit became more democratic in the west, which attracted those who did not prosper in the plantation country, where good lands could no longer be found, and where great capital was necessary to attain success. Poorer Virginians, including indentured servants whose time had been served, streamed steadily to the west, seeking their fortunes. They joined the great tide of men who built the heart of the nation on land claimed by Virginia and which became the states of West Virginia, Kentucky, Ohio, Indiana, Illinois, Michigan, and Wisconsin.

It may have been the challenge of the unexplored expanse of the colony that lured Joshua Fry, the partner of Jefferson's father in a famous map-making enterprise, from the faculty of the College of William and Mary. However, other faculty members remained in Williamsburg, and the college continued to monopolize education in Virginia, drawing all who wished higher learning except for the minority able to enter colleges in the northern colonies or in England.

But Williamsburg's history during the eighteenth century was by no means a mere process of instructing colonial leaders. Life was often vivid and exciting, highlighted by scenes of historical interest and significance. There were occasional spectacles: Blackbeard's pirates were herded in to be hanged; General Edward Braddock passed on his way to a wilderness ambush; the Stamp Act provoked a mob scene before a coffeehouse; the swarming troops of the armies of the Revolution occupied the town; George Rogers Clark came begging for aid to conquer the Northwest; and finally the net was drawn about Cornwallis at nearby Yorktown, a memorable scene witnessed by many civilians, some of them no doubt from Williamsburg.

Virginia's leadership survived generations of severe testing before the revolutionary era, in which it was to make such remarkable contributions to American history. The challenge of building and organizing was endless: a college, a city, a palace, a capitol, new counties, a frontier defense, the Anglican church and new sects of dissenters, new land laws, tobacco laws, laws on inheritance, new means of taxation, a system of currency, America's first public mental hospital and its first theatre, a new postal system, new trade relations with other colonies. As government grew more complex, Virginians, though stoutly affirming themselves to be Englishmen, became continually more insistent that they were free Englishmen.

In succession the generations of Virginians learned to cope with governors strong or weak, irritable and grasping or benevolent and humane, creative and farsighted or plodding and bumbling. For the first half of the eighteenth century they saw the rights and privileges of the colonists defended chiefly by the Council, which was so powerful that it could often defy governors. After the French and Indian War the increasing power of the House of Burgesses introduced a new factor in Virginia political affairs, an almost imperceptible movement toward democratic processes.

The little city was a training ground where veteran county officeholders like Edmund Pendleton could complete their mastery of Virginia politics, at the bar, on the bench, and in the House of Burgesses. Here a very young Jefferson learned much from the veteran parliamentarian, his cousin Peyton Randolph, who became so influential as attorney general and speaker of the House that he was a logical choice for president of Virginia's conventions of the revolutionary era, and finally as first president of the Continental Congress.

Since the chief industry of the place was always politics, when the official machinery was in use, men from all parts of the colony crowded the public buildings, streets, and taverns. For in Virginia, Williamsburg was the one place to do official business. The seat of power was unchanged from 1699 to 1780, and centralization was virtually complete; the one court of appeal was in London, weeks away. In addition, men came to gamble, or to trade or speculate, or on matters of life and death. Much of their most vital private business could be transacted nowhere else; anything from a law suit or a land grant to crop controls over tobacco or militia commissions might be at stake.

Under these circumstances Virginians learned to govern themselves through a process generally unrecognized by Great Britain until it was too late. An early governor, Alexander Spotswood, who arrived in 1710, complained of the liberties assumed by Virginians "which, by a lost custom, without any lawful foundations, they have been used to." He warned that they would submit to no authority, "civil or ecclesiastical," except that established under their own laws. It was to be a plaint of governors down to the last one before the Revolution, Lord Dunmore.

The government of Virginia involved vast problems unknown to Europeans of that era, and of these, the conquest of a constantly receding frontier and the settlement of a beckoning continent were perhaps the greatest. The westward expansion never ceased, and its cost in money, lives, and human energy was immense. It brought death to isolated settlers and years of wracking toil to governors like Robert Dinwiddie; its increase was shared by the United States for generations afterward.

It is striking to note that Washington recorded fifty-five visits to the city in the generation before the Revolution, but it is more instructive to trace his progress through those years, as he learned his several trades—

surveyor, soldier, land speculator, and member of the House of Burgesses for sixteen years. He was not an orator or a pamphleteer, but when he spoke he was forceful, and he did not easily change his position. He came to write defiantly of British abuse of authority, and was among the first Virginia leaders to speak of war. Washington's association with Williamsburg covered an important part of his life. There is no doubt that Washington drew on the lessons of Williamsburg in his later public life, both as a soldier and a statesman.

To a greater or lesser degree, most of the eminent men of pre-revolutionary Virginia had the same sort of exposure in the small capital, and during the years that led to revolution, these gifted colleagues gathered here, each contributing his talents to a movement that would sweep the colonies and change the history of the world.

Informal portraits of twenty of these men are sketched in the following pages. Because the emphasis in each sketch is on the subject's association with Williamsburg, the chapters are arranged chronologically, in order of the appearance of the men in Williamsburg. (However, an exception to this arrangement is made in presenting the royal governors.)

The subjects themselves range from the world-famous, like Washington, Jefferson, Patrick Henry, and George Mason, who have become symbols of Virginia's prodigious production of great men in the revolutionary era, to less well-known, but hardly less important builders of Virginia and America, men like the irascible executive of church, school, state, and retail merchandising, the Reverend James Blair; or the urbane and charming Governor Francis Fauquier, at whose Palace table Jefferson heard "more good sense, more rational and philosophical conversations, than in all my life besides"; or Judge St. George Tucker, who left one of the most interesting diaries of a revolutionary campaign, installed Virginia's first bathtub, and experimented with rapid communication.

The lives of these men influenced, some of them profoundly, the course of American history. Though these twenty lives are only a sample of the rich and colorful story of Williamsburg in the eighteenth century, they were not chosen at random. Together they reveal in variety the resolution, self-reliance, and vigor so remarkable in leaders of their era. These lives have become part of a heritage more universal than the men could have dreamed of during their crowded years on the tiny stage of the colonial capital, Williamsburg.

FRANCIS NICHOLSON

THE British Empire had a new ruler, Queen Anne.

The opening of this era in English history was celebrated with colorful pageantry at the College of William and Mary, a ceremony by turns doleful and joyous. Virginians crowded against the two thousand militiamen who had formed a hollow square in the college yard. Musicians played from the three balconies of the Wren Building as Commissary James Blair preached a funeral oration for the dead king. Bugles blared from the upper balcony, joined by oboes and violins from below, and when the proclamation of King William's death was called out, they played "very movingly and mournfully."

Governor Francis Nicholson was clad in black during the somber morning scene, but in the afternoon he led his people in rejoicing for Queen Anne. The governor now wore a dazzling blue uniform trimmed with braid and when the crowd had cheered the new queen and cannon had been fired in her honor, Nicholson entertained "right royally," though "the ordinary persons" in the crowd got no more than a glass of rum or brandy.

The next day some Indian guests bested colonial musketeers with their bows and arrows, as well as with rifles. An Indian queen also entertained the governor's guests: "the queen danced so wonderfully, yea barbarously, that everyone was astonished and laughed. It has no similarity to dancing. They make such wonderful movements with body, eyes and mouth, as if they were with the evil one . . . it is impossible to describe this mad and ludicrous dance."

Note: There is no known portrait of Francis Nicholson.

The holiday was interrupted by an outburst from the governor, who was walking with one of his naval guests on the second floor of the college when the captain asked Nicholson for the money he had promised to help send the fleet back to England. There was a roar: "the Governour flew out into such a Passion against the Commissioners of the Navy calling them all the basest Names that the Tongue of Man could express, & with such a Noise, that the People down in the lower Roomes caime running up Stairs."

One of the captains, who was one-legged, jumped from his bed on the floor above and stumped down the steps without his wooden leg, fearing that the building was on fire, only to be astonished by the "Folly & Passion of the Governour, saying *Bedlam* was the fittest Place for such a Man."

The ceremony opened a new phase of conflict between the governor and the commissary. Nicholson took offense when Blair praised the "mildness and gentleness" of the late king's reign, thinking it was an indirect criticism of his own administration. And there were complaints that the governor had entertained too elaborately, spending £500, calling reluctant militiamen from great distances, and causing public drunkenness in the capital.

These tumultuous scenes, though characteristic of this mercurial governor, were strange footnotes to the administration of one of the most creative and influential of Virginia's colonial executives. It was Francis Nicholson who founded Williamsburg and directed its city plan, one of America's first. He was largely responsible for the location of the Capitol on the site of the old Middle Plantation, so that it might be near Bruton Parish Church and the college. He was a founder of the College of William and Mary and of St. John's College in Maryland, and the author of the city plan of Annapolis, as well.

In a long career in America he was to act as governor of five colonies and as supervisor or military consultant to others. As one biographer wrote, he was "almost the only Englishman of his time who might be called a professional colonial governor." Despite the fury of his temper, Nicholson's enthusiasm for education and religion, his productive energy, and his broad vision made him one of the most effective colonial officials of his day.

He served two terms as Virginia's governor, and in the second of them had the misfortune to incur the wrath of a powerful man who was equally as resolute, and as high-tempered, Commissary James Blair, head of the Anglican church in Virginia, rector of Bruton Parish, president of the College, and member of the Council. Between them Nicholson and Blair were to write lively passages in Virginia history.

Francis Nicholson, for all his prominence in the planning and early building of Williamsburg and Annapolis, remains an obscure figure. His parentage is uncertain, his contemporaries left no known record of his physical appearance, and the accounts of his personality bear the obvious marks of prejudice. There is little doubt that his displays of temper were spectacular at times; an Indian who observed Nicholson in a tantrum said that he had been "born drunk."

No one questioned the governor's bravery. When a French pirate ship, *La Paix,* entered Hampton Roads in April, 1700, with a crew of 140 men, Nicholson went aboard an English man-of-war, the *Shoreham,* with other volunteers, determined to see the buccaneer taken. At 4 A.M. the next day the *Shoreham* crept near the pirate ship, kept to her windward during the day, and shot her to pieces in a gun duel at close range. The battered *La Paix* ran aground and surrendered. Nicholson had stood on the quarter deck of the *Shoreham* through hours of fighting, though one volunteer was killed at his side.

Nicholson was born on the Bolton estate near Richmond in Yorkshire, England, in 1655. There is a tradition that he may have been a son of the Duke of Bolton, but he was probably the son or grandson of a Francis Nicholson who had aided a former owner of the estate in a legal matter. In any event the Duke of Bolton launched young Nicholson's career by making him a page to his wife. Francis entered the British Army when he was twenty-four and spent several years in Tangier, where he was a courier and aide to the governor. He came to America in 1686 as captain of an infantry company under Sir Edmund Andros, governor of New England, and two years later became lieutenant governor of that dominion. He was living in New York when word came of the end of the long reign of the Stuarts in England and the coming of William and Mary, in the "glorious revolution" of 1688. Nicholson was so outraged that he refused to proclaim the new monarchs and was forced to return to England.

In spite of his defiance of the Crown, Nicholson was sent to Virginia as lieutenant governor in 1690, and in his brief first administration of two years made firm friends in the colony. He rented a small cottage, where he kept bachelor quarters, and often invited prominent citizens to dine. He established a system of athletic contests, which the early Virginian historian Robert Beverley rather scornfully styled "Olympick Games." In every county men shot, wrestled, raced, and dueled with broadswords for cash prizes, but the only eligibles were "the better sort of Virginians onely who are batchelors."

Nicholson governed Virginia with vigor and wisdom. He visited the frontiers, which then lay along the fall line of the rivers, from Maryland to Carolina, inspecting Indian towns and trying to reassure uneasy settlers. He found the militia poorly equipped and requested arms for these troops. He inspected defenses on the coast and proposed building forts along Virginia rivers as protection against pirates. He not only visited other colonies, but sent an agent to inspect and report on those as far north as Massachusetts. He also established a postal system.

Nicholson's relations with councilors and burgesses were warm, and in his first session laws were passed encouraging trade, taxing imported liquors, opening trade with the Indians, and establishing a college and free lower school.

When Blair and other clergymen proposed that the long-planned college be built, the governor opened the subscription drive with a generous pledge of £150. The Assembly sent Blair to England, where he spent almost two years before he got a charter and support for the college, and a lifetime position as its president. Nicholson was a trustee, but by the time the cornerstone of the first building was laid, the governor had left Virginia, having been assigned to the colony of Maryland.

Nicholson continued his creative work in his new post. In 1696 he directed the move of the capital from St. Mary's City to Annapolis, whose plan was probably drawn by Nicholson himself. Nicholson's successor in Virginia was his old commander in New England, Sir Edmund Andros. The newcomer soon ran afoul of Commissary Blair, who was overcome with nostalgia for Nicholson. The Blair-Nicholson controversies were soon to bring turmoil to Virginia, but now Blair wrote to London in praise of the departed governor, saying that he had always befriended the church, even going so far as to pay the living costs of new ministers until they were settled in their parishes, and had left a surplus in the treasury.

The colony was now treated to a ludicrous conflict. Nicholson returned from Annapolis to attend meetings of the college trustees, and each time he was greeted with insults by Andros. As Blair described it,

"At first Sir Edmund tried to make him weary by dryness, and frowns, and asking uncivil questions." Andros would ask: "Why did you leave your government?" or "How do you plan to amuse the people of Virginia?" When these tactics failed, Andros induced Colonel Daniel Parke, "a complete sparkish gentleman" with a reputation as an expert swordsman, to challenge Nicholson to duels. At one meeting of the trustees in Jamestown, Parke slashed the unarmed Nicholson with a horsewhip, and before others could part them, Nicholson had struck Andros with his fist. The affair ended with blustering about a threatened duel across the colonial line, in Carolina. Andros once went so far as to put Nicholson under arrest on a flimsy pretext, but ordered him released within an hour or so.

Blair soon brought this to an end; he went to England, complained to the Bishop of London that Andros was an enemy of religion and education, and urged his recall. Andros lost his post almost immediately, and Nicholson was sent back to Virginia to replace him.

Nicholson's return was due largely to the influence of Blair, who supported him in London, but it was a different Nicholson who returned to become full governor of Virginia. Nicholson's friends in England had been concerned over his intemperate behavior in Maryland, and when Blair returned from London he carried to Nicholson letters from the Archbishop of Canterbury and others, urging him to control his temper.

Blair described the ensuing scene, as the governor read these letters:

"What the Devil do they mean to recommend moderation to me?" Nicholson asked.

"Your friends are all of the opinion that it's the best advice you could have," Blair said, explaining the reaction of the men in England to stories of Nicholson's uncontrollable temper, and adding that his enemy, Andros, would make capital of them.

"God, I know better how to Govern Virginia and Maryland than all the Bishops in England. If I hadn't 'hampered' the people in Maryland and kept them under, I should never have been able to govern them."

"Sir, I don't pretend to understand Maryland but if I know anything of Virginia they are as good natured tractable people as any is in the world and you may do what you will with them by the way of civility but you will never be able to manage them . . . by hampering and keeping them under."

The warnings went unheeded, Blair said; within six weeks, when the commissary told him that he was in danger of losing control of the Assembly, Nicholson said that he could govern without an Assembly. In reporting this to London, Blair wrote: "in a great passion he commanded me never to speak to him more in any matters relating to ye Government but to let him alone and to meddle with my own business." Blair thought that the governor was "so furious, imperious and menacing" when he lost his temper that he was like a "mad man" in looks, walk, and gestures; he called leading men of the colony "the vile names of rogues, rascals, villains & cowards" and threatened to cut their throats. Blair said that he had been slow to conclude that Nicholson's case was hopeless, "recollecting his charitys, his constancy in publick prayers, his vigour & diligence in stirring about & driving on the business of his Government."

It was not a one-sided squabble. Twenty-four Virginia clergymen publicly protested Blair's behavior, charging that he had been "troublesome under every Government" and that he could no more give up "venting his Gall" against Nicholson than he could give up breathing. One visitor wrote home to an English bishop to report that Blair was resented in the colony and that prominent Virginians, including members of the Council, had asked: "Don't you think there may be in England amongst the English, a clergyman fit to be Commissary and Counsellor and President of our College?"

Three lawyers who commented on the noisy quarrel published their opinions in London: "As Governour *Nicholson's* Aim has been always known to be for the publick Good, and it being impossible for *Blair* and his Relations to carry their private Ends in *Virginia* under such a Governour, they used all Endeavours to ruine his Reputation in *England*."

Blair continued the campaign against Nicholson throughout his second administration, accusing him of a variety of outrages, among them crowding the colony's offices into the college building and not only holding meetings of the House of Burgesses there but "public treats," which disturbed the students; of hurrying the building to completion by hiring unskilled workmen and using unseasoned lumber; of spending money pledged for scholarships on the building. Endlessly, Blair complained, Nicholson insulted the commissary: he armed the schoolboys with pistols and had them lock Blair out of their hall, and once tried to break into his quarters at night.

Miraculously, in the midst of such petty and malicious squabbles, the building of Williamsburg began. Since the burning of the statehouse at

Jamestown by the rebel Nathaniel Bacon, some Virginians had thought of moving the capital to Middle Plantation, since it was known to be "healthy, and agreeable to the constitutions of the inhabitants . . . having the naturall advantage of a Serene and temperate aire dry and champaign land" with sweet springs and two convenient creeks nearby. When the statehouse burned again in 1698, the need for a new building became urgent.

There was precedent for putting the capital at Middle Plantation where the Assembly had met fifteen years earlier, in the same house where Bacon and his followers had gathered at the opening of the rebellion. Middle Plantation had also been a natural site for the location of the college, which Nicholson and Blair had worked so hard to establish during their first, and peaceful, years together. Under Nicholson's direction and supervision Theodorick Bland drew a plan of the small city, with an area of 283 acres, including two ports on College Creek and Queens Creek. The main street, some seven-eighths of a mile long and ninety-nine feet wide, ran from the college on the west to a site on the east which Nicholson reserved for a capitol—he seems to have first used the term himself. The main street was named for Queen Anne's son the young Duke of Gloucester, and the parallel streets (Francis and Nicholson) for the governor; cross streets honored kingdoms of the empire, Scotland, England, and Ireland, and famous people, King and Queen, Prince George, Henry, and Nassau Streets. Careful restrictions prescribed the size of houses, their distance from the street, lot sizes, a time limit on building residences, and mandatory fencing.

The governor also had a major part in designing and planning the Capitol, a twin structure of striking originality that was about twice the size of the old statehouse at Jamestown. The act providing for its erection was exceptionally detailed, and records of its construction so complete that the building could be faithfully duplicated on its old foundations in the twentieth century. In the spring of 1704, when the General Assembly sat there for the first time, Nicholson's fate had been sealed by Blair, who had campaigned against him in England so effectively that the governor was soon recalled. When he had gone Blair added the final humiliation by removing from the Capitol ornamentation designed by Nicholson, including the governor's coat of arms; these were painted over and supplanted by the arms of Queen Anne.

The Public Gaol was also built in Nicholson's regime, another of the notable group of structures completed in the first years of the city, buildings to which it owed its existence as a capital. London had frequently prodded Nicholson to build a governor's house, but though he in turn urged the burgesses to act, they pled poverty, the colony being in "very low and needy Circumstances," and the efforts to build "a convenient house" endured into other administrations. Nicholson could do little more than acquire sixty-three acres for a site.

Virginia's gossips found the forty-three-year-old Nicholson's romance with teen-aged Lucy Burwell the most fascinating phase of the Blair-Nicholson controversies. Lucy, the daughter of the influential planter, Major Lewis Burwell of King's Creek, was apparently the only love of Nicholson's life, and he was extremely jealous. One day he called in the commissary and charged that his brother, Archibald Blair, had been courting Lucy. Blair denied it. The governor, "thundering . . . out as loud as he could roar" and "with hands & eyes lifted up to heaven," shouted: "Sir, your brother is a villain & you have betrayed me. Mr. Blair take notice, I vow to the Eternal God, that I will be revenged on you & all your family."

The governor often threatened that if Lucy married someone else, he would cut the throats of the bridegroom, the minister, and the justice who gave the license. Blair maintained that this unhappy love affair turned Nicholson against him and was the cause of their difficulties. The incident was soon common talk in London, where it became such an issue that Nicholson afterward wrote to the Board of Trade that the romance had ended and that Blair and his friends had "no reason now to endeavour my ruine," since a rival, Captain Edmund Berkeley, "hath got the gentlewoman." The governor wanted to hear no more of the matter: "they may both be at quiet, if they please." There was damage to the governor's purse, as well as to his heart: "I think, while I courted Major Burwell's daughter, I did not put him to 5 pounds charge, but one way or another it hath cost me as many hundreds."

Even the Bishop of London tired of hearing echoes of the distant courtship in Virginia, and wrote to Blair when he discovered t̶ at Nicholson had recovered "from his Love-Fit" that he longed for peace in Virginia: "still you keep up your Feud against him . . . let me beg of you to lay aside all Prejudice and Passion, and as a Wise, as well as a Good Churchman, seek all Means of Reconciliation and good understanding. They say here, that you concern yourself in the politick Affairs at Council: I desire you to be tender in that point. . . ."

But it was not in Blair's nature to be "tender," and the storms continued to buffet the colony.

In 1703 five of the Council joined Blair in a petition to the queen, accusing Nicholson of a variety of sins in addition to wickedness and maladministration: he had falsified records, browbeat judges, juries, and lawyers; set up a private spy system; and was highly unpopular in Virginia. The queen passed the matter to the Board of Trade, which asked Nicholson for a reply to the charges, and the governor staged a remarkable scene in the House of Burgesses, declaring his innocence.

The governor denied tampering with records, said that the people supported him and that he would resign willingly if one five-hundredths of them were against him. Rather than be the kind of governor depicted by the Blair faction, Nicholson said, he would prefer to be jailed and live on bread and water. The burgesses debated the question until dusk, refusing admission to three of the Council who came to be heard, and passed a resolution twenty-seven to eighteen, saying that Nicholson had "a great respect for the welfare and prosperity of this country" and that "the better part" of the population supported him. The next day the House passed six other resolutions in the governor's behalf and sent them to Queen Anne.

Most of the Virginia clergy also backed Nicholson and joined ministers of Pennsylvania and New Jersey in sending resolutions to England supporting him. It was in vain. Blair won his case in London, and was able to have Edward Nott appointed in Nicholson's place.

After his downfall in Virginia, Nicholson's career prospered. He was made a Fellow of the Royal Society and was sent back to America as a soldier. He failed in an attempt to conquer Canada in 1709, for lack of troops, but the next year captured Port Royal and brought Nova Scotia under British control. Queen Anne appointed him lieutenant general of forces in North America, and then general, also commanding in Nova Scotia and Newfoundland. He served as governor of Nova Scotia for two years, but when George I became king he was recalled, and spent about six years in England, as consultant on colonial problems.

Nicholson's last post as governor was in South Carolina, which he ruled from 1720 to 1725. Trouble followed him there, and, after a dispute with Charleston merchants over the issue of paper money, he was recalled. He died in England in 1738, his role in developing Virginia largely forgotten and his American monument, the capital city of Williamsburg, little known to his countrymen.

Commissary James Blair, by J. Hargreaves. In the collection of The College
of William and Mary in Virginia and reproduced with its permission.

COMMISSARY JAMES BLAIR

IT is astonishing to hear what contrary Characters are given of the Country of *Virginia,* even by those who have often seen it, and know it very well; some of them representing it as the best, others as the worst Country in the World. Perhaps they are both in the Right. . . . as it came out of the Hand of God, it is certainly one of the best Countries in the World. But on the other Hand, if we enquire for well built Towns, for convenient Ports and Markets . . . for well improv'd Trades and Manufactures, for well educated Children, for an industrious and thriving People, or for an happy Government in Church and State . . . it is certainly, for all these Things, one of the poorest, miserablest, and worst Countries in all *America,* that is inhabited by Christians.

In these words, almost a century after the founding of the colony, the Reverend James Blair, one of the dominant figures of its early eighteenth-century life, began his loving, but critical, description of *The Present State of Virginia.* He had as co-authors Edward Chilton, the former attorney general, and Henry Hartwell, a member of the Council of Virginia, but the views were largely those of the resolute, capable, contentious, and sometimes overbearing man who for more than fifty years was to influence powerfully the course of Virginia. In his long career Blair disposed of three governors who resisted him and engaged in endless controversies and petty quarrels, but he was a builder: founder and highly successful promoter of the College of William and Mary; a major influence in moving the capital to Williamsburg; champion of the Anglican church; one of the colony's leading businessmen; and the master Virginia politician of his day.

From his arrival at the age of thirty, a young Scottish clergyman who had already fled a religious controversy, Blair was an imaginative, resourceful architect of Virginia's future. He began as rector of the country parish of Varina in 1685, and within two years had allied himself with one of the leading plantation families of the colony by marrying Sarah Harrison, daughter of Colonel Benjamin Harrison of Surry County. It was said that the bride (who had been promised to three others by her father) was somewhat reluctant, and made the ceremony a nightmare for the minister, one Mr. Smith: "When she was to say *Obey,* she said, *No Obey;* upon which he refused to proceed, *&c.* The second Time she said, *No Obey;* and he then refused again to proceed. The third time she said, *No Obey;* yet the said Mr. *Smith* went on with the rest of the Ceremony." That, at least, was the version of Blair's nuptials in an anonymous pamphlet circulated during one of his stormy struggles for power. It is one of the few glimpses of his unhappy wife left to posterity. (Governor Nicholson charged that Blair married "a woman already contracted for," and then forced her to work in his store, without shoes and stockings.)

Four years after his coming, Blair was promoted to commissary, or representative of the Bishop of London, the first post of its kind in the colony; he was now effectively in charge of the church in Virginia. He made brisk reforms of the poorly organized institution, called regular meetings of its leaders, fought for higher salaries and free houses and land for ministers, and imported men for the vacant parishes. Since many of the new ministers were from Scotland, Blair's critics were soon active: "The Clergy," one aroused rector said, "is composed for the most part of Scotchmen, people indeed so basely educated, and so little acquainted with the excellency of their charge and duty, that their lives and conversation are fitter to make heathens than Christians." As for Blair, he had "cast an odium upon himself by his great worldly concerns." But though even his bishop was to chide him for political activity, Blair did not swerve from his purpose. He had only begun.

In 1691, Blair led the church to ask for a college in Virginia. The Assembly approved and sent Blair to London to obtain a royal charter and support for the college. He spent almost two years unraveling red tape, outwaiting busy monarchs and reluctant officials—and raising money. When he was delayed, Blair ingeniously raised money by private subscription. At the death of the wealthy scientist Robert Boyle, he secured a grant from his estate for an Indian school at the college. When he learned of the plight of three Virginia pirates who were in England seeking a pardon and restoration of some of their plunder, he persuaded the buccaneers to contribute £300 toward the college endowment, in return for a pardon.

Queen Mary liked the idea of the college "extraordinarily" and helped to persuade King William, who told Blair: "Sir, I am glad that that colony is upon so good a design & I will promote it to the best of my power."

As Benjamin Franklin later told the story, there was opposition even then. The attorney general objected when he was told to draw the college charter and provide for an endowment of about £2,000 from Virginia revenues. England was at war, the money was needed for other purposes, and he saw no reason for a college for the tobacco plantations in Virginia. Blair argued that it would educate young men for the ministry, and begged him to consider "that the people of Virginia had souls to be saved as well as the people of England." The official replied, "Souls! Damn your souls! Make tobacco!"

Blair won every point, including confirmation by the General Assembly of his appointment as president "during his natural life." Not only would the college have its £2,000, it would control the office of surveyor general in the colony, with all fees, acquire twenty thousand acres of Tidewater lands, have a representative in the House of Burgesses, and receive a coat of arms by the College of Heralds, the only one granted to a college in America.

Blair took his spoils to Virginia in 1693, and the Assembly ordered that the college be "built as neare the church now standing in Middle Plantation old fields as convenience will permitt." Two years later the foundation of the Wren Building was laid and the College of William and Mary rose not far from Bruton Parish Church, which had long stood near the middle of the old log palisade built across the peninsula to guard Middle Plantation from the Indians. The city of Williamsburg had begun to take form.

By then Sir Edmund Andros, an old soldier, had replaced Nicholson as governor; he almost immediately clashed with Blair, who had become a member of the Council. When Blair became ill and was unable to preach, Andros appointed a minister to take his place as rector at Jamestown, and Blair reacted with such violence that Andros suspended him from the Council. The king restored him some months later, and the Blair-Andros feud was on in earnest. Blair complained that the governor had suspended him upon a "frivolous Occasion," because he had charged Andros with obstructing plans for the college. He openly accused Andros of being an enemy of the college and church, and said that the Governor "notoriously dispised and undervalued" the commissary, as representative of the Bishop of London.

Specifically, Blair said, Colonel Philip Ludwell, who had been asked to build the college, refused a contract because he saw "no possibility of carrying it on in this Governors time." Andros had also "seduced" some of the workmen imported from England to raise the building and had ordered the brickmaker to produce bricks for him rather than for the college. Andros retorted that he had done all he could for the college, but that Blair "could not be obliged by all Endeavors nor containe himself within bounds." It was Blair's "restless Comport," the governor said, that had brought upon him the wrath of the whole Council, resulting in his suspension.

Governor Nicholson, who had moved to Maryland, returned to Virginia on occasion to aid Blair in his troubles with Andros—and was once arrested by his successor. In short, Blair said, the church was in danger under Andros: "Never so many affronts were publickly thrown upon the Clergy as during this Government, all which pass unredressed . . . it is carefully buzzed into the people's ears that they must not encourage the coveteousness of the Clergy, nor be priest ridden. . . ."

Blair's formal protests led to a hearing at Lambeth, the home of the Archbishop of Canterbury in London, where William Byrd II pleaded the case of Andros and Blair spoke for himself. Andros was recalled and, at Blair's request, Francis Nicholson was returned to govern Virginia.

The former allies quarreled almost at once; heated controversy was to mark Blair's remaining career.

James Blair was born in Scotland in 1665 or 1666, the son of Robert Blair, also a minister. The details of his early life are little known. He studied at Marischal College in Aberdeen and became a master of arts at the University of Edinburgh in 1673. He was ordained in 1679 and served in the diocese of Edinburgh for two years, until he became embroiled in the controversy over the Test Act of 1681; Blair refused to take an oath to acknowledge the supremacy of the king in all matters, both in church and in state, and went to London, where he worked in the office of the Master of the Rolls and became acquainted with Henry Compton, Bishop of London. It was Compton who interested young Blair in America and sent him to Virginia.

In the six years before he returned to London to plead for his college, Blair had not only married Sarah Harrison and become commissary in Virginia; he had begun to acquire land, including a 100-acre tract in Rich Neck plantation from Colonel Philip Ludwell. He may also have entered the mercantile business with Ludwell about this time. By 1705 he was in partnership with his brother, Dr. Archibald Blair, and Ludwell, operating a store on Duke of Gloucester Street in Williamsburg. It was, as Governor Spotswood said later, "one of the most considerable trading stores in this country." Dr. Archibald Blair managed the store with great success; by the time of his death in 1733, the stock was valued at £7,000.

Thus, as the administration of Andros ended and Francis Nicholson returned to Virginia, Blair, now in his early forties, was already a powerful figure, prospering as a merchant, building the college and reforming the church by his own plans, largely without interference, and gathering political strength with ties of friendship, kinship, and business interests in the Council. (Benjamin Harrison and two sons-in-law, Blair and Philip Ludwell, were on the Council, and two Harrisons were burgesses.) He had given up his remote parish at Varina and become rector at Jamestown, where he remained until 1710, when he moved to Bruton Parish, a post he held for life. His growing stature in Virginia was increased by the recently proved powers of his influence in London. He was a man to be reckoned with, as Andros had learned.

His clashes with the returning Nicholson were immediate, violent, and enduring. Power may have corrupted Blair or perhaps as the historian Robert Beverley said, Nicholson returned as a troubled man, without "that smoothness on his brow" that he had worn in his first Virginia regime. Whatever the cause, the governor and the commissary joined their private warfare as if they would tear the colony apart. It began when Blair returned from his triumph over Andros in England and gave Nicholson letters from the Archbishop of Canterbury and other officials, warning him that he should control his temper and cease the irrational behavior of which his people in Maryland had complained. The governor then ordered Blair out of his sight, the commissary said, and swore that he would rule Virginia without an Assembly. Soon afterward the mercurial Nicholson, in a strange pattern he was to follow during the six years of his second term, wrote the Bishop of London of his appreciation for being entrusted with his post, and for giving him "most wise and paternal advice" how to manage both it and himself.

Their quarrels did not prevent Blair and Nicholson from cooperating to develop the college and to move the capital of the colony from Jamestown to Middle Plantation. At the May Day ceremony of 1699 at the college, undoubtedly staged with Blair's assistance, a speaker extolled the attractions of Middle Plantation: "the beginning of a town, a church, an ordinary, several stores, two mills, a smiths shop, a grammar school, and above all, the Colledge." He also made the plea that the college "will help to make the Town," adding one hundred people to the population. Furthermore, "the prime Youth of the Country being here, it will occasion a great resort hither of parents and other friends." Blair and the governor joined in the speechmaking, and the Assembly soon agreed to put the public buildings "somewhere at Middle Plantation, nigh H.M. College of William and Mary."

Blair had begun to concentrate his interests in the new city. For the first five years of the city's life he worked at close range with burgesses, Council, and General Court, all of which met in his college. He also used the hall of his building as a chapel. With a rare flash of humor he once told a pious visitor that the hall was the most useful place in the college: "Here we sometimes preach and pray, and sometimes we fiddle and dance, the one to edify, and the other to divert us."

Blair did not resist the accomplishments of Nicholson's new administration—the attempted reform of the land grant system, preparation of the first accurate rent roll, a postal system, defense against pirates, and banning of some industries in the colony.

It was usually over trifles that Blair and Nicholson clashed. Just before Christmas, 1702, boys of the college grammar school locked out their teachers in an effort to lengthen their holiday, as they had done in the past. In other years Blair had joined the celebrations of the boys when they had enforced their demands, but the Battle of 1702 was more serious. Blair had servants batter down the door, and boys fired at them with pistols loaded only with powder. Blair, suspecting that Nicholson had incited the students to riot, sent them to the governor to determine their holiday; the irritated Nicholson ordered them back to their books, and Blair complained to London that Nicholson had furnished the boys powder and shot in hopes that they would shoot their president. Denials by students, teachers, and Nicholson did not quiet the furor.

A major source of the quarrels between the stubborn leaders was Nicholson's vain courtship of young Lucy Burwell, which led the unstable governor to curse Blair and accuse him of conspiring against his romance. Nicholson's consequent neglect of his business and his growing irritability led to Blair's final effort to drive the governor from his post.

The commissary wrote the Archbishop of Canterbury that Nicholson governed Virginians as if they were "a company of galley slaves by continual roaring and thundering, cursing and swearing, base, abusive, billingsgate language . . . utterly incredible to those who have not been the spectators of it." Despite many resolutions of support for the governor, Blair had his way and Nicholson was recalled. But there was an epilogue. One group of ministers asked, "shall a Scotch Commissary have the making and unmaking of our governours? He was not . . . pleased with the last, nor is with this, and will be as little with the next."

The clergymen were prophets. After the one-year term of Governor Nott, who died of fever, and two interim governors, Alexander Spotswood arrived in 1710, a vigorous soldier and executive also destined to feel Blair's wrath. Spotswood attempted reform of the land laws, wrote a new tobacco law, and tried in vain to break the hold of influential families upon the Virginia government. By 1714 both burgesses and Council had turned against him, when he opposed efforts to keep Virginia revenues at home rather than sending them to England. When he insisted upon reform of the muddled accounts kept in the offices of Philip Ludwell, the deputy auditor, and William Byrd II, the receiver general, Blair and his relatives turned upon the governor. Archibald Blair and Ludwell's son-in-law, John Grymes, led the opposition in the House of Burgesses.

Mr. Blair clashed openly with Spotswood over the issue of appointing ministers. It was an angry, complicated dispute between vestries, clergymen, and the governor that ended in a test case in court: Was Blair legally rector of Bruton Parish Church, since he had not been approved by the governor? The case posed a dilemma for Blair, who sought to remove clergymen from control by their vestries, but who also wanted a more sympathetic governor to make church appointments. The governor thought the commissary and his allies were to blame, and reminded the

Board of Trade that "a Blair and a Ludwell" had originated the complaints that disposed of both Andros and Nicholson. In the end, Spotswood, too, was recalled, and the case was dropped.

Meantime, the governor charged that Blair used his entrenched position for private advantage. Spotswood wrote the Board of Trade in 1718 to complain that the Assembly had offered Blair's brother, Dr. Archibald Blair, £4,000 of public money to lend at 4 per cent, and that he was to have half of the profit from the enterprise or to use the money without charge if he did not choose to lend it. "I have resolved to reject that bill," Spotswood said, adding that the Council was controlled by "a great majority of the relations of those Gentlemen."

The protest was in vain, and powerful Virginians continued to control Virginia, through changing administrations. Blair also continued to build his college, having overcome the opposition of two governors, the indifference of leading Virginia families, and a disastrous fire in 1705. By 1729 he had its property transferred from the trustees to the faculty, removing the danger that opponents might try, as they had in the past, to seize college lands through private grants. He moved into the new President's House in 1732, and by the time of his death there were three fine buildings on the campus. His persistence in face of all obstacles made the college a growing force in the colony. A later historian praised Blair as "the creator of the healthiest, and the most extensive intellectual influence that was felt in the southern group of colonies before the Revolution."

By the time of the arrival of the next strong governor, Sir William Gooch, in 1727, Blair was aging. He was past seventy, and his personal empire was thriving. He was alone now; his wife had been dead for fourteen years. The commissary was hospitable to the new governor, taking him into the college during his first days. He was, as Gooch wrote to England, "very courteous and kind," but the governor doubted the old man's sincerity and a few months later had discovered that Blair covertly pushed every possible handicap into Gooch's path, since he was not his chief adviser. But Gooch, determined to keep peace outwardly, treated Blair with tact and patience throughout his regime. He left the old man in his accustomed exercise of power, though, as William Byrd II noted, "the country is a little dissatisfied, with being Governd by an Ecclesiastick," especially since Blair was becoming so old and infirm. The aging commissary hung on grimly. He not only acted as governor during the absence of Gooch on a campaign against the Spanish at Cartagena, in South America, but continued to hold every office of which he was capable.

"His understanding is still good," Byrd conceded, but the old man was stone deaf and could no longer sit as chief justice of the General Court. So Byrd took his place, while Blair sat nearby, occasionally nodding off to sleep.

As he neared the end of his life, Blair became less of a problem to Gooch, who had long before concluded that the commissary was "a vile old Fellow" who must be handled gingerly. Gooch once wrote of him: "He is an unaccountable spark, hated abominable by all men but his countrymen [Scots], and when he can't advise nor direct, he's inclined to perplex, but as yet we are good Friends and I intend to keep so if I can, which will be difficult."

Blair had long been in poor health, though he gave no sign of his affliction. On April 18, 1743, he died in the President's House of the college, where he had lived since its completion ten years before. Gooch wrote to the Bishop of London:

> The deceased has had a Rupture about forty Years, a secret to every Body save one acquaintance, and that turning to a mortification killed him; but such was his Constitution that he struggled with the Conqueror ten days after the Doctor had declared he could not live ten Hours. He has left his Books and £500 to the College and to his nephew and his Children near £10,000, besides other small legacies.

Blair left property to John Blair's four children, dividing among them the £3,000 value of his stock in the Blair-Prentis-Cary Store.

He was buried in the churchyard at Jamestown, beside the grave of his wife, who had lain there for so long. It was very near the spot where he had first come ashore sixty-eight years before, when the island village had been the capital of that long-gone Virginia which, as much as any man of his time, he had been responsible for shaping and changing. In a tempestuous passage of years he had been the unquestioned storm center of the colony's life.

Alexander Spotswood, attributed to Charles Bridges. Colonial Williamsburg.

ALEXANDER SPOTSWOOD

COLONEL William Byrd II, who was given to uneasy nights, wrote in his diary for June 21, 1710: "I dreamed I saw a flaming star in the air at which I was frightened . . . I fear this portends some judgment to this country or at least to myself."

It may have been an omen, for that afternoon Byrd learned that a new governor had landed in Hampton Roads, a man with whom the master of Westover was to contend for power for more than ten years. The governor was Alexander Spotswood, at thirty-four a veteran soldier who was to become one of the most able and versatile leaders in Virginia history—architect, town planner, frontier fighter and friend of the Indians, promoter of western expansion, iron miner, foe of greedy landowners, and, at last, a landed Virginian himself.

Byrd, who saw Spotswood the next day, found him courteous and "a very good man," a judgment he would amend.

The new governor came from a Scottish family prominent in religion and politics. One of his ancestors had been a close associate of John Knox, and Alexander's grandfather, a well-known lawyer, had been executed for his loyalty to Charles I. Alexander was born at Tangier, the son of a British Army surgeon, and had been in the army himself since the age of seventeen. He kept as a souvenir the cannon ball that had struck him at the Battle of Blenheim.

Spotswood had pleasant features, a long face with high forehead and a small mouth, which turned up at the corners, at least when he sat for his portrait. Virginia's officials who watched as he took his oath in Williamsburg thought him affable indeed. He wrote home his private thoughts of his new situation: "The life I am likely to lead here is a perfect retir'd Country life; for here is not in the whole Colony a place that may be compar'd to a Brittish village." He complained that everyone lived "disperst up & down at their Plantations," where they had all necessities.

Spotswood began hopefully, however: "I have a fair prospect of a good Agreement with the People, & believe I shall live very contentedly here; for if I have not the Diversions of London (which I do not in the least hancker after) neither have I the perplexitys of that Town." Like most chief executives of colonial Virginia, Spotswood was officially lieutenant governor; the nonresident governor, in London, was Lord Orkney. Spotswood's salary was £2,800, of which he paid Orkney £1,200, but, as Spotswood said, there were also "perquisites."

He was to discover that, in season, life in the small capital could furnish "perplexitys" enough, during the vigorous and creative era he inaugurated. Spotswood straightened the streets and drew new boundaries, but much remained to be done. As he urged the Assembly: "I wish you Joyned in Opinion with me, that to Give Some Assistance to this Infant Town, towards building a Market House, bettering the Landings, and Securing the few Publick Springs, would not only Redound to the Credit of the Country when Strangers Resort hither, but would likewise be for the benefit of all those whose business calls them to the Assemblys And Generall Courts."

Spotswood had the city incorporated, with a mayor and aldermen and a representative in the House of Burgesses. He provided for Wednesdays and Saturdays as market days and for semiannual fairs. It was Spotswood who added to the town plan the axial green before the Governor's Palace; he designed the cruciform Bruton Parish Church, the Powder Magazine, a major addition to the public jail, completed the Palace and its gardens— all told an exceptional group of public buildings.

Bruton Parish Church was in such disrepair that a new building was necessary. When the Assembly asked him to plan a church, Spotswood modestly thanked the House for the confidence they had in him and said that though he had never done such work, he would do his best. The result was today's Bruton Parish Church, a model of fine proportion. "It would be wrong," the architectural historian Marcus Whiffen wrote, "to say that in designing Bruton Parish Church Spotswood called Geometry to his aid; he practically handed the job over to her."

Spotswood designed and built the Powder Magazine in order to store a large shipment of arms and ammunition sent to the colony by Queen Anne. Its thick brick walls were built as an octagon, the walls and the roof of equal heights, the proportions once more dictated by geometry. Spotswood's addition to the jail, designed for debtors, was much larger than the original of 1704, and featured a detail new to Virginia, a flat roof; he later enlarged the jail a second time, to the form of its present restoration.

The completion of the Governor's Palace set off one of his first struggles with the powerful Virginia Council, dominated by men like Commissary James Blair and Colonel Byrd. Spotswood arrived when the Palace was structurally complete, but little more than a shell, and at once he directed the burgesses to furnish money to finish the building and grounds: "This is a Matter in which Your Own Honour is now so far Engaged, That I no ways Doubt of your Ready complyance."

The Assembly appropriated money to finish the Palace, build a wall, outbuildings, and garden, and install furniture—but this was merely the beginning of a controversy that dragged on for years. One contractor was hired and discharged, and burgesses began to complain of the money being spent on Spotswood's home (it was first called the Palace officially in 1714). When a committee called on Spotswood to talk over the building, he scolded the burgesses: "Some of those I See here present being Accustomed to Speak very irreverently of the Kings Governours should I enter into Conversation with them may perhaps forget what House they are in and be apt to speak to me in their usual rude Termes."

Soon afterwards, William Byrd, in England to complain about Spotswood, reported that in completing the Palace the governor "lavishes away the Countrys money." Spotswood replied that he had spent little more than £200 a year, that he had agreed to pay for the fish pond and terraced gardens himself, and that the burgesses had deliberately complicated laws and accounts to make him appear extravagant. Largely because of such squabbles the Palace was fourteen years in the building.

Spotswood contributed many distinguishing features to the Palace, including the designs of the garden, walls, and gates and even such details as the muskets displayed in the hall.

But the governor seldom found leisure to pursue architecture. Within three months of his arrival the Tuscarora Indians wiped out a new settlement at New Bern, North Carolina, killed two hundred whites and terrorized the Carolinas. Spotswood sent militia to the border to prevent

Virginia Indians from joining the war. In a colorful ceremony he met with Indian leaders at Nottoway Town on the Carolina border, persuaded some Tuscaroras to make peace and to send two boys from each village to the College of William and Mary as hostages. The Indians agreed, but intermittent Indian troubles continued.

Spotswood pacified Virginia Indians by settling the colony's nine tribes on reservations (they numbered only 700, with about 250 warriors). Each group was to have "a large tract of land to hunt in, a body of English to live among them, and to instruct their children . . . to bring them to a more civilized and plentiful manner of living, and to establish a constant intercourse of trade." The Indians came to the Council Chamber of the Capitol to sign Spotswood's treaty in February, 1714. That summer, in a further effort to protect the colony, Spotswood spent six weeks in the backwoods of the frontier, planning the new Indian reservations and setting up Virginia's border defenses. He also acquired for himself lands on the upper Rappahannock that were rich in iron ore.

The governor was not only humane toward the Indians, but was aware of the aggressions of Virginians on the frontier, many of them former indentured servants who played on the Indians' love of rum, "first making them drunk and then cheating them of their skins, and even of beating them in the bargain." Only when they had suffered "notorious" injury did the Virginia Indians strike, the governor reported to London.

Spotswood tried to expand trade by forming the Virginia Indian Company, supervised and financed by the colony, but open to private stockholders. It conflicted with the interests of William Byrd II and a few others who had monopolized the rich trade, and the king was persuaded to abolish this corporation. Meanwhile Spotswood built a flourishing outpost at Christanna on the Meherrin River, with a fort, ammunition magazine, warehouse, and an Indian school with an English teacher, Charles Griffin, who was so admired by the Indians that the Saponi tribe tried to make him its king. Later, Griffin directed the Indian school at the College of William and Mary, which Spotswood improved. He supported the school by levying a tribute of furs upon Indians and ended the cruel practice of filling it with captive boys taken in tribal warfare.

The Indian School flourished under Spotswood's direction, with about twenty Indian students "all decently cloathed after the English manner" and apparently happy in Williamsburg. The queen of the Pamunkeys, when she saw how well the boys were cared for, voluntarily sent more, including her son.

At almost every step the governor was resisted by the burgesses—who, as he complained, were elected by the "mob of the country"—because they had promised to levy no taxes, irrespective of the public need. Spotswood found the burgesses and the Council stubborn in other respects; since 1706 they had been developing their own form of government, setting their own precedents in law and practice, and they defended them fiercely against Spotswood's efforts to apply his powers.

He reported that the Council did not feel itself bound by the oath of office it took, and that it acted contrary to the king's interests "when these interfere with the ease of the people or the libertys which, by a long custom, without any lawful foundation, they have been used to." These men, the governor saw, would submit to "no jurisdiction, civil or ecclesiastical, but what is established by laws of their own making."

Further, the governor saw that they looked down on him as an interloper, if not an inferior: "These are the men that look upon all persons not born in the Country as foreigners, and think that no other qualification is necessary for an imployment . . . but that of being born in the Country." It was one of the earliest plaints of a newcomer that Virginians looked upon themselves as a race apart.

Spotswood tried to break the power of the numerous Burwell family on the Council by naming three new men to vacancies, but the coalition of wealthy planters remained, and its chief spokesman was James Blair, who as president of the Council, commissary of the Bishop of London, and president of the College of William and Mary, was a formidable foe.

It was almost certainly Blair who, working behind the scenes in London, undermined the influence of Spotswood at court. Spotswood saw the combination of Virginia planters and London merchants as an economic monopoly. Each move, he thought, was dictated from London: the conspiracy should be broken up. "I think it is doing little honor to the Government to have its Council appointed in the Virginia Coffee House." He resented the selection of Virginia officials by merchants who had "no other rule to judge of a man's merit than by the number of his tobacco hogsheads."

For all his efforts to bring freer trade to Virginia, Spotswood remained a Tory, with little faith in the ability of the common people to govern themselves. He wrote home of his regret "that I must always have to do with the representatives of the vulgar people, and mostly with such members as are of their stamp and understanding, for so long as half an acre of land . . . qualifys a man to be an elector, the mean sort of people will ever carry the elections."

Spotswood's efforts at reform soon turned to Virginia's land laws, which had been subverted over the years so that, rather than the 50-acre grants originally intended for each immigrant, the average grant for more than half a century had been almost seven hundred acres, and they often ran to as much as twenty thousand acres. William Byrd, who "tried to soften" Spotswood on the land-grant issue, found him "a gentlemen that means well, yet he is too obstinate." The governor persisted, trying to prevent most of the colony's lands from coming under control of specula-tors who did not settle families on their tracts. He insisted that laws requiring the settling of tenants or building of houses and grazing of cattle on land grants be enforced; he also sought to force landowners to pay quitrents, then generally being evaded. The governor's reform of the colony's bookkeeping was so obnoxious to Colonel Byrd that he resigned the lucrative office of collector of revenue.

Despite the Assembly's revision of the laws and discovery of "con-cealed lands" bringing in no quitrents to the colony, Spotswood was defeated. The Council simply interpreted the new law as it wished in its role as the General Court, and previous patents remained undisturbed. Spotswood finally gave up his attempt and in the last years of his administration joined the land rush himself, acquiring more than eighty-five thousand acres in a county named for him, Spotsylvania.

The energetic governor also attacked the knotty problems of the tobacco trade, then blighted by overproduction, fluctuating prices, and inferior leaf. He found that planters were sinking more deeply in debt to London factors each season and, unable to fill their needs with income from tobacco, were raising other crops to sustain their families. The law proposed by Spotswood ended a chaotic system but his victory was temporary.

Tobacco, which was used as legal tender, was taken to official ware-houses set up by Spotswood, inspected, and graded, and inferior leaf destroyed by colony agents. The remaining hogsheads of good tobacco were accepted as cash. In this way collecting, loading, and shipping

Virginia tobacco was simplified, and tobacco itself became a more stable form of currency. It was a spur to the Virginia economy, and Spotswood was proud of this law as "the most extraordinary one that ever passed a Virginia Assembly."

The governor was chagrined to learn that the king had disallowed both the tobacco act and the Indian act of 1714. The rejection of the latter dissolved the Virginia Indian Company and ended Spotswood's efforts to do justice to the tribes. This reversal, too, was probably due to the work of Commissary Blair at court, in retaliation for the governor's interference in the political, economic, and religious life of the colony. Blair found that he had unexpected allies in the powerful London merchants, who were determined to keep the profits they had been squeezing from an unregulated tobacco trade, and resented Spotswood's reforms.

Spotswood met other defeats, even in such a project as trying to build a lighthouse at Cape Henry, but he steadily improved Virginia's defenses and relations with Indians and brought a degree of order into financial management of the colony. He proposed making tar and pitch in Virginia, to supply the British Navy in case of war.

He is best remembered for his contribution to the early movement of settlers to the west.

In June, 1716, Spotswood told the Council that Virginia rangers had found a pass "over the great mountains to the westward of this Colony," and that he would send a larger expedition in August to explore the new country. The governor decided to lead it himself.

The governor went to Germanna, a rude settlement of German-Swiss he had established on the Rapidan, riding with a young Huguenot visitor, John Fontaine, who left a record of the journey in a diary. The expedition assembled at Germanna, "several gentlemen of the Colony," twelve rangers and two of their officers, and four Meherrin Indians—in all, Spotswood said, sixty-three men, seventy-four horses, and some hunting dogs. Among the "gentlemen" of the company to become known as "The Knights of the Golden Horseshoe" were James Taylor, the great-grandfather of President Zachary Taylor; George Mason, father of the author of Virginia's Declaration of Rights; Robert Brooke, grandfather of a Virginia governor; the historian Robert Beverley; and Colonel William Robertson, clerk, and Austin Smith, member of the Council.

Their route to the mountains cannot be traced in detail today. According to one version, it followed the south bank of the Rapidan River almost to its source, then the south branch of the river to a point near the present town of Stanardsville, then up Swift Run Valley along the tortuous course of Swift Run, up the hills to Swift Run Gap. Here the adventurers found the source of the stream "where it runs no bigger than a man's arm from under a big stone." The party then probably followed Elk Run down the mountain, to the site of the present town of Elkton on the Shenandoah River, a stream they called Euphrates. Another version of the route says the Knights went northwest from the Robertson River, through Milam's Gap, and, passing Fork and Double Top Mountains, came near present Big Meadows Lodge, and descended Tanner's Ridge to the Shenandoah. They were more than two hundred miles from Williamsburg.

When they reached the summit of the Blue Ridge on September 5, Spotswood and his company "drank King George's health, and the Royal Family's, at the very top of the . . . mountains." These toasts, it developed, were mere preliminaries. Each day was filled with adventures. They began at seven each morning with a bugle call and lived off the country, cooking bear steaks (which Fontaine thought as good as veal), venison, and wild turkey. They slept in tents on beds of boughs, after one experimental night on the ground. A guard was posted before Spotswood's tent. Rattlesnakes were plentiful, and a bear once attacked a rider and would have killed him except for the brave dogs, who drove off the beast despite a savage mauling.

Fontaine wrote: "we had a rugged way; we passed over a great many small runs of water, some of which were very deep, and others very miry. Several of our company were . . . down with their horses, others under their horses, and some thrown off." They passed thickets so "tightly laced together" that their clothing was torn to ribbons. Two men who came down with measles were left behind with hunters to care for them; hornets stung several horses and one man, whose face "swelled prodigiously." Fontaine had malaria, but cured his aches and raging fever with quinine bark.

When they reached the river Shenandoah, where they saw sign of elk and buffalo, Fontaine cut his name into a tree and Spotswood buried a bottle with a paper enclosed "on which he writ that he took possession of this place in the name and for King George the First of England." They named the highest peak in sight Mount George and the second highest

Mount Alexander (today these are called High Knob and Saddleback—
or perhaps Fork Mountain and Double Top). Fontaine wrote of the
ceremony at this place:

> We had a good dinner . . . got the men together, and loaded all their
> arms, and we drank the King's health in Champagne, and fired a volley
> —the Princess's health in Burgundy, and fired a volley, and all the rest
> of the Royal Family in claret, and fired a volley. We drank the Gover-
> nor's health and fired another volley. We had several sorts of liquors,
> viz., Virginia red wine and white wine, Irish usquebaugh, brandy, shrub,
> two sorts of rum, champagne, canary, cherry punch, water, cider, etc.

Spotswood sent some rangers farther west, across the Shenandoah
Valley, but the main party turned back toward Williamsburg and reached
the capital on September 17. The expedition had lasted not quite a
month, and Fontaine reckoned that they had traveled 438 miles.

Since the horses, which never wore shoes in sandy Tidewater, had
been shod at Germanna to protect them against the stony soil of the west,
horseshoes became a symbol of the expedition. The governor presented
each of his companions with a golden horseshoe inscribed on one side:
"*Sic juvat transcendere montes*" and on the other side "The transmontane
order."

Spotswood later said: "The Chief Aim of my Expedition . . . was to
satisfye my Self whether it was practicable to come at the Lakes . . .
From the pass where I was It is but three Days' March to a great Nation
of Indians living on a River w'ch discharges itself in the Lake Erie."

He also had a more serious purpose, as he wrote the Board of Trade.
He feared that "The French are endeavoring to settle a communication
between Canada and their lake settlements on the Mississippi by the way
of the Lakes." To forestall this, Spotswood urged that Virginians be
granted land only on one side of the James, so that westward settlement
would be hurriedly pushed across the path of the French.

Six years after his famous journey to the Shenandoah, Spotswood ended
a conference with chiefs of the Five Nations at Albany, New York, by
giving their spokesman a Golden Horseshoe, and had his interpreter
explain that it would help him to pass over the mountains "and that when
any of their people should come to Virginia with a pass they should bring
it with them."

In 1722 the Council, led by Commissary Blair, had Spotswood removed from office. The energetic governor had found, as one historian said, that "it was futile to contend against a Virginia nationalism."

Virginians loved him still. In October the deposed Spotswood rode into Williamsburg, apparently from his Germanna plantation. He was met several miles out of town by his successor, Governor Drysdale, and many leaders of the colony. "From thence he was conducted by a Train of Nine Coaches, and about 200 Gentlemen on Horseback, to the Governor's House, where he was saluted with a discharge of the Cannon." There were bonfires at night, illuminations, and "other publick marks of that Respect and Value which this Country has for a Gentleman, who has so long, and with so much Prudence and Justice, presided in the Administration of this Government."

Two years later the forty-nine-year-old Spotswood went wife-hunting to England, but he did not desert his vast holdings in Spotsylvania County or his iron mines, which were now productive. He married young Anne Butler Brayne of St. Margarets, Westminster, "a young lady said to be wonderfull pritty but no money," and brought her to Virginia in 1728. Spotswood had now been appointed postmaster general of the colonies, and attacked new problems with his customary vigor; he soon had postal routes along the Atlantic Coast, with their southern terminus in Williamsburg.

William Byrd, by then on friendly terms with the former governor, visited the "enchanted castle" of the Spotswoods at Germanna in 1732, and was charmed by Mrs. Spotswood's aplomb in the midst of wilderness life: she calmly observed a pair of tame deer romping through her house, even when they broke one of her pier glasses. Byrd also found that the ironworks were in trouble. Spotswood blamed himself for their mismanagement by one of his cousins, a mathematician, saying "he was rightly serv'd for committing his Affairs to the care of a Mathematician, whose thoughts were always among the Stars."

When war between England and Spain broke out in 1739, Spotswood raised an American regiment and was made major general, second in command of an expedition to sail against Cartagena. Busy with the embarkation, he died in Annapolis in 1740. The London *Daily Post* said he "was taken suddenly with a Fit of the Stone that carried him off in a few Hours. The Death of this Gentleman, on Account of his Conduct and personal Bravery, is very much lamented in that Country."

SIR WILLIAM GOOCH

THE Capitol was on fire.

Despite danger people ran in and out of the building, as the fire raged overhead, and saved virtually all of the records of the colony of Virginia, which had been stored there since 1704. Someone salvaged the portraits of the royal family.

The blaze leaped to the cupola. The two bells melted and fell with the ruined town clock. The roof and its timbers collapsed; the second floor and then the first were consumed. Only the massive charred brick walls were left standing. They were sound, except for a few small cracks in the curved ends of the building.

On that last Friday in January, 1747, the city itself was saved only by a change in the wind, for, though "fleaks of fire . . . flew about plentifully," they were borne away from the town, into woodlands about the Yorktown road.

Governor William Gooch suspected arson, though he could not understand how any rational person could commit or even imagine "so flagitious a Crime." But, as he told the House of Burgesses, the smoke that had crept through the shingles had come from a room without a chimney, and the interior of the roof had been found ablaze, in sheets of fire that could not have resulted from accident. He attributed the loss to "the horrid Machinations of desperate Villains, instigated by infernal Madness," but he knew it must have been the work of an outsider: "such superlative Wickedness would never get Admittance into the Heart of a Virginian."

As for the future, Gooch told the burgesses that they should think of

Note: There is no known portrait of Sir William Gooch.

"restoring that Royal Fabric to its former Beauty and Magnificence."
Meanwhile the Assembly would meet at the College of William and
Mary, as it had done about half a century earlier.

Benjamin Waller, a member of the building committee, soon had his
workmen grubbing among the Capitol's ruins, salvaging the old iron, lead,
and bell metal; he was to pay the costs from their sale, and "pay the
Overplus into the Treasury."

Whatever the cause of the devastating fire, it very nearly ended the
forty-eight-year career of the city of Williamsburg as the capital of the
mammoth colony of Virginia—whose western border, as Gooch said,
included "the Island of California." The burgesses made an unexpected
response to Gooch's exhortations. They appealed to the governor's political ambitions with a grander plan than mere replacement of the Capitol:
"To lay the Foundations of a new City, to raise this Building in a Place
commodiously situated for Navigation, will compleat the Glory of your
administration, and transmit your Name with the highest Lustre to the
Latest Ages."

This was the work of burgesses from distant places, who were not sorry
to see the building burn. These men sought a more central location for
the capital and also envied the situation of ports like Norfolk, which
could be reached directly by ocean-going ships. Gooch was so far persuaded that he recommended to the Board of Trade that the capital be
moved. He was refused, despite strong sentiment in the Assembly for a
change. The House of Burgesses was rebellious on the point. It voted
down a bill to rebuild the Capitol on its old site and passed another for
establishing a new city on the Pamunkey River. This was rejected by the
Council and the House of Burgesses offered a compromise, a study
commission to inspect possible sites on the Pamunkey and the James.
When this was also defeated, Governor Gooch dismissed the Assembly,
saying that he hoped they would think over the problem seriously and
return to "cordially unite, either in repairing the old, or in building a new
Capitol."

When the legislators returned eighteen months later a committee of
the burgesses reported that Williamsburg was "very remote from the far
greatest Part of the Inhabitants of this Colony, and by Experience has
been found altogether unfit for Trade and Navigation"; and that a town
"be established on some convenient Place on York River." By now Gooch
had become "an Advocate for building upon the old Foundations," but he
needed all his influence to keep Williamsburg alive. A bill for rebuilding

the Capitol on its original site passed its second reading by two votes and squeaked by the third by the same margin. Gooch signed the bill as one of the last important official acts of his twenty-two-year regime in Virginia. He had barely saved the second capital.

Sir William Gooch had been lieutenant governor of Virginia since 1727, and his administration had been marked by peace and prosperity based on the thriving tobacco trade; it had been a time of the building of great manor houses on Tidewater rivers, a golden age of colonial development. The governor had won a reputation for amiability, and for unswerving friendship to Virginians, whose cause he had supported against grasping London merchants.

His regime began auspiciously, and with special ceremony, since his arrival coincided with celebrations of the crowning of a new king, George II. Gooch's commission was read in the General Courtroom in the Capitol and he took his oath in the Council Chamber. As a gesture of good will he pardoned a convicted pirate, an act said to be "very fit to begin his administration." He then joined the president of the Council for a ride down Duke of Gloucester Street in the state coach; cannon fired salutes at the Capitol, Market Square, and the College of William and Mary. An entertainment at the Palace in the evening was made merry by three great bowls of arrack punch, and guns were fired as healths were drunk, until midnight.

Councilor William Byrd, who was not easy to please, liked the new governor: "By a great Accident we have a very Worthy Man to represent Lord Orkney. It is Major Gooch, brother of an eminent Clergyman of that Name. He seems . . . to maintain the Character of a very just Man, and has a remarkable share of good Sense, good Nature, and good Breeding. How long he may hold his Integrity I cannot warrant because Power and Flattery corrupt many a Hopeful Ruler." Nine years later the House of Burgesses gave public testimony that Byrd's cynical suspicions had been unfounded: "You have not been intoxicated with the Power committed to You by His Majesty; but have used it, like a faithful Trustee, for the Public Good, and with proper Cautions . . . You never propose Matters, without supposing Your Opinion subject to the Examination of Others, nor strove to make other Mens Reason blindly and implicitly obedient to Yours."

An even more influential Virginia official was looking over Gooch with care: James Blair, president of the college, commissary of the Bishop of London, and a member of the Council. Blair wrote the Bishop about Gooch: "The Country is all in peace and quietness and seems to be mighty well satisfied with their new Governor. He is a sober serious and well tempered man, obliging and courteous to all, never swears, nor gives way to passion, which examples no doubt will do a great deal of good. . . . There is a perfect good understanding betwixt him and me."

But from the start Gooch was wary of the powerful man who had already ousted governors with whom he could not agree. However, Gooch was so adept at handling the powerful cleric that he did not incite him to open warfare, and by his patience and tact kept the colony at peace. He outlived Blair, who died in 1743.

Other problems of his early years in Virginia required more than tact. Like other lieutenant governors, he was forced to share income with the nonresident governor in England, and Gooch complained of the high cost of living in the Palace. He had spent the large sum of 300 guineas on the voyage to Virginia, bringing his wife, her sister, and his son, William Gooch, Jr. Official functions also cost the new governor dearly. The first year there were celebrations involving the royal family, including the observance of the birthdays of His Majesty and Prince Frederick. The friendly Assembly helped him out: the Council with £300 from the quitrent collections, and the burgesses with £500 from general revenues.

Gooch responded with vigorous and loyal support of Virginia interests, and provided the Virginians the kind of leadership they had expected of him. Gooch had been a soldier for most of his life. He was born at Yarmouth, England, and entered the army very early. He fought in Europe under Marlborough, and was present at the great English victory at Blenheim, which capped Marlborough's career. Gooch married Rebecca Staunton, of Hampton, Middlesex, whose family name was to be perpetuated in that of a Virginia city.

Virginia made important advances under Gooch. He ordered a survey of the Virginia–North Carolina border, thus ending an old irritant by removing a no-man's land that had become a haven for debtors and tax evaders of the two colonies. A few months after his arrival, Gooch reported to the Bishop of London that the College of William and Mary need wait little longer for long-neglected improvements: "We are going to build the Chappel as fast as we can." He was interested in all needs of the church, and once wrote to England suggesting that the king or queen be asked to provide an organ for Bruton Parish.

The chief development during Gooch's administration was the westward expansion of Virginia. He arrived only eleven years after Governor Spotswood and his Knights of the Golden Horseshoe had visited the Shenandoah Valley. The first Assembly that Gooch met with created Goochland County, which extended to the Blue Ridge. Within six years three other enormous counties were created, generally following the westward course of the great rivers from the Potomac to the Roanoke. The Greenbrier Company, which made the first substantial settlement west of the Alleghenies, was formed in 1745, and the Ohio Company, with its grant of half a million acres, was formed before Gooch left Virginia.

Gooch favored the new, liberal, land-grant laws passed by the Assembly and defended large grants as more effective in rapidly settling new territory. He pointed out that Spotsylvania County with its large grants, had developed more quickly than Brunswick, with its small ones. The large grants, the governor said, had "given encouragement to the meaner sort of people to seat themselves as it were under the shade and protection of the greater."

When Gooch left Virginia, the colony had forty-four counties, fourteen of them added under his regime. The results of this expansion were to shape the colony's history, influencing the French and Indian War and creating a new type of Virginian whose interests often clashed with those of the Tidewater aristocracy. Unlike his successor, Robert Dinwiddie, Gooch did not seem to sense the prospects of profit in the western lands; he invested in an iron mine, whereas Dinwiddie joined the Ohio Company.

The most difficult of Gooch's problems was the regulation of the tobacco trade, by which Virginia lived. Prices were subject to violent fluctuations, and, even when prosperous times followed periods of depression, overproduction of the leaf was ruinous to planters. London merchants preyed upon the growers, forcing them to assume risks of transport and all costs, even the failure of purchasers to pay for shipments. Taxes reached almost £20 per hogshead in 1733. All efforts to stabilize prices and correct inequities had failed when Gooch called the Assembly in 1728, chiefly for the purpose of revising the tobacco law. In the same year John Randolph, sent to London to plead Virginia causes, was able to persuade Parliament to repeal a law requiring tobacco to be shipped on the stalk, a practice which increased problems of growers, added to the shipping costs, and enabled unscrupulous merchants to sell inferior tobacco in England.

When the law of 1728 proved ineffective, Gooch successfully urged the Assembly of 1730 to pass a new act. It was so sound that it remained in effect throughout the colonial period with few changes. Gooch enforced his law firmly and defended it against the "Most turbulent" planters, some of whom burned tobacco warehouses so that they might continue to cheat the public with inferior tobacco. Gooch's act effectively removed "bad and trash tobacco" from the market, ended fraud in customs collections, and established inspection in public warehouses.

Not only did the tobacco crisis move Gooch to decisive action against rebellious planters, but it also inspired him to write a fable: "A Dialogue Between Thomas Sweet-Scented and William Oronoco, Planters . . . and Justice Love-Country, who can speak for himself." This homely fable stressed the simple economic facts involved in an orderly sale of tobacco through warehouses, with inspection and consequent higher prices. Resistance to the act soon faded, and, as Gooch told the Board of Trade in 1734, Virginia was blessed with "peace and plenty."

The governor could not win all his struggles against the London merchants, who lobbied against Virginians and inspired frequent royal vetoes of colonial acts. He supported a law to build a lighthouse at Cape Henry, to be financed by a tax of one penny per ton on shipping; it was repealed because of the opposition of English merchants, and no lighthouse was to be built on the important headland until the eve of the Revolution. Other acts which laid duties on slaves and liquor were also repealed. The repeal of all Virginia's laws on trade was prevented only by the protest of Gooch and the Council that the result would bring chaos to the Virginia economy.

Gooch also struggled with a crime wave, caused largely by the importation of English convicts as plantation laborers. There were several acts of violence, including the burning of Mount Pleasant, the home of Magistrate Thomas Lee in Westmoreland County. The Assembly met the threat by providing the death penalty for those found guilty of burning or plundering warehouses. Gooch thought this law necessary in a country "so much crowded with convicts."

In 1740, Gooch was ordered to raise troops for the War of Jenkins' Ear against the Spaniards, and at the suggestion of Attorney General Edward Barradall he drafted all the idle men in Virginia who were "able-bodied persons, fit to serve his Majesty, who follow no lawful calling or employment." The Assembly's act exempted indentured servants, as well as all of those eligible to vote in elections for burgesses. Gooch raised four hundred men for the war against the Spaniards. The commander, former Governor Alexander Spotswood, died suddenly on the eve of embarkation, and Gooch was called upon to command the unsuccessful expedition against Cartagena, a Spanish stronghold on the northern coast of South America. He was seriously wounded there when a 24-pound cannon ball passed between his ankles, injuring both legs. He also contracted fever, and a year later reported to the Bishop of London, "I am still weak in my knees, and very lame." When he returned to Virginia in July, 1741, after an absence of ten months, he found that he had been missed. His homecoming was observed with gun salutes, bonfires, and illuminations.

The next year the death of his son added to the decline of the governor's health. In spite of ill health he took an active part in planning defenses against the threatening French and sent two Virginians to Lancaster, Pennsylvania, in 1744, when Maryland, Pennsylvania, and Virginia signed an important and lasting treaty with the Six Nations; Virginia acquired Indian lands and gained allies in the coming wars. When King George's War began soon afterward, the king chose Gooch to command troops from all the colonies in a futile effort to conquer Canada, but the aging governor declined, saying that he was "fitter for a hospital than a camp." He reminded the king of his long service: "I am next October sixty six years of age and have served the Crown forty five of them."

A few months later, in November, 1746, Gooch was created a baronet, and three years later, as Sir William Gooch, he resigned his governorship and returned to England, where he died at Bath in 1751. His widow, Lady Gooch, left to the College of William and Mary a folio Bible in four volumes and two pieces of silver, which were later entrusted to Bruton Parish Church. His contribution to Virginia was acknowledged in August, 1736, when the speaker of the House of Burgesses declared that he was a wise and prudent ruler, vigilant and painstaking, for "those who have differ'd from you in opinion, far from being revil'd or despis'd for their Integrity, have been treated with that Regard and Civility, which are due to the Representatives of a People. This is the Source of many good Things that have been done, during Your Government, and the true Cause that has banish'd all Factions and Parties out of this Colony; and in this, Your Example may instruct those who shall come after you, in the best Methods of Governing the King's Subjects here. . . . You have shew'd how easy it is to give universal Satisfaction to the people under Your Government."

William Byrd II, by an unknown artist. Colonial Williamsburg.

WILLIAM BYRD II

I HAVE a large family of my own, and my doors are open to everybody, yet I have no bills to pay, and half-a crown will rest undisturbed in my pocket for many moons together. Like one of the patriarchs, I have my flocks and my herds, my bondmen and bondwomen, and every sort of trade amongst my own servants so that I live in a kind of independence of everyone but Providence. . . . we sit securely under our vines and our fig trees without any danger to our property. We have neither public robbers nor private . . . . Thus, my Lord, we are very happy in our Canaans if we could but forget the onions and fleshpots of Egypt.

Thus did William Byrd II, one of the most gifted and beguiling Americans of his time, in a letter to an acquaintance in England describe his life in Virginia in 1726.

He was handsome, haughty, amorous, earthy and ribald, shrewd, and highly responsible in business, politics, and most personal affairs. His father, a wealthy trader, left him some 23,000 acres, which he increased to more than 177,000 acres. He was at home as a London dandy, in drawing rooms with the wits and beauties of society or carousing in taverns or on the streets. He was equally at ease as master of vast plantations, marching with survey teams through the wilderness and sleeping on the ground "for fear of getting too tender."

He was a physical culturist and almost every morning of his life "danced his dance," his own form of exercise. He walked and skated a great deal. For a time, he plunged into the James River twice weekly, the year 'round, "without once being discouraged by frost or snow," to adjust his body to changes of temperature. He took the medicinal root ginseng in an effort to lengthen his life and sometimes ate bear meat to promote virility.

As a youth he sometimes hunted with bow and arrow; later he hunted for minerals and mockingbirds' nests. He grew hemp and grapes and experimented with many seeds and plants. He encouraged Mark Catesby, the artist and naturalist. Because he was surgeon and doctor to his family and servants, he hunted for cures for chills and fevers; once, when he had malaria, he kept a complete clinical record of symptoms and treatment.

Byrd often wrote in his shorthand diary of his dreams, omens of death and disaster like flaming swords in the sky and falling stars. Once he dreamed of the death of Benjamin Harrison (who died a few days later), and at another time he dreamed of the death of his wife. He was a prophet, forecasting the end of slavery in Virginia, the war with France, and movement toward colonial independence.

He opposed slavery, urged the British government to halt the trade, and spoke scathingly of "Saints of New England" who ran rum and Negroes into the South; no one, he thought, "could slip through a penal statute" like New Englanders. He deplored cruel treatment of slaves, and, among its other evils, he thought slavery made whites proud and disdainful of work.

He made abstracts of laws and court cases, wrote a natural history of Virginia, and is believed to be the author of a treatise on the plague, published anonymously in London. His diaries, covering most of the period from 1709 to 1741, have been compared with those of Pepys—and to the works of Rabelais. His love letters and a short satire, "The Female Creed," are examples of the uninhibited writing of the period. His secret writings, most of them undiscovered until the twentieth century, are a matchless mirror of the life of Virginia's early plantation society.

For all his confessed vices, Byrd was a devout and practicing churchman. Above all he was a consummate politician. A member of the Council for nearly forty years, he finally succeeded James Blair as president in 1743, after having often allied himself with Blair in the complex maneuvering for position between leaders in Williamsburg and London. He was in many ways a model for the Virginia gentlemen who were to follow him; yet he was unique and, though cultivated and urbane, a natural, free, and independent spirit.

William Byrd II was born March 28, 1674, at the present site of Richmond, by the falls of the James where his father's caravans of Indian traders left for the wild backcountry with their goods and brought their bales of precious furs. His mother was Mary Horsmanden, who, by family tradition, traced her lineage to Charlemagne.

Young Byrd was sent to England for his education when he was seven, and spent twenty-three years in school, studying law at the Middle Temple and learning business with a firm of London merchants. He led a zestful and licentious life in London, yet remained a Virginian at heart.

At the death of his father in 1704, Byrd returned from England to inherit the vast lands, slaves, servants, and family enterprises. He assumed the post of receiver-general or collector of revenues of the colony and a place on the Council.

In 1706 he married Lucy Parke, a high-spirited daughter of Colonel Daniel Parke. Byrd rashly assumed the debts of his father-in-law's estate in an effort to gain the Parke lands, and set off an intricate train of financial involvements which ran for years, once endangering ownership of Westover, his own home. Mrs. Byrd died in London of smallpox in 1716. Some years later, on a visit to England devoted to acquiring a rich wife, Byrd married Maria Taylor of Kensington. To his regret, she did not bring a dowry to Virginia when they returned in 1726.

Before 1730 he completed Westover, the elegant Georgian mansion on the bank of the James, perhaps on the site of an earlier house built there by his father. He lavished upon it his money, energies, good taste, and enduring patience, for he had begun twenty-one years earlier with his workmen making brick and raising walls and chimneys; stonemasons built the library chimney in 1714. The spacious house, especially its river façade, resembles somewhat the Governor's Palace in Williamsburg (completed about 1720), and may owe something in its design to that fine public building.

Characteristically, Byrd gave attention to details: the *rocaille* ceilings; seven marble mantelpieces imported from England or Italy; great entrance gates on the land side, unique in America, made in a London foundry; stone eagles to surmount the garden walls; magnificent paneling on the walls of the large downstairs rooms. Outbuildings got the same careful attention from Byrd, even the brick necessary houses, complete with fireplaces and lordly views over sloping lawns to the James.

He returned to the life of country gentleman on a grand scale, seized with a new hunger to accumulate land. In the 1730's he settled Richmond and Petersburg and brought Swiss immigrants to develop his lands on the Roanoke River. That venture ended in tragedy with the wreck of a shipload of newcomers in the Virginia surf; there were few survivors. The twenty thousand acres of new land on the Dan River, which he bought from the North Carolina commissioners of the boundary-line survey, he called "The Garden of Eden," incorporating a pun on the name of the Carolina governor, Robert Eden.

In his later years Byrd continued to make Williamsburg his second home. His visits were frequent, on social as well as state occasions when the Council or Court demanded his presence. He owned three lots in Williamsburg, where the Charlton House and King's Arms Tavern now stand, but whether he lived there during his visits or rented the property is uncertain.

As one of Virginia's richest men, with much to be affected by laws on trade, lands, and taxes, Byrd was often involved in struggles for power within the Council and without. As a fledgling lawyer, he had tried to best Commissary Blair by pleading a colonial cause for friends in London. However, Byrd met the most stubborn of his adversaries in the veteran Scottish soldier, Colonel Alexander Spotswood, sent to govern Virginia in 1710.

Since the time of Sir William Berkeley, Virginia had known weak governors. In practice, the Council ran Virginia as it pleased, and had undermined at least two previous governors. Spotswood recognized the oligarchy at once. Half of the twelve councilors, who controlled every phase of the colony's life, were related by blood or marriage. Their enormous land holdings gave them almost imperial power, one result of which was to drive poorer men and newcomers to other colonies (chiefly North Carolina) to seek their fortunes. Colonel Ludwell once raised a patent from two thousand to twenty thousand acres merely by adding a zero to the records, and his influence in the Council prevented action against him.

Spotswood moved to curb the Council's power by reforming laws involving settlement on large tracts, the collection of quitrents, the sale and trading of tobacco, and the addition of new courts. Much of this struck at Byrd, who collected the Crown's quitrents through local sheriffs. Byrd fought back, with varying success, and at last sold his post as receiver-general, saying of Spotswood that an officeholder "must either be a slave to his humor, must fawn upon him, jump over a stick whenever he was bid. . . . In short, such a man must be either the governor's dog or his ass; neither of which stations suit in the least with my Constitution."

Byrd went to London to fight the involved causes before the Board of Trade and other bodies, acting as agent of the House of Burgesses. One effect of these struggles was to unite Virginia's leaders even more completely and to make them realize that they were Virginians first, with their own interests at heart. This interest was power, and not democratic principles, and the confirmed aristocrat, Byrd, was able to lead these tough-minded Virginia empire-builders from London. Spotswood, with some feeling, called him "that implacable man Byrd." In later years, however, long after their troubles had ended, Byrd and Spotswood became fast friends.

As he neared the end of his life, pressed for money despite his great land holdings, Byrd vainly sought more public offices, as governor or collector of customs for the southern colonies. He was unsuccessful.

Although Byrd never returned to England after 1726, the place must have been much in his thought. He corresponded faithfully with old friends in England, among them distinguished men of the era: Sir Hans Sloane, a physician and botanist who was head of the Royal Society to which Byrd belonged; Charles Boyle, the Earl of Orrery; Lord Egmont; and Sir Robert Walpole, the prime minister. At Westover he created a "picture gallery," with portraits of relatives and several well-known English friends.

The study habits begun when he was a child in England were lifelong. He continued reading in Latin, Greek, Italian, and other languages almost daily, studying the familiar classics of his youth and reading new books. It was not unusual for him to read two hundred verses of Homer before breakfast. His library at Westover, more than thirty-six hundred volumes, was the finest in the southern colonies at the time.

William Byrd II found time to write two histories (one of them secret) of the running of the North Carolina-Virginia boundary, an account of a journey to his new land on the Dan River, and another of a trip to mines in western Virginia. These vivid and humorous books contain passages reminiscent of Swift, and are more like the work of Franklin than are those of any other American writer.

His gibes at North Carolinians became famous:

> Surely there is no place in the world where the inhabitants live with less labor than in North Carolina . . . . The men, for their parts, just like the Indians, impose all the work upon the poor women. They make their wives rise out of their beds early in the morning, at the same time

that they lie and snore . . . . To speak the truth, 'tis a thorough aversion to labor that makes people file off to North Carolina, where plenty and a warm sun confirm them in their disposition to laziness for their whole lives.

He was also irreverent of Virginia history. He described the Jamestown settlers, whose council "were always engaged in Factions and Quarrels, while the rest detested Work more than Famine." Of their landing at Jamestown, he wrote, "like true Englishmen, they built a church that cost no more than Fifty Pounds, and a Tavern that cost Five hundred."

But Byrd did not write out of malice; during his lifetime his prose was read only by friends to whom he entrusted the manuscripts. He had perhaps moved too long in the urbane literary circles of London to publish without laboriously polishing his works. When asked why he did not publish them, he wrote, "Twould be a pity to spoil so much paper."

He took great care to keep the contents of his diaries secret. They were written in his version of a popular shorthand of the day, and, in addition, the identity of many of his friends was elaborately disguised. He wrote proverbs, recipes, rules for good health, verse (some of it bordering on obscenity); he repeated gossip about others and anecdotes of all kinds. But his diaries were not mere jottings. They reveal a perceptive observer of life all about him, with a keen interest in almost everything; above all, he revealed himself.

Byrd spared few details of his love life, personal habits, opinions of others, and the ways of men and women in London, Williamsburg, and the plantations. All was put down without self-consciousness. He once wrote of his amorous nature: "Never did the sun shine upon a swain who had more combustible matter in his constitution. . . . Love broke out upon him before his beard, and he could distinguish between the sexes long before he could the difference between good and evil."

Throughout his life Byrd was boyishly unpredictable, as his private confessions illustrate: He tossed a mischievous "lampoon" into the House of Burgesses, poking fun at some members, and was not discovered until George Mason (grandfather of the author of the Declaration of Rights) revealed the secret; he admitted cheating at cards to beat his wife; skinned a muskrat; he tried to buy for himself the office of governor of Virginia; he flirted outrageously with wives of friends; he opened the grave of his father years after death, found him too "diminished" for recognition, and then calmly recorded that he had fish for supper.

He remained the lively *bon vivant* of his youth, even in his sixties, though he never again recorded such an affair as that of November 2, 1711, when, after a busy day, he and some companions rounded up a couple of fiddlers, found some willing ladies, and staged an impromptu ball in the Capitol. He continued to play games, indoor and outdoor. He tried to control his gambling, by swearing off when he had lost as much as £50 at billiards, piquet, whist, or cricket.

He said daily prayers, or confessed when he forgot them. He often entertained and talked with clergymen of the colony, especially the well-educated Reverend Peter Fontaine, of Huguenot descent, who became minister of Westover Church, which Byrd had bought. The diaries comment often on sermons, usually favorably.

Byrd died August 26, 1744, of causes unknown today, and was buried in the garden of Westover of which he was so fond. The last known entry in his diary was for August 31, 1741:

I rose about 5, read Hebrew and Greek. I prayed and had tea. I danced. The weather was cold and clear, the wind north . . . wrote letters till dinner when Doctor Monger came and I ate a fish. After dinner we talked of several matters and then the Doctor went away without a fee because he came not in time. I walked in the evening and at night talked with my people and prayed.

JOSHUA FRY

ONE late July morning in 1732, having had only two buildings after more than a generation, the College of William and Mary in Virginia began a third, the President's House.

The contractor's bricklayers were standing by impatiently, but the president, the Reverend James Blair, made the moment of beginning into a ceremonial occasion. There was no cornerstone, but five academic amateur masons each laid one of the first bricks in the foundation. Blair laid the first brick, followed by the Reverend William Dawson, who was destined to succeed him in office. The third was laid by Joshua Fry, the thirty-two-year-old professor of natural philosophy and mathematics, who was to play a unique role in opening Virginia to the west, in setting the continental course of British America, and in depicting the colony to the world. (The "masons" who followed Fry were William Stith, a governor of the college who later wrote a history of Virginia, and one Fox, presumably a member of the faculty.)

Fry had come to Virginia from England about ten years earlier; he had been born about 1700, at Crewkerne, in Somerset, and for at least a year had studied at Wadham College, Oxford. Still in his early twenties, he quickly gained prominence in Essex County, Virginia, where university-trained men were rare. He became a vestryman and a magistrate and married a wealthy widow, Mary Micou Hill, the daughter of a Huguenot physician.

Commissary Blair had called him to Williamsburg as master of the new grammar school, which was to prepare future students for the

Note: There is no known portrait of Joshua Fry.

college. He spent only two years with these young men, for in 1731, a few months before his work on the foundation of the President's House, Fry was promoted to the college faculty.

As a trained mathematician and surveyor, Fry saw the need for an accurate survey of Virginia, which had remained largely uncharted since its beginnings in 1607, except for the coastal map of Captain John Smith and running a portion of the boundary with North Carolina. In 1737, Fry and two others asked the House of Burgesses to commission a survey of the colony and to publish a map, so complete that it would show "the bays, navigable rivers, with the soundings, counties, parishes, towns and gentlemen's seats, with whatever is useful or remarkable." After a debate that dragged on for five years the Assembly finally rejected the idea.

By then Fry had given up and "gone to the back settlements in order to raise a fortune for his family," and was living not far southeast of the present site of Charlottesville, when Albemarle County was carved out of Goochland County. He immediately became the county's leading citizen, and a member of the House of Burgesses, so that he often returned to Williamsburg. He was also the first presiding justice of the county, commander of the militia, and surveyor. As surveyor, one of his assistants was Peter Jefferson, then in his late thirties and the father of two-year-old Thomas. The two became close friends, and worked together until Fry's death.

Peter Jefferson was a legendary strong man, one of many Virginia frontiersmen of whom it was said that he could stand between two hogsheads of tobacco as they lay on their sides and raise each upright. He and Fry, at any rate, led the Albemarle militia and worked together on surveys of tracts, of which Fry made scores in the next few years, helping to bring order to land records of the region.

The imperial domain of the Fairfax family, including the whole of Virginia's Northern Neck, had never been surveyed along its western border, between the Potomac and the headwaters of the Rappahannock (though William Byrd II and a party had made a beginning east of the Blue Ridge thirteen years before.) In 1746, by orders of the Council, this western line was surveyed. Colonel Joshua Fry was one of the commissioners and as a surveyor he chose Peter Jefferson; they set off in a party of forty men in September on a harrowing adventure of exploration.

For seven weeks men and horses struggled up and down the Alleghenies, threading swamps choked with laurel and rhododendron, clambering up slopes where horses had to be led and pushed, sometimes running out of food, and often losing sight of the sun and sky. Several horses were killed, and those that survived came back as walking skeletons. Two of the worst spots on the journey were named Purgatory and the Styx, the latter "enough to strike terror into any human creature." At last, when they had returned to their starting place by the Fairfax Stone of the boundary, Jefferson carved his initials, "PJ," on a ridge atop the Alleghenies.

Three years later, in 1749, Fry and Jefferson were hired by Virginia to complete the boundary line between North Carolina and Virginia, which Colonel Byrd's party had run 237 miles inland from the sea to Peters Creek, in Patrick County, Virginia. (Fry and Jefferson never found the end of this old line, but reckoned their position by the stars.) This expedition was as full of hardship as the Fairfax survey, according to Jefferson family tradition; the men were attacked by wild animals by day and forced to sleep in trees at night. Several of the party fainted from hunger and fell out of the march, but Jefferson (and apparently Fry) ate raw meat and "did not once flag," until the line had been run westward as far as Steep Rock Creek. They had gone ninety miles over rough mountain country, including a crossing of New River.

When their report and a map of the area reached Williamsburg, the Council paid Fry and Jefferson £300 each, beyond expenses, a handsome fee, whatever their privations.

Thus this surveying team was well known in Williamsburg when a vigorous new president of the Board of Trade and Plantations, the Earl of Halifax, took office in London. Halifax pressed immediately for a clearer picture of the bounds of Virginia. He ordered an accurate map, for vital reasons: he wanted information on "English settlements . . . and of the Encroachments, if any have been made by the Subjects of any foreign Prince on this Colony."

Acting Governor Lewis Burwell knew just the men for the job, and commissioned Fry and Jefferson as "the most able persons." Fry, as the senior partner, had apparently found Peter an apt pupil during their years of work together. As Peter's son Thomas wrote, "My father's education had been quite neglected, but . . . eager after information, he read much and improved himself."

The remarkable map produced by Fry and Jefferson on the basis of their years of surveying in the west was presented to the Council late in

1751, and the cartographers were paid £150 each. Burwell was so delighted, especially with Fry, that he sent it off to the Board of Trade saying, "considering that we are yet a Country of woods, it is Surprising how he could draw so beautiful a map of it." The Earl of Halifax had it printed in London, probably in the spring of 1752, as "A Map of The Inhabited Part of Virginia."*

Their work contained surveys made by earlier map makers, especially eastern Virginia, and there were some errors. (The Youghiogheny River, for example, was shown as flowing south into the New River, and not northwest.) The original London engraver, Thomas Jeffreys, seems to have cut off part of western Virginia from the manuscript map, since the Cumberland River, mentioned in Fry's report, does not appear in the published version.

The map was the greatest contribution from Fry or Jefferson (excluding the famous son of the latter). It stood for many years as the most valuable map of Virginia, and was the ancestor of many others. New material in the map chiefly concerned southwest Virginia, a territory previously unknown in detail; and Fry's observations sketched the beginnings of the westward movement across the Alleghenies. Fry's lengthy report, attached to the map, reviewed Virginia history from the Jamestown settlement and included material from several histories (among them that of his fellow brick mason of the President's House, William Stith) and lore of western Indian tribes, as well as a report on the territory of New France.

In the year of the map's publication Fry was chosen, with Lunsford Lomax and James Patton, to make a treaty with the Six Nations, as well as the Shawnee, Mingo, and Delaware tribes, in an effort to open up the Ohio country. They met the Indians near the forks of the Ohio River. Frenchmen had been there before them, but, after many days of bargaining, Fry and his companions persuaded the chiefs to sign the treaty of Logstown (or Lancaster), which permitted the English to build two forts on the Ohio and to settle southeast of that river. As a result of this treaty the warriors of the Six Nations, an important force, sided with the English during the French and Indian War.

* The first edition of this famous map is exceedingly rare; the two known copies are in the Tracy W. McGregor Library of the University of Virginia and the New York Public Library. Several later versions exist, and the Fry-Jefferson map was the basis for the Virginia region in the later John Mitchell map of America, said to be the greatest example of American cartography.

The short-lived peace on the Ohio was shattered in 1753 by a French invasion. Determined to drive out the French, Virginia, now governed by Robert Dinwiddie, once more turned to Colonel Fry. In May, 1754, Fry got a commission from the governor: "You are by me appointed Commander in Chief on the expedition," the purpose of which was to complete an outpost on the Monongahela and Ohio.

Troops from Georgia, South Carolina, New York, and North Carolina accompanied the 300-man Virginia regiment, making about eleven hundred in all. Since some of the troops were commanded by British officers, Fry was warned to "show due regard" for their authority. The advance party was led by Fry's assistant, Lieutenant Colonel George Washington, who was irritated by the colonel's tardiness.

Delayed by dilatory contractors, reluctant volunteers, deserting Indian allies, and lack of transport, Fry was long in Alexandria. Washington wrote him from his wilderness camp: "If there does not come a sufficient reinforcement, we must either quit our ground and retreat to you, or fight very unequal numbers which I will do before I will give up one inch of what we have gained."

Washington soon fought a skirmish, defeating a party of Indians under a French officer, Joseph Coulon, the Sieur de Jumonville, for which Governor Dinwiddie sent out medals from Williamsburg to Washington, Fry, and the Indian leader, Half King. There was little else to celebrate from the expedition.

Fry and his party at last reached Fort Cumberland, the present site of Cumberland, Maryland, with an absurdly small provision train of five rickety wagons and a cart. It was near there, at Wills Creek, that Fry died, badly injured by a fall from his horse. He was buried May 31, 1754.

He was probably attended by the only doctor in his regiment, Dr. James Craik, who was to become Washington's physician and medical officer of the armies of the Revolution. One historian found a manuscript in the Fry family papers describing the burial, attended by Washington and the little army; Washington is said to have carved an inscription on a large tree over the grave: "Under this oak lies the body of the Good, The Just and the Noble Fry."

Command of the expedition fell to the twenty-two-year-old Washington, who led the troops westward, met the French and Indians, and was driven off in defeat. It was a failure that prompted the British Parliament to a major effort to rid the continent of the French, and led to the shipping of Braddock's troops to America a few months later.

Back in Albemarle County, Fry's successor was Peter Jefferson, who inherited from him the posts of member of the House of Burgesses, commander of the militia, and county surveyor. Peter himself died three years later, passing on his surveying tools, half a dozen maps, and books, as well as land and slaves, to his son Thomas, then fourteen. Among the maps was probably a copy of the Fry-Jefferson map, which is known as "the best one that anybody made of Virginia in the eighteenth century."

Within ten years after the old Williamsburg schoolmaster Fry went to his grave in the Maryland hills, the continent had been made safe for British rule and the Virginia he had mapped was secure. Within another generation, the son of his companion of wilderness surveys had played a major role in changing American destinies once more.

Fry has not been celebrated by historians; as one early chronicler of his life wrote: "I know of no other person in our history of like social position, wealth, capacity, character and public services . . . about whom there is so little to be found in print, and that little so scattered. . . ."

Robert Dinwiddie, attributed to C. Dixon. Colonial Williamsburg.

ROBERT DINWIDDIE

MAJOR General Edward Braddock, a veteran of European wars, entered the Governor's Palace at dusk of a Sunday in February, 1755, smelling faintly of snuff. The handsome sixty-year-old Guardsman was splendid in a red coat with gold lace, a ruffled cravat, a broad crimson sash, and a rosette on his cocked hat. He had ridden up from nearby Hampton after a stormy and "very fatiguing" seven-week voyage from England.

The general was on his way to the disaster in the wilderness that would mark his place in history and add to the fame of a new American hero, George Washington.

In his four years as governor, Robert Dinwiddie had known no more welcome visitor, for the general and his two regiments of troops, which were soon to arrive at Hampton, were London's answer to Dinwiddie's pleas. Only British regulars, he thought, could protect the western frontier of Virginia, now suffering "horrid murders and barbarities" in Indian raids. It was Dinwiddie who had sent Washington to the Ohio country the year before and to a defeat that helped to set off a worldwide struggle between France and England. Young Washington's surrender of a remote palisade called Fort Necessity had only aroused the fighting spirit of the Scottish governor in Williamsburg.

Dinwiddie at sixty-one was paunchy and heavy jowled. The son of a Glasgow merchant, he was a tax-collector and administrator, not a military man. But, as Virginia's House of Burgesses could attest, the governor was stubborn, with an indomitable will. He had taken up the war with the French as if the future of the British empire were bound up in the American continent, and as if the Ohio were his private domain. He had prepared for Braddock's arrival with all his energies, badgering Virginians and other colonial governors to raise men and supplies for an expedition. He wrote a friend, "These 12 months past I have been a perfect slave," but he had hopes that his sacrifices would not be in vain: "If I live to see the French drove off the British lands and confined to their bounds in Canada, it will fully answer any trouble I have had about them."

Braddock had been none too hopeful about the enterprise. On his last night in England he had shown a woman friend a map of North America, tracing his route across mountains in the wild country, and said, "We are sent like lambs to the altar." But the general had a reputation for bravery; he had once fought a duel with both swords and pistols with a brother officer. He was also known as a confirmed gambler and spendthrift.

Dinwiddie must have smiled when Braddock revealed his orders from the king: The colonies were to raise money for the invasion of the west, to furnish provisions and wagons, and to fill out his battalions to seven hundred men each. Dinwiddie was ready. The Assembly had voted him a sum of £20,000, and he had accumulated enough beef, pork, salt, flour, and dried fish to sustain an army of three thousand men for eight months. He had contracted for eleven hundred head of cattle to be delivered during the summer, enlisted one thousand men, and ordered sixteen wagons. Other colonies had pledged money, except for Pennsylvania, which was dominated by Quakers and Germans; "they are not a fighting people," Braddock said.

The two planned the thrust against the French at Fort Duquesne; they would hold the weary troops aboard the transports until they were ready to sail up Chesapeake Bay and the Potomac to the new town of Alexandria. They would march upstream to Wills Creek, the site of present Cumberland, Maryland, the rendezvous for the march over the mountains to the French fort. Braddock was astonished to find that the final leg of the route was not a brief, leisurely march, as he had thought, but more than 110 miles, over some of the most forbidding terrain on the continent. He would need a road twelve feet wide to pass his wagons, heavy guns—and a carriage he had brought from London. The army faced a major engineering feat before it met the enemy.

The general spent several weeks in Williamsburg, living at the Raleigh Tavern, where his expedition excited so much interest that the proprietor, Alexander Finnie, announced that he would go along to supply provisions. The expedition's quartermaster, Sir John St. Clair, gave a dinner party at the Raleigh for Braddock, his officers, and several prominent

Virginians, including George Washington, who was to march with Braddock as an aide, without a commission.

Dinwiddie sailed with Braddock to Alexandria, where he spent a month, conferring with the general and other governors, still urging help in supplying the troops. He spent the spring collecting medicines, money, arms, bayonets, and powder, and gave so much of Virginia's stores that, as he wrote Governor DeLancey of New York, the Williamsburg powder magazine was "quite bare."

The governor soon found Braddock unwilling to listen to his advice. Dinwiddie urged speed in moving westward, the use of many Indian allies, and the informal marching order of colonial troops; Braddock insisted on long, thorough preparation; he distrusted Indian warriors and used much "ceremony and formality" in handling the troops. The general also refused to send his light troops ahead of the artillery and wagons, which had to be pulled laboriously up the mountains. Dinwiddie felt no rancor: "He and I live in great harmony," he wrote, "and I think him a very fine officer." But Braddock, wearied of the endless effort to get proper aid from the colonials, was writing privately: "I am in the folly of Mr. Dinwiddie and the roguery of the assembly."

At last, in early June, the army of about three thousand was ready to move, and Braddock, who disdained his local troops, "whose slothful and languid disposition renders them very unfit for military service," rejected all warnings of the dangers of an ambush in the overgrown mountain country ahead. Benjamin Franklin, who visited Braddock at Frederick, Maryland, gave him a prophetic warning: "The only danger . . . to your march is from ambuscades of Indians . . . and the slender line, near four miles long, which your army must make, may expose it to be attacked by surprise in its flanks, and to be cut like a thread into several pieces, which from their distance, cannot come up in time to support each other."

Braddock's reply would soon assume a tragic irony: "These savages may, indeed, be a formidable enemy to your raw American militia, but upon the King's regulars and disciplined troops, sir, it is impossible they should make any impression."

The army marched, often making no more than two miles a day as engineers blasted stones and cut trees from the trail. Enemy scouts saw and heard them most of the way; on July 9 the vanguard was ambushed after it had crossed the Monongahela River, within a short distance of Fort Duquesne. A party of French and Indians, about 800 strong, cut Braddock's force to pieces, killed the general, took his artillery, and killed or wounded 977 men. Many of the wounded left on the field were thought to have been scalped or tortured. Washington had two horses shot from under him and four bullets passed through his clothing.

Dinwiddie had called the Assembly into session on the day of the massacre, in great hopes that General Braddock was already in possession of the fort on the Ohio. The governor first got word of the disaster from Colonel James Innes of the militia at Fort Cumberland, but could not believe it. He put it down as the report of a panic-stricken deserter and sent for more details. The news merely became worse. Colonel Thomas Dunbar, who commanded a wing of Braddock's army, fell back to Philadelphia, though his 1,600-man force was far superior to the enemy's. He left the frontier unguarded and the newly cut road open so that raiding Indians could easily strike at the heart of the colony. Dinwiddie offered Dunbar more men and supplies, and was astonished to learn that the colonel had burned his stores and ammunition and retreated to winter quarters. Dinwiddie commented bitterly that he had gone into winter quarters in August. He was also critical of Braddock for "leaving half his army forty miles behind" and for failure to clear the woods with scouting parties, but the governor was not discouraged by the defeat. He urged Virginians to greater efforts.

The governor became eloquent in his appeal to his Assembly, pointing out the dangers facing the colony. He asked for a bounty for enemy scalps and new funds for defense, and added: "The natural bravery of our countrymen, if ever questioned, is now established beyond a doubt, by those Virginia forces, who purchased, with their lives, immortal glory to their country and themselves, on the banks of Monongahela." The Virginia companies had been almost wiped out.

It was to the twenty-three-year-old Washington that Dinwiddie turned at the collapse of frontier defenses. He made him colonel of the Virginia regiment and commander in chief of all forces of the colony: "And you are hereby charged with full power and authority to act defensively or offensively, as you shall think for the good and wellfare of the service." He also ordered Washington to make headquarters at Winchester, where the frontier post Fort Loudoun was built, and, as a parting admonition, wrote: "I sincerely desire that you will inculcate morality and virtue among your men, to punish drunkenness and swearing."

Parties of Indians, each led by a French officer, were soon striking down the Braddock road, killing and burning as far as the Shenandoah Valley. In response the Assembly voted to build a string of forts among the western hills. This defense was to occupy both Dinwiddie and Washington until the governor returned to England, when its demands had strained their friendship and written a bitter chapter in colonial history.

By 1755, Robert Dinwiddie was already a veteran administrator, one of the senior royal representatives in America. His career in the colonies had begun in 1721 in the West Indies, where he later made a reputation as a vigilant customs officer by uncovering frauds in collections. In 1738 he was promoted to surveyor general of customs for the southern colonies, a domain extending from Pennsylvania into the Caribbean. Within the next year or two Dinwiddie settled in Virginia. (The site of Dinwiddie's early home in Virginia is unknown, but an official report on the Council of 1744 showed that he lived forty-six miles from Williamsburg.)

The vigorous Scot attacked his problems, public and private, with businesslike efficiency. During his term of more than ten years as surveyor general, he busily inspected most of the colonies, sailed to England to settle his troublesome Barbados affairs, and purchased an interest in a shipping vessel. He was responding to family tradition and lifelong habit. Dinwiddie was born at Germiston, near Glasgow, to a family engaged in trade for many generations. He was educated at the University of Glasgow, and married Rebecca Affleck, the daughter of a minister; they had two daughters. He apparently had been trained in the family counting house and in a pottery business before he went to Bermuda at the age of twenty-eight.

The new surveyor general of the customs got a cool reception from Virginia leaders. The Council refused to seat him as a regular member, as his predecessors had been. Dinwiddie was told that he could sit only as an "extraordinary" member, a mere consultant. He protested to London that he could not conduct the king's business properly without the powers he had expected, including a vote in the upper house of the Assembly and a seat on the General Court. He argued that only with full membership could he influence legislation, especially any attack by Virginians on the laws of trade, which had been in effect for a century, though unenforced. Colonials were always aware of these laws, since they were London's device for control of trade, and for striking at the American purse.

The Council, jealous of its position in Virginia, also appealed to the Board of Trade, urging that Dinwiddie be denied. But London sided with the surveyor general and ordered him seated as an ordinary councilor. For many years Dinwiddie worked so effectively with the colony's leaders that he became the logical successor to Governor Gooch at his retirement.

The Scot served the Board of Trade well. His extended reports on colonial trade covered American territory from Newfoundland to the Barbados and were models of their kind, with details of shipping, products, population, militia strength, the condition of slavery, and many other facts. As he wrote, he had gone to much trouble and expense to inform himself of the trade of His Majesty's American empire.

Dinwiddie later made himself unpopular by clashing with Virginians over taxation, which he did not seem to recognize as a major irritant that might lead to revolt, but he was quick to see that Englishmen living in America were passionately fond of their liberties: "Next to the blessing of heaven on the industry of the planter and the richness of the soil . . . they are happy in the constitution, in having a power to make laws for their government, which is more than their neighbouring colonies are indulged with."

The surveyor general seemed to respect this independence of spirit in Virginians during his early career, and though he was a forthright, plain-spoken official, unsparing of himself or his friends where public duty was concerned, he played the unpopular role of tax collector without stirring controversy.

Dinwiddie left Virginia by early 1749, resigning as a customs officer, perhaps in order to give his full time to trade, and was in London two years later when, at the retirement of Governor William Gooch, he was called to return and administer the colony. Although he arrived at a time when the currents leading to revolution had begun to run (there would be strife over the power of Parliament to tax the colony, wars on the frontier, the use of a royal veto, and a revolt against the Anglican church), the beginning was harmonious enough.

Dinwiddie and his family landed at Yorktown in late November, 1751, and went to Williamsburg, where he was met by several old friends, including John Blair, Philip Ludwell, Colonel William Fairfax, and other members of the Council, and the mayor and aldermen of Williamsburg. Dinwiddie was entertained at a ceremonial dinner at Wetherburn's Tavern, where many toasts were drunk. Cannon roared a welcome from Market Square. The Council went with the new governor to his house, the present-day Carter-Saunders House on Palace Green, which the colony bought to use as Dinwiddie's residence while the Palace was being extensively renovated.

The new governor "produced his Commission with a handsome Speech declaring his Purpose of studying the Welfare of the Country, relying on the Assistance of the Council," took his oath of office, and returned to Yorktown for the night. John Blair noted in his diary that he dined with the Dinwiddies that week and that "many Ladies and Gentlemen visited them in the Afternoon, and were highly pleased with them."

The governor took an active part in the life of the colony. He joined the Ohio Company and acquired a stake in the western lands for which a war was to be fought. He welcomed the twenty-year-old George Washington to his home, and the visit began a friendship which, though sometimes stormy, was to play a role in fighting that war and in shaping the American future. In February, 1752, Dinwiddie faced his first Assembly, which met at the College of William and Mary—the Capitol was being rebuilt. He said he was happy to be back in Virginia, which he referred to as his country, among people with whom he had lived in "domestic felicity" and friendship. The burgesses replied by praising Dinwiddie's "social virtues" and forecast for his regime "an equitable and well ordered government."

The conscientious governor and the Assembly then began the struggles which were later to be recognized as the prelude to revolution. They were allies in the first skirmish with London. The king had vetoed ten acts of the Assembly and approved fifty-seven others, all of them passed earlier in a revision of the colony's laws. The burgesses protested bitterly. Men of the Privy Council in London could not sensibly judge the merits of a law forbidding wooden chimneys in the Virginia village of Walkerton, although the House explained that the purpose was to guard tobacco warehouses against fire. They also protested that the veto of a new law governing the General Court threw their affairs into chaos, since it nullified recent decisions. The veto brought further confusion, by reviving previous laws which the newer ones had supplanted. Worst of all was the king's tardy approval of the fifty-seven acts. The burgesses complained that they could not pass tentative laws, waiting for months or even years to put them into effect until royal approval finally came.

Dinwiddie agreed to help press the case in London and proposed the appointment of an agent, James Abercromby, to petition the king. The effort was largely in vain; two laws were reinstated, but as late as the end of 1759, when Francis Fauquier had become governor, Virginians still lacked royal approval of their land laws. When John Mercer made the first abridgment of the colony's laws in 1758, he complained that it was hard to tell which laws were in effect.

The first session ended with such warmth between governor and Assembly that Dinwiddie was voted £500 "as a grateful acknowledgement for his regard to the interest and welfare of this Colony." A new county was named in his honor. The honeymoon was soon ended, by a long, noisy squabble that became known as the "pistole fee" controversy.

Dinwiddie had found piles of land patents waiting for his signature, more than seventeen hundred in all, plus about one thousand surveyors' certificates on which patents should have been issued. These were not merely official papers, but represented about a million acres of land in western Virginia. In the past, such grants had been issued free to settlers and speculators. Dinwiddie thought it fair, and businesslike, for the governor to be paid for his trouble in signing and stamping the Virginia seal on these documents for free land, and proposed to charge applicants a small fee. The Council agreed that this was reasonable and set the fee at one pistole, a small Spanish coin then in circulation. (A pistole would buy "a good cow and calf" in Virginia at the time, a matter of importance to small farmers.) Dinwiddie kept the fee secret until the Assembly had adjourned, and even when it became public, the governor claimed that most Virginians were "very easy and well satisfied till an evil spirit entered into a high priest, who was supported by the family of Randolphs." The "high priest" was the Reverend William Stith, whose mother was a Randolph, and whose influential cousins included Peyton Randolph and Richard Bland. Stith had been chosen president of William and Mary over Dinwiddie's opposition. (The governor charged that Stith was unorthodox in religion and a troublemaker in politics, that he was ruled by his violent temper, and lived too far from Williamsburg, in Henrico Parish.)

Stith conceded that he was one of the first to protest. He was fond of proposing a toast at his table, "Liberty and property and no pistole," which became popular in many parts of Virginia. His phrase became a rallying cry for men who regarded the fee as a tax, and was echoed in a pamphlet by Richard Bland: "Liberty and property are like those precious vessels whose soundness is destroyed by the least flaw." Bland urged the "opposing in a legal way every attempt of this sort which like a small spark if not extinguished at the beginning will soon gain ground and at last blaze out into an irresistible flame."

Petitions of protest began to come in from several counties, and the burgesses faced Dinwiddie resolutely: had the governor ordered this fee himself, and by what authority? Dinwiddie explained that the action had the Council's blessing and said that he had not exceeded his authority.

The reply of the burgesses, couched in dignified but reproachful terms, was one of the early documents of the revolutionary movement. The House, it said, had every right to "enquire into the grievances of the people," and it added: "The rights of the subject are so secured by law, that they cannot be deprived of the least part of their property, but by their own consent: Upon this excellent principle is our constitution founded. . . . The demand of a pistole, as a fee for the use of the public seal, being not warranted by any known and established law, is, we humbly conceive, an infringement of the rights of the people, and a grievance highly to be complained of."

Dinwiddie refused to back down. The Crown lands, he insisted, had no relation to the affairs of local government. The burgesses appointed Peyton Randolph as an agent of the House to present its case in London, and voted £2,500 from the public treasury for his expenses. The outraged Dinwiddie dismissed Randolph from the office of attorney general and named George Wythe in his place. The controversy dwarfed even the growing Indian troubles of the frontier. After another session of the Assembly tempers cooled and the House and governor cooperated to prosecute the Indian war, and peace was made in the capital. The House voted £20,000 for the war and Peyton Randolph and Dinwiddie resumed their friendly relations. London compromised by limiting the fee to tracts of more than one hundred acres and exempted those settled by families imported, as well as all those "beyond the mountains." The crisis passed without rancor, largely because of Dinwiddie's impersonal view of the controversy; he did not hold grudges.

Historians have found Dinwiddie's stubbornness in this dispute an enigma. He was under contract to pay the non-resident governor of Virginia, the Earl of Albemarle, more than half of his salary, but Dinwiddie was a wealthy man, and the small fee could not have been of vital importance. In the end he wrote wryly that if he had known the affair "would have created so much uneasiness to me, and trouble to my friends at home, I would not have taken that fee."

The war on the frontier now demanded the energies, and financial resources, of Virginia's government. On instructions from London, Dinwiddie sent twenty-one-year-old Major George Washington as a messenger to the French, who were penetrating the Ohio and Mississippi valleys.

Washington was to warn the intruders that they were on English soil. The major was already a district militia adjutant, and in Dinwiddie's eyes the young man was already "a person of distinction." Washington justified the governor's trust, making his way through hundreds of miles of wilderness to deliver the message to the French commander and taking careful note of the strength of the enemy and signs of coming invasion. One party of French officers in a frontier fort, after a bout of drinking wine, exposed their war plans: "They told me," Washington reported, "that it was their absolute design to take possession of the Ohio, and by G—— they would do it."

When Washington returned to report that the French were ready to invade the western territory with fifteen hundred men, Dinwiddie ordered a fort built at the present site of Pittsburgh and sent out two detachments of troops, one of them under Washington. The French drove the Virginians from the fort and seized control of the region west of the Alleghenies. Dinwiddie was moved to greater exertions, largely on his own, since he could not persuade other governors to help him. When Braddock arrived from England in response to his pleas, the governor gave him all the support he could wring from the Assembly, and not even the defeat of that expedition discouraged Dinwiddie. For the remaining two years of his administration the governor devoted himself to frontier defense.

He championed Washington, but their relationship was strained and, during a period when both men were ill, was marred by mutual suspicions. Washington complained that he and his officers were discriminated against because they lacked regular commissions; they were underpaid, short of men and equipment, and weary of the life in frontier posts. Dinwiddie's letters became angry retorts, and more than once he gave Washington peremptory orders to make ill-advised military moves.

Things reached such a pass that Washington once charged that Dinwiddie would be happy to hear that he was in trouble, however undeservedly; such, Washington felt, were Dinwiddie's dispositions toward him. Washington thought of himself as "in a manner an exile." On one occasion Dinwiddie scolded his militia commander: "My conduct to you from the beginning was always friendly, but you know I had good reason to suspect you of ingratitude . . . I had reason to be angry." And Washington wrote in reply: "I do not know that I ever gave your Honor cause to suspect me of ingratitude, a crime I detest and would most carefully avoid." On the eve of Dinwiddie's departure from Virginia, Washington asked permission to leave his Winchester headquarters to ride to Williamsburg and settle his accounts, but he was refused sharply: "You have been frequently indulged with leave of absence. You know the fort is to be finished."

On such a hostile note the long collaboration between the governor and his young colonel came to an end, and affairs on the frontier suffered.

London was so concerned over the course of the war that Lord Loudoun was sent to America to plan its defense. He called a conference of governors in Philadelphia, and it was there that the aging Dinwiddie asked for relief. He was worn with long labors, had some form of paralysis, and had contracted malaria. He asked William Pitt for a leave of absence in England, hoping to recover his health at Bath.

Dinwiddie's last meeting with the Council was in January, 1758, a few days before he sailed for England. The Council got him immediate passage, by paying £300 to have a ship's captain remove fifty hogsheads of his tobacco cargo to make room for the Dinwiddie family and its baggage. He did not return to Virginia, but in the twelve years left to him he never lost interest in the colony. As he wrote Pitt before his departure, Virginia had been more obedient and cooperative in the Crown's work "than any one Colony on this continent."

The Corporation of Williamsburg praised Dinwiddie's devotion to duty in a formal farewell, and John Blair, the Council president who served as interim governor, wrote London to express the hope that the incoming Francis Fauquier would make up their loss in his predecessor.

From England, where he worked to see that Virginia got her share of a war appropriation by Parliament, Dinwiddie wrote to his friend Richard Corbin that he was aware of his Virginia critics, who complained that his defense funds had been spend in other colonies: "It surprises me they should mention that money, as it was sent me for the King's Service in general, and not for the Collony of Virginia." He added: "I hope my Character is above their reach to hurt me, and their endeavours shall not prevent my doing everything in my power for the Service of Virginia."

Despite his tireless prosecution of the war against the French, and his long and fruitful association with Washington, Dinwiddie's reputation suffered from their final bitter exchanges; his quarrels with the Assembly over finances were magnified, and the old governor was depicted as fussy and arrogant, an inefficient and unpopular executive whose departure was not regretted in Virginia. He died in Bristol in 1770, at the age of seventy-eight, on the eve of a greater war that was to see all the vast territory he had helped to save from France lost to Great Britain forever.

Francis Fauquier, by Richard Wilson. Reproduced by permission of the Governors of the Thomas Coram Foundation for Children, London, which has the original in its collection.

FRANCIS FAUQUIER

WILLIAMSBURG was crowded, and noisy, and stirred by an excitement rare even for a time when General Court was in session. The city was lively enough on any public occasion, as a French traveler had noted in his journal in the spring: "Never was a more disagreeable Place than this at Present. In the Day Time People hurrying back and forwards from the Capitoll to the Taverns, and at Night, carousing and drinking in one Chamber and Box and Dice in another, which continues till Morning commonly."

But on the crisp autumn Wednesday of October 30, 1765, a more ominous game was being played. For five months, since Patrick Henry's impassioned oratory had stirred the colonies against the Stamp Act, Virginia had been waiting. The new Stamp Act was to take effect on November 1. The revenue stamps were expected in the colony at any moment, and the tax was certain to be resisted.

Governor Francis Fauquier foresaw the halting of all courts in Virginia, "the total stagnation of business," and a "dreadful calamity." A few days earlier the justices of two counties had warned that they would not serve after the stamps came. The governor was a man not easily alarmed, but he had heard rumors that "at the time of the General Court parties would come down from most parts of the country to seize on and destroy all Stamped Papers."

Unluckily, Virginia's shipment of the stamps arrived that Wednesday, brought by Colonel George Mercer, a respected veteran of frontier fighting. He had left the stamps aboard ship at a Hampton wharf and come to Williamsburg, unaware that he was entering a hornet's nest. When

Fauquier heard of Mercer's coming he hurried to Mrs. Vobe's Coffee House (later Christiana Campbell's Tavern), on Waller Street. It faced the Exchange, a kind of open-air clearing house where merchants and other businessmen gathered during court sessions to settle accounts and trade in currency. If violence was brewing over the Stamp Act, the merchants would be in the thick of it.

Fauquier waited on the porch of the coffeehouse, he said, so that he "might be an eyewitness of what did really pass." He was watching the crowd expectantly when someone shouted "One and all!," and at this signal the traders hurried off, looking for Mercer. They found him outside the Capitol and surrounded him.

The governor would have called "this concourse of people" a mob if he had not known these men, the leading merchants and county officials of Virginia. As the governor watched, the crowd held Mercer at bay, shouting to him: Did he intend to distribute stamps, or to resign as agent? Mercer was not cowed. He said that he had to discuss the matter with friends, since it was "an affair of great moment."

He promised an answer by ten o'clock Friday morning and told the merchants to meet him there at the Capitol steps. He then pushed through the crowd, eastward across the green toward the coffeehouse, where Fauquier sat with members of the Council. Speaker John Robinson stood in front of the governor as the crowd rushed after Mercer, still badgering him for a reply.

Mercer went up the steps of the coffeehouse, where the governor and Council gave him a warm welcome, evidently in hopes of impressing the crowd. Fauquier studied the merchants below them and concluded that "to judge by their countenances, they were not well pleased," but the men were silent for a time until someone shouted: "Friday's too late. The Act takes place then. We'll have an answer tomorrow."

The mob seemed unsure of itself, but was in no mood to leave. Leaders sent messages to Mercer on the porch, but the colonel repeated his reply each time: "I've already given an answer, and I'll have no other extorted from me."

Fauquier described the next moments, in which the first violence of the pre-revolutionary movement in Virginia was narrowly averted: "After some little time a cry was heard, 'let us rush in.' . . . we that were at the top of the steps . . . to repell those who should attempt to mount them, advanced to the edge of the Steps."

"I immediately heard a cry, 'See the Governor, take care of him.' "

The men pushing up the steps fell back, leaving room before Fauquier —out of love and respect for him, the governor thought. Mercer's friends then urged him to give in to the crowd, and he agreed reluctantly to give them his answer the next afternoon at the Capitol. Fauquier thought that the danger had not yet passed:

> The crowd did not yet disperse; it was growing dark, and I did not think it safe to leave Mr. Mercer behind me, so I again advanced to the edge of the steps and said aloud I believed no man there would do me any hurt, and turned to Mr. Mercer and told him if he would walk with me through the people I believed I could conduct him safe to my house and we accordingly walked side by side through the thickest of the people, who did not molest us, tho' there was some little murmurs.

Mercer and the governor talked for a long time at the Palace, and Fauquier gave the perplexed agent candid advice. If he feared for his life, the governor offered no suggestion, but if he were not afraid, he should keep the office. Mercer kept his appointment the next day and found the crowd greatly swollen by men who had been called in from nearby counties overnight. The colonel backed down. He read a formal statement, saying that he had been appointed agent after he had gone to England and that he had not understood the Stamp Act Resolves of the House of Burgesses as official. He made a final promise: "I will not, directly or indirectly, by myself or deputies, proceed in the execution of the act until I receive further orders from England, and not then without the assent of the General Assembly of this colony."

He was interrupted by cheering. The Stamp Act crisis in Virginia was over, and the new tax was soon to be repealed. The farsighted Fauquier was not deluded by the quiet which fell upon the town. He wrote his superiors in London that "a state of general outlawry" existed in the colony, and he made a gloomy forecast: "What other consequences may follow from these, are so buried in obscurity that it requires a sagacity . . . much superior to my own, even to guess at them. . . . But it seems to me that disorder, confusion and misery are before us."

Fauquier promised to do his duty about the stamps, but he could not promise to save them from destruction. He also reminded the Board of Trade that it had sent him no instructions to guide him "through the wilderness." In fact, he had never been notified that a Stamp Act had been passed, and it had become an issue in Virginia only when Patrick Henry had set off the clamor in May.

The governor had foreseen some such trouble. Almost five years before he had warned William Pitt that any taxation on the colonies by Parliament would lead to serious disturbances. He had also tried to explain to the Lords of Trade that these unpredictable Americans were not of the same breed as Englishmen at home: "Whoever charges them with acting upon a premeditated concerted plan, don't know them." He found that Virginians were "Expedient-Mongers in the highest degree," though their haphazard methods were very costly to them. Even the apparent waywardness of the House of Burgesses, which often reversed itself, was a key to the behavior of Virginians: "The incertitude of the proceedings of the General Assembly . . . seems to be so inherent in the nature of the Members, as to be characteristic of the People."

This resolute and sensible governor, who was remembered by Thomas Jefferson as the ablest of all Virginia executives, was an accomplished Englishman of sixty-two, then in his eighth year as head of the colony, an urbane man of advanced ideas. He had proposed a graduated income tax to finance British war debts, one of the early schemes of its kind; he kept Virginia's first records of weather observations; proposed America's first public mental hospital; opposed slavery; and he ordered that an autopsy be performed after his death so that doctors could study any strange fatal disease and that he might "become more useful to my fellow Creatures by my Death than I have been in my Life."

He was a musician who held regular concerts in the Palace with a small group of other amateurs; he had a microscope, telescope, and other scientific instruments. Early in his administration he added a fillip to the education of the young law student Jefferson by holding intimate dinner parties in the Palace for Professors George Wythe and William Small and the nineteen-year-old Thomas. In his old age Jefferson recalled those evenings where, he said, he heard "more good sense, more rational and philosophical conversations," than at any time in his life.

Fauquier was descended from a French family of the Bordeaux region. His father, Dr. John Francis Fauquier, who probably fled to England to escape the persecution of the Huguenots after 1685, was naturalized by an act of Parliament and married a wealthy Englishwoman, Elizabeth Chamberlayne. As deputy master of the Mint, the doctor served under Thomas Neale, the predecessor of Sir Isaac Newton. He was director of the Bank of England and left a large estate at his death in 1726.

Francis Fauquier, the eldest son, was born in London in 1703. Although details of his education are unknown, he developed interests in science, music, and the arts. In one surviving portrait by Hogarth, Fauquier appears in a family group wearing a fashionable wig with long curls. (A frequently published miniature said to be of Governor Fauquier has probably been erroneously identified. It is perhaps a portrait of his son William; the miniature depicts a handsome, thin-faced young British officer, in appearance quite unlike the Governor Fauquier of the family portrait.)

Young Fauquier came into a fortune when he was twenty-three, at the death of his father, his estate including £25,000 in stock of the Bank of England and the South Sea Company. About four years later he married Catherine Dalston, by whom he had two sons. He became a director of the South Sea Company and a fellow of the Royal Society.

In 1756, at the opening of the Seven Years' War with France, which was to settle the fate of the North American continent, Fauquier published *An essay on ways and means for raising money for the support of the present war, without increasing the public debts,* which was of such originality that it won the attention of British leaders and went through three editions. His theory was that every tax on necessities was inevitably passed on to the ultimate consumer. As a substitute he proposed (in vain) a graduated income tax.

His tax pamphlet and his standing in London financial and political circles may have led to his appointment as lieutenant governor of Virginia when Robert Dinwiddie resigned the post in 1758. His patron at Court in winning the governorship seems to have been the Earl of Halifax, to whom Fauquier left a substantial token of gratitude in his will, "one single Stone brilliant Diamond Ring of the value of one hundred Guineas at least."*

* The early Virginia historian John Burk established Fauquier's reputation as a reckless gambler with a story that Admiral Anson, returning from a voyage around the globe, met Fauquier and "in a single night's play he won at cards the whole of his patrimony . . . afterwards, being captivated by the striking graces of this gentleman's person and conversation, he procured for him the Government of Virginia." Burk may have been misled by Fauquier's dedication of the tax pamphlet to Anson, but the tale sounds false or greatly exaggerated. It was fourteen years after Anson's celebrated voyage that Fauquier went to Virginia; a generation after the allegedly ruinous card game, he was still collecting handsome dividends on his English properties. Fauquier left so large an estate at his death that his Virginia executors were bonded for £50,000.

Later historians improved on the story and saw Fauquier as a pioneer in Virginia vice: "He introduced a passion for high play that ruined many a fine old family, encouraged hard drinking and a mania for racing, delighted in having the clergy and favored students join him in his all-night revels." There is plentiful evidence that Virginia needed no indoctrination in these pastimes.

The departed Governor Dinwiddie, who reached London before Fauquier sailed for Virginia, sent to Williamsburg a favorable report on his successor: "He is a gentleman of good sense and Interest here, and I hope he will be agreeable to the people and make a good Governor." Fauquier came to Williamsburg in June, 1758. A striking contrast to Dinwiddie, he was an affable and elegantly dressed London sophisticate with polished manners and with a broad knowledge of modern sciences and the arts. He felt at home with the colony's leaders, in whom he saw "a character compounded of the same elements as his own." Fauquier praised Virginians as "very zealous in his Majesty's service and very strenuous to support the common cause."

The new governor found Virginia in the final phase of the French and Indian War. Two regiments on the frontier, commanded by Colonel George Washington and William Byrd III, were part of an army struggling over the mountains toward Fort Duquesne, at the site of modern Pittsburgh. Fauquier had hardly settled in the Palace before he had a warm letter from Washington: "Although but a poor hand at complimenting . . . permit me, nevertheless to offer your Honor my congratulations . . . ," but both Washington and Byrd complained to the governor about the commander of their expedition, General John Forbes of the British Army.

Washington protested the long delay caused by Forbes, who insisted on building a road through Pennsylvania, rather than using the route of the ill-fated Braddock expedition of three years before which had been cut "at the expense of so much blood and treasure." The young colonel once wrote: "All is lost! . . . Our enterprise ruined!" This frustration was reflected in the first Assembly of Fauquier's regime in September, 1758. Its members, angry over expensive delays and suspicious of their Pennsylvania rivals, voted to disband one regiment, and only a desperate stand by older members saved the troops. The burgesses set a deadline: if the troops were not back in Virginia by December 1, their pay would stop. The little army raced against time over mountain passes in November to an incredible and bloodless victory.

The French had burned and abandoned their fort at the forks of the Ohio, leaving charred chimneys and a few supplies.

Washington wrote that the taking of this fort was "a matter of great surprise to the whole army"; this was only the first of many British victories in the year to come. Within nine months Fauquier reported to

London that the French and Indians were being defeated, that "the whole country between the Sea and the Lakes is clear."

Fauquier's first Assembly was also the first for Washington, who had been elected a burgess from Frederick County as an absentee candidate while he was fighting in the west. When the colonel came home to marry Martha Dandridge Custis and attend the House session, Fauquier offered Colonel Byrd command of the army: "Colonel Washington has resigned his command of the Virginia forces (and is married to his agreeable widow)." A few months later Fauquier rode out to Winchester to visit Byrd and his troops, hoping to raise a regiment of "healthy active likely young fellows," but was forced to buy two loads of convicts to fill the ranks. Byrd said they would be as good as any recruits he could find in Virginia.

The Assembly of spring, 1759, was progressive despite the problem of financing the war. There was an act "encouraging arts and manufactures" to attract immigrants and new businesses; there was drought relief for a disaster area in southwest Virginia, in the form of free corn for the people; mill owners on the Rapidan River were forced to open a way for spawning fish to pass upstream, an early conservation measure; and a new county was named for Fauquier.

The governor found that he could not do all that London asked, however. He had orders to divide the posts of treasurer and speaker of the House, now held by the portly, dignified John Robinson. The governor saw at once that Robinson would not be an easy victim, and within a week of his arrival wrote to London: "I am afraid [the proposed reform] will meet with great difficulty as it has been a custom of so long standing and the Present Gentleman so popular and so sure of the Chair." As time passed Fauquier found Robinson even more formidable, as he told the Board of Trade, "the darling of the Country, as he well deserves to be for his great integrity, assiduity and ability in business." Fauquier found Robinson so useful in pushing bills through the Assembly that he urged that he be left alone. Years later this lenient policy proved to be costly for Virginia, for on Robinson's death his slipshod business methods were revealed; scores of prominent Virginians were in debt to him for money he had taken from the public treasury to help his friends.

In all the ten lively years of Fauquier's administration he faced nothing more vexing than the furor over the salaries of Anglican clergymen in Virginia. Before his arrival, they had been paid in tobacco, at the rate of sixteen thousand pounds a year. But in a year of a short tobacco crop, when the price of the leaf zoomed upward, the Assembly passed a new law called the Two Penny Act: debts could be paid in currency, rather than tobacco, and ministers were given their small salaries in cash at the rate of two pence per pound of tobacco. They had complained bitterly, saying that they were forced to serve their large parishes winter and summer for a pittance, and that even these salaries were usually a year and a half in arrears.

Again in 1759 a shortage of tobacco threatened, and the new Two Penny Act was passed, with Fauquier's approval. He defended it to the Board of Trade on the grounds that it was a temporary law and that it would have been improper for a governor who was "an entire stranger to the distress of the country" to oppose the strong public demand. The preachers began a bitter campaign against him and the act. Ministers who came to Fauquier found that he spoke as politicians often speak: With him it was not a question of whether the law was just or unjust, "but whether the people wanted it."

Fauquier now faced wily veterans of many Virginia squabbles. For years the clergy and the College of William and Mary had been involved in strife; the Tory faculty of the college had battled the Board of Visitors, composed of political leaders who represented the public. Ministers of the established church fought the rising power of the Presbyterians and Baptists; the Anglican clerics had also squabbled among themselves. These frictions had often involved governors, two of whom had been driven from Virginia by Commissary James Blair, the early leader of college and church in Virginia. The ministers now turned on Fauquier and the Assembly.

The first attack came from the Reverend Jacob Rowe, professor of philosophy at the college, who wondered in public how many burgesses were to be hanged and vowed that he would not administer the Sacrament to any member who voted against the clergy. The House passed a resolution against these "scandalous and malicious" words and forced an apology, but there was more to come. Rowe and another professor, Goronwy Owen, a gifted young Welsh poet, were often "scandalously drunk" on the streets, uttered "horrid oaths and execrations in their common conversation," and stirred trouble between the president and faculty of the college.

Fauquier acted vigorously; he sent Owen to another parish and voted with the Board of Visitors to dismiss Rowe—who continued his mischief by leading college students against town boys in "a pitched battle with pistols and other weapons" and once drew a pistol on Peyton Randolph. As the faculty journal put it, Rowe was "unanimously desired to remove himself and his effects from the College by Monday the 29th instant."

The governor's trials with the preachers had only begun. Angry ministers chose the argumentative Reverend John Camm, an ousted professor of divinity at the college, to take their case to London. He was to plead the plight of the impoverished clergy and, even more seriously, to charge Fauquier and the Assembly with violating royal orders by passing their "pretended laws." With the aid of the Bishop of London, Camm won a complete victory in England; the Bishop convinced the Privy Council that Fauquier and the burgesses were undermining the authority of church and Crown, and were guilty of treason. The king vetoed all the acts involved, ordered ministers paid in tobacco on the most favorable terms, and warned Fauquier to obey instructions to the letter on pain of "our highest displeasure and being recalled."

Camm himself was made the royal messenger to carry the news to Virginia, but he was in no hurry; he stayed in England for eighteen months, sent word of his triumph to Virginia, and ordered his lawyer to bring suit for his back salary. Two able pamphleteers, Richard Bland and Landon Carter, attacked Camm personally and denounced the principle of royal interference in Virginia affairs.

Camm came back at last, bearing the orders from London—copies of which by now had been seen by hundreds in Virginia. Camm stopped in Hampton for a week or so to visit a friend, the Reverend Thomas Warrington. In late June, 1760, accompanied by Warrington and the Reverend William Robinson as witnesses, the king's messenger appeared at the Palace. The scene lived long in Virginia memory.

Fauquier had worked himself into a rage over Camm's insolence in sending the orders through the colony before bringing them to the Palace. He thought this a "step unprecedented" and "a high insult on majesty." Camm and his two witnesses at last faced the governor, and Camm handed over the papers. Fauquier inspected them scornfully: "Open, dirty and worn out at the edges and folds"; he saw that they bore an old date, and that one of them was not the original, but a copy.

"Were these papers delivered to you open?"

"Yes, sir."

"In whose possession have they been in all this time?"

"In mine, sir."

"I shall write to the Board of Trade and Lords of Council to inquire about these things."

"Your Honor may do as you please."

"I am well acquainted with the calumnies you have thrown on me."

"I am willing to face your Honor's Informers."

"I am above board and quarrel with people to their face."

"Your Honor never quarrelled with me to my face before, and I do not come to quarrel with your Honor now."

"You thought proper to visit Mr. Warrington before you waited on me. . . . You are very Ignorant or very impudent, take which alternative you please. You are a foolish Negotiator; and I order you never to enter my doors again."

The ministers moved toward the door, but Fauquier called a servant: "Westmore, call my Negroes. Call all my Negroes." When servants came Fauquier pointed to Camm: "Here, look at him, look at him; that you may know him again. If ever he should come to ask for me suffer him not to enter my doors."

The ministers left the Palace.

As Mr. Robinson told the story, Fauquier "in Countenance, words and Gesture shewed himself to be in a most violent passion. Mr. Camm bore his treatment with the greatest patience."

Fauquier made no effort to conceal his impatience with the clergymen; he once told a group of them in the Palace "that the Clergy were well enough in their own sphere but when they turned politicians they were arrant fools."

During these clamors with the clergy Fauquier became more popular because he sided with the public. It was also during this time that he became more intimate with young Thomas Jefferson, who frequented the Palace at dinners and musicales with his professors, George Wythe and William Small, a gifted mathematician. When Jefferson said, much later, that Williamsburg was the finest school of manners in early America, he was paying tribute to Fauquier, from whom he heard such stimulating conversation. Jefferson may also have acquired his views on freedom of religion from Fauquier and have seen in the cultivated governor some of the spirit of the Renaissance. Jefferson was so impressed by Fauquier's weather observations that he later began a similar record himself. (Fauquier reported to the Royal Society on the most interesting of his weather observations, a hailstorm of July, 1759, which broke every window on the north side of the Palace. The unusual stones, he said, were of oblong, square form, up to an inch and a half long, some with half-inch spikes. He used the stones to chill wine and freeze some cream.)

Another of Fauquier's interests which must have won the admiration of the future President was a proposal for a mental hospital. The governor once found four insane people penned in the Public Gaol, and urged the House of Burgesses to care for the "poor unhappy set of people who are deprived of their Senses and wander about the Country, terrifying the Rest of their Fellow Creatures." The governor inspired the nation's first public mental hospital, in Williamsburg, "A legal confinement" for the insane: "Every civilized Country has an Hospital for these People, where they are confined, maintained and attended by able Physicians, to endeavour to restore to them their lost Reason."

When he was once reprimanded from London for siding with the colonists in public affairs, Fauquier explained that he always sought "to preserve an entire harmony," especially with the Council and the House, "to keep them in good humor with each other." He suggested that London might overlook some "improper or indecent" expressions in the legislature, as "the sallies of a young people in a progress towards politeness." Sometimes, he confessed, he was caught in such a dilemma in his efforts to satisfy both the burgesses and the Board of Trade, that he was forced to hoodwink the Virginians, "and at last have acted out of character, having made use of more art, than I ever practised with them before."

Even when the first Stamp Act crisis came and Patrick Henry stampeded the House into passage of his Resolves, the governor was sympathetic; he wrote of the "hot and giddy" leaders who had taken the defiant step, after a copy of the act had "crept into the House." He deplored the near-violence of the mob's rush upon Colonel Mercer in October, 1765, and thought from that moment that the colonies were resolved to make serious trouble for the Crown. But he was obviously happy when, in June, 1766, he issued a proclamation announcing the repeal of the Stamp Act.

A British traveler who passed through Williamsburg about this time noted Fauquier's relations with Virginians in the capital: "The people are well-bred, polite and extremely civil to Strangers—The Governour's

House is handsome and commodious, and he himself very happy, and the people so in him."

He was also an exceptionally vigorous executive. He called eleven sessions of the Assembly during one period of three years and nine months. He not only visited the Virginia frontier and the northern colonies, but he sailed to Augusta, Georgia, in 1763 to attend a peace conference with southern Indian tribes. In the same year he made an extended report on Virginia, estimating its population at about 121,000, equally divided between white and Negro, with an increase of more than 16,000 in the past three years.

Little is known of Fauquier's family life in Williamsburg. His wife and son left the colony for England in May, 1766, just before the proclamation of the Stamp Act repeal, but his wife is not mentioned in records of social events of the time.

In the last few years of his life Fauquier developed an unknown ailment, "a tedious illness," and by 1767 had "numerous infirmities which embittered the latter Part of his Existence." His will reflected the judgment and unselfishness which had dominated his life. He not only ordered an autopsy on his body, but he asked that he be buried "in the Earth or Sea" as he should "happen to fall, without any vain funeral Pomp and as little Expence as Decency can possibly permit."

He mourned the existence of slavery and added to his will instructions to provide for his own slaves: "a part of my Estate in its nature disagreeable to me but which my Situation made necessary for me, the disposal of which has constantly given me uneasiness . . . I hope I shall be found to have been a merciful Master to them and that no one of them will rise up in Judgment against me in that Great Day when all my Actions will be exposed to public View." To make their lot easier, he directed that his slaves be allowed to choose their own masters, to have six months to make their decisions, and to be sold below their value if necessary to accomplish this.

His will bore other examples of Fauquier's liberality and common sense. He left each of his servants a year's wages, except his faithful cook, Anne Ayscough, who was left £250 for her fidelity and attentions during his illnesses because of the "great Oeconomy with which she conducted the expences of my Kitchen . . . when it was in her power to have defrauded me of several hundred pounds."

The governor bore his afflictions with patient fortitude until, at 2 A.M.

of March 3, 1768, at the age of sixty-four, he died in the Palace. The *Gazette* wrote of his last days: "Though his End was accompanied with uncommon Anguish, yet no Sigh or Complaint issued from his Bosom, no Pain interrupted the Serenity of his Mind."

President James Horrocks of the college mourned Fauquier's death as "no small misfortune" to his friends, and, more important, to the colony. His administration, Horrocks thought, had been conducted with a "fair and even hand" between the rights of England and Virginia, so that Fauquier "highly merited the Esteem and Affection of the People here."

The *Gazette* echoed Horrocks: "As a faithful Representative of his Sovereign; he was vigilant in Government, moderate in Power, exemplary in Religion, and merciful where the rigours of Justice could by any Means be dispensed with." His personal life had also been admirable: he was warm and humane, punctual in keeping engagements, "munificent to Indigence," and "truly paternal" in his domestic affairs. In all, "His life was a Pattern worthy of Imitation," and governors who came after him should find their way easier, because of the plain footsteps left by "this upright Man."

Fauquier was buried in the north aisle of Bruton Parish Church with more ceremony than he had wished. The Williamsburg militia turned out, and mourners included the president and all members of the Council who could reach the city, Speaker Peyton Randolph, Treasurer Robert Carter Nicholas, Attorney General John Randolph, and other leading local citizens.

An admirer, writing in the *Gazette*, expressed the colony's affections in a farewell:

> If ever virtue lost a friend sincere,
> If ever sorrow claim'd Virginia's tear,
> If ever death a noble conquest made,
> 'Twas when FAUQUIER the debt of nature paid.

Norborne Berkeley, Baron de Botetourt, by William Hoare. Reproduced by permission of His Grace the Duke of Beaufort, K.G., Badminton, Gloucestershire, England, who has the original in his collection.

NORBORNE BERKELEY,
LORD BOTETOURT

THE governor was expected.

Virginians had read in their *Gazette* three weeks before, on October 6, 1768, among the freshest news from London, an item that dated back to July 30: "Yesterday Lord Botetourt kissed His Majesty's hand at St. James's on being appointed Governour of Virginia."

Even the next report from London failed to prepare the colonials for the splendor in store for them: The prosperous tobacco merchants in London, who were among the world's leading men of trade, had given "an elegant entertainment" at the George and Vulture Tavern for the court favorite Norborne Berkeley, Baron de Botetourt. In the farewell party were "several Noblemen and other persons of distinction."

The coming of the new immigrant was not a mere social event to Virginians, who had been without a governor since the death of Francis Fauquier, more than six months before. And those were rather uneasy times. The Stamp Act crisis was only three years past, and new taxes, under the Townshend Acts, had aroused the colonies. A few months earlier the Virginia Assembly had expressed sympathy with the people of Massachusetts, who had sent out a circular to protest the newest taxation; the Virginians had announced their "fixed resolution" to join other colonies in this struggle.

Thus, on October 25, 1768, when the 60-gun man-of-war *Rippon*, eight weeks out of Portsmouth, dropped anchor in Hampton Roads, the colony was prepared to welcome its new ruler with more than passing interest. The next morning, when he went ashore at the plantation house Little England on York River, a few cannon banged in salute. About noon, when His Lordship had stretched his legs for a few hours, he went on upriver and reached Williamsburg near sunset.

The town turned out to greet him. He was met by the Council, Speaker of the House of Burgesses Peyton Randolph, Attorney General John Randolph and Treasurer Robert Carter Nicholas, and went to the Capitol, where he sat in the Council Chamber while his commission was read, took his oath of office, swore in the councilors, and went with them to a banquet at the Raleigh Tavern. The town was illuminated in his honor, and as the *Gazette* said, Virginians liked Botetourt at first sight: "All ranks of people vied with each other in testifying their gratitude and joy that a Nobleman of such distinguished merit and abilities is appointed to preside over, and live among, them."

The governor called the Assembly into session almost immediately, and presented such a spectacle as his coach rumbled from the Palace toward the Capitol that he was known among generations of Virginians as a "man of parade." Williamsburg saw him in all this magnificence by the grace of King George III, who had donated the coach and horses— clearly intending that Virginians see what a proper governor should look like.

People stared at the coach, "a clumsy machine, and enormously heavy," the weight of two ordinary farm wagons. It was gilded everywhere, even to the rims of the iron tires on its wheels, and bore the arms of Virginia on each side. The driver and footmen were English servants. The horses were gray Hanoverians, wearing silver-mounted harness.

The governor's ceremonial manner did not cease when he reached the Council Chamber of the Capitol. One Virginian thought his speech "pretty long," but his "deportment was dignified and his delivery was solemn." Men who had seen George III on ceremonial occasions thought Botetourt's manner like that of his monarch: "He spoke very slow, with long pauses. His costume was . . . handsome and rich; the coat of a light red color, of gold thread tissue . . . His Lordship . . . was in much greater state than any Governor of Virginia had ever before displayed."

Then about fifty, Botetourt was of the family of the early Virginia governor Sir William Berkeley and was said to be of "amiable character" and remarkable for his devotion to duty. He had missed few sessions of the House of Commons in twenty years, before his rise to the House of Lords.

There was more in Norborne Berkeley's recent life than Williamsburg knew. He had left as the storm center of a court scandal, and, while he crossed the Atlantic in the *Rippon,* letters in London newspapers lampooned him. He had speculated in an unincorporated brass company, and, when this firm came near bankruptcy and Botetourt's private estates were endangered, he tried to save himself by having the company hastily incorporated.

Lord Chatham, who was Keeper of the Privy Seal, resisted this effort to defraud creditors illegally and Botetourt then attempted blackmail. If Chatham did not comply, he said, he would call for an investigation of his lax administration. The frightened Chatham then agreed to resign his Seal to others temporarily so that Botetourt might avoid ruin. Members of the House uncovered the scheme, however; the metal firm went bankrupt, and Botetourt lost his fortune.

The acidulous Horace Walpole, at the time of the farewell party in London, said Botetourt was "like patience on a monument, smiling in grief. He is totally ruined." Walpole thought Williamsburg was in for an experience. His comment went far to explain Botetourt's regal airs in the Virginia capital: "To Virginia he cannot be indifferent; he must turn their heads somehow or other. If his graces do not captivate them, he will enrage them to fury." Walpole also saw beneath Botetourt's benign exterior. "I take all his douceur to be enamelled on iron."

George III rescued his favorite from poverty by giving him the governorship of Virginia, as a replacement for the nonresident incumbent, Sir Jeffrey Amherst. This change set off a newspaper offensive against the minister, Lord Bute. One jingle in the *Chronicle* assailed Bute:

> Then thus unto a Scribe he spoke
> (A man at top o' th' trade)
> Lord Bow-at-Court has serv'd me well,
> 'Tis fit he should be paid.

But of these things, Virginians knew nothing. They were unaware of London gossip that the sociable bachelor had once been married to a Miss Christie, a ceremony ruled illegal because it had been performed in the Roman Catholic Church; he was said to have a son by this marriage.

In Williamsburg all was serene. Botetourt wrote the Board of Trade that conditions in Virginia left little to be desired: "in appearance nothing can be better," and he was "at present upon the very best Terms with all. I like their stile exceedingly and augur well of every thing that is to happen." Williamsburg officials thought they had done rather well in preparing the Palace for Botetourt's coming: "Many pieces of furniture are in the best taste, and we believe most of the liquors are good in their kind. The Slaves are reckon'd orderly and valuable. . . ."

But Williamsburg was not London and Norborne Berkeley was accustomed to better things, as he confided to the Board of Trade: "As my Servants cou'd not keep up with me and the Palace was Totally unprovided with every thing, I have been asked every day to dinner by the principal Gentlemen. . . ." Botetourt soon found that he had been mistaken in bringing his white servants, and "found it convenient and necessary" to buy and hire slaves to attend him in the Palace and "do the Drudgery without doors."

The honeymoon with the Virginians continued. Botetourt exchanged speeches and greetings with the mayor and aldermen and common council of Williamsburg on public occasions, with the Assembly, and with the president and professors of the College of William and Mary. The college was a special favorite:

> The college of William and Mary does honour to this great country, ages unborn will feel its effect, and . . . you cannot oblige me more than by marking out any plan by which I may be enabled to contribute to its advancement and prosperity.

He and the college soon devised a likely form of patronage, and Botetourt gave two gold medals annually "for the honour and encouragement of literary merit"—the first of their kind in America.

Botetourt had been in office hardly six months before the spell was broken. The spring session of the Assembly opened in May, and its members were in a defiant mood. Massachusetts had ignored a Parliamentary ban on its Townshend Acts circular to other colonies, and in retaliation Parliament had invoked an ancient British law: Those accused of treason outside the kingdom should be taken to England for trial. This quarrel was in the minds of Virginians, though they gave no sign of it as the Assembly opened. The ceremonial forms were more elaborate than ever.

The burgesses took oaths of office before the governor in the Council Chamber and returned to the House, only to be recalled to the chamber by Botetourt, who directed them to go back and elect a Speaker. Back in their own chamber the burgesses elected Peyton Randolph unanimously. The symbolic mace was taken from beneath the big table and placed on its top. Then the burgesses went back to inform Botetourt, who approved their choice. Speaker Randolph then intoned the customary address, claiming the rights and privileges of the House, including exemption from arrest and protection of their estates and especially freedom of speech and debate. Botetourt gave his promise to observe and defend these rights. The governor's speech included an assuring passage: "I have nothing to ask, but that you consider well, and follow exactly, without Passion or Prejudice, the real Interests of those you have the Honour to represent; they are most certainly consistent with the Prosperity of Great-Britain. . . ." In short, what was good for the Crown was good for Virginia.

Thomas Jefferson, who was serving his first term in this Assembly, was assigned to write a response to the "very affectionate" message of the governor. He ended it with the hope that "Providence, and the royal pleasure, may long continue His Lordship the happy ruler of a free and happy people." This memorial suffered a revision by Robert Carter Nicholas, largely because it was too brief, and the older burgess did his work, as Jefferson said, "with amplification enough"; the final message lacked the grace of the original, but Jefferson was not yet acknowledged as the most inspired of Virginia pamphleteers.

There were other important men in this Assembly: Patrick Henry, Richard Bland, Edmund Pendleton, Richard Henry Lee, Benjamin Harrison, Thomas Nelson, Jr., and George Washington, a burgess from Fairfax County who had come with a proposal for action written by George Mason.

The Assembly proceeded uneventfully until, on the ninth day its manner changed. As burgesses had done before them in the Stamp Act controversy, they passed a set of resolves. They denied the right of Parliament to tax the colonies, since that power was reserved for the Assemblies themselves. They insisted upon their right to petition the king and their freedom to communicate with other colonies on common problems without interference. They assured the king of their complete loyalty, but begged that he intervene to avoid "dangers and miseries" that would follow if Americans were dragged to England for trial.

Botetourt had no alternative. Like every other royal governor in America, he had been ordered to dissolve any Assembly that so much as approved the circular from Massachusetts. Botetourt did this duty with restraint.

When he heard what was happening in the House, the governor hurried from the Palace to the Capitol, apparently once more in the awesome coach. He sent the Clerk of the Council, Nathaniel Walthoe, to the House of Burgesses. Since the House had not completed its resolutions, Walthoe was barred for a few minutes until action was complete.

The burgesses, called to the Council Chamber, found the governor this time in a plain scarlet suit, surrounded by the Council. Peyton Randolph stopped at a respectful distance, with other members behind him. An onlooker described the brief scene: "A solemn pause of a minute or two ensued, when the Governor, with an assumed stern countenance and with considerable power said: 'Mr. Speaker, and Gentlemen of the House of Burgesses, I have heard of your Resolves, and augur ill of their Effect. You have made it my Duty to dissolve you; and you are dissolved accordingly.' "

The former members of the dissolved House moved along the street to the Raleigh Tavern and went into informal session in the Apollo Room, where they named Peyton Randolph moderator and organized a boycott of British goods. The body drew up an "Association," agreeing not to import or use British goods until the unpopular duties had been repealed. The action was largely based upon the proposal Washington had brought, which was drawn by his neighbor George Mason. It was signed by eighty-nine delegates.

Even this association did not seem to strain relations between Botetourt and his people. In the same month he presided over a Queen's Birthday Ball at the Palace, attended by "a very numerous and polite company of Ladies and Gentlemen." The governor also continued his friendly visits with Williamsburg leaders. One burgess overheard Botetourt in a conversation in the home of Robert Carter Nicholas one evening, saying that he would write Lord Hillsborough, who was Secretary of State for the Colonies, and tell him that unless the "obnoxious acts" were repealed, he wanted to be recalled.

Whatever His Lordship's true feelings, his people were loyal and affectionate, and saw him in some charming moments. Botetourt seems to have been a lonely man in the Palace. One August evening in 1769, when the town belle, Anne Blair, was singing on the steps of her family home with friends, a figure came up the street with a candle lantern and stopped at the gate to listen. The singers fell quiet, and then heard the governor's voice: "Charming! Charming! proceed for God's sake, or I go Home directly." Botetourt then sat on the Blair steps with the amateur chorus for half an hour before the party broke up and all went home in the dark.

Two months later, on the king's birthday, the governor gave "an elegant ball at the Palace, where there was a numerous and very brilliant assembly of Ladies and Gentlemen."

Near the end of the year, the governor attended a very different kind of ball. This one was given in his honor by the House of Burgesses at the Capitol, and to make the point that the Virginia boycott against imported British goods was in effect, about one hundred ladies wore homespun gowns, a performance that led William Rind in the *Gazette* to a patriotic cry: "It were to be wished that all assemblies of American Ladies would exhibit a like example of public virtue and private economy, so amiably united."

The Assembly that winter gave no sign of rebelliousness, and Botetourt's opening address was all geniality and forgiveness. He predicted that Parliament would remove taxes on glass, paper, and colors (he failed to include tea), and made jokes at the expense of the ministers in London who were not, he reminded, immortal; their successors might be more lenient.

Botetourt then said he would willingly be declared "infamous" if he failed to plead the cause of the colonies on every occasion, whatever the issue. He won the burgesses completely, and young Jefferson, at least, thought His Lordship was sincere. The Assembly replied that Botetourt's devotion to the colony had endeared him to them all, but that his generous and noble declarations demanded their warmest and most grateful acknowledgements. The governor was applauded throughout Virginia. Only in London did officials remark that he had gone too far; he had managed to sound much like a potential colonial rebel himself.

At the height of his popularity, when he had been in office not quite two years, Botetourt became ill, "indisposed, for some days, with a fever." He seemed to recover, but within two weeks, about 1 A.M. of October 15, 1770, Norborne Berkeley died. By tradition, his last words were spoken to his intimate friend Robert Carter Nicholas.

Some months before, Nicholas had said: "My Lord, I think you will be very unwilling to die."

"Why do you say that?"

"Because, you are so social in your nature, and are so beloved, and have so many good things about you, that you must be loath to leave them."

On the night of his death, Botetourt is said to have sent for Nicholas, who came into the governor's bedroom:

"What is it, Sir?"

"Nothing," Botetourt said, "but to let you see that I resign those good things that you spoke of with as much composure as I enjoyed them."

He then grasped Nicholas by the hand "with warmth, and instantly expired."

The *Gazette*'s obituary spoke for the colony: "Suffice it then to inform such Parts of the World as were strangers to his transcendent Merits, that Virginia, in his Fall, sorely laments the Loss of the best of Governors, and the best of Men."

Botetourt's funeral was the grandest Williamsburg had seen. More than ten years earlier His Lordship had made a will, asking that he be buried, very simply, in England's Stoke Church, "and carried to my grave in the most private manner by my Servants." The ceremony of Friday, October 19, 1770, was not simple.

At 1 P.M. the bells of Bruton Parish Church, the college, and the Capitol began tolling, and an hour later invited mourners assembled at the Palace. At 3 P.M. the hearse led the procession along Palace Green to the church, between ranks of militiamen from the city and adjoining counties. Two mutes walked in front, and three on each side of the hearse, in their traditional role as mourners. Alongside the mutes were the pallbearers, including six members of the Council and Speaker Peyton Randolph and Richard Bland of the House of Burgesses.

Botetourt's servants came next, followed by clergymen and college professors, the church clerk and organist, the college faculty, and the mayor, aldermen, and councilmen of the city, with the mace borne before them. After them came "Gentlemen of the Law, and Clerk of the General Court, Ushers, Students and Scholars, of William and Mary college, all having white hatbands and gloves," and then the general crowd behind, "two and two."

The coffin was carried into the church, where the altar, pulpit, and the governor's pew were draped in black. Mr. Woolls conducted the service, and his text, "Put thy trust in God," as the *Gazette* reported, "joined to the deep affliction felt by the whole audience for the loss of such an excellent man, and so good a Governour, drew tears from many."

The procession then moved to the college, where the governor was buried in a vault as the militia fired three volleys. The remains were enclosed in three coffins, one of lead, an inside one of some inferior wood, and one of black walnut. Crimson velvet covered the exterior, and there were eight silver handles and sixteen silver escutcheons. A large silver plate was engraved with the governor's name, date of death, and age.

The next year the burgesses ordered "an elegant Statue" of Botetourt from the well-known London sculptor Richard Hayward, whose works had been placed in Westminster Abbey. Hayward used a wax likeness of Botetourt as a guide in carving His Lordship's face and achieved what Virginians thought a "very strong" likeness. Hayward's work created a stir among the "Curious and Artists" of London, and was finally shipped to Virginia in 1773.

Hayward's assistant, John Hirst, set up the statue between the wings of the Capitol, surrounded by an iron railing, and the ornate work was "universally admired." Even during the Revolution, when statues of George III were demolished in America, the figure of Botetourt escaped harm. Revolutionary Virginia leaders cared for the statue and had it cleaned regularly until 1779, when the capital was about to move to Richmond.

In 1786 the statue was still in good condition, but during the nineties it was "shamefully defaced"; vandals knocked off Botetourt's head, nose, and one hand. In 1801 the college moved Botetourt to its grounds and repaired the figure, though the right hand was lost. On the eve of the Civil War, when the Wren Building burned, the statue was still in place, and "the mossy coat of old Botetourt . . . unscathed." The figure stood briefly before the mental hospital during the Civil War period, but was finally returned to the College of William and Mary. It stands in the Earl Gregg Swem Library of the college today, its inscription still proclaiming the spirit that Virginians found in Norborne Berkeley during his brief term as Governor: "Let Wisdom and Justice preside in any Country, The People will rejoice and must be happy."

John Murray, fourth Earl of Dunmore, by Sir Joshua Reynolds. Reproduced by permission of the owner, Mrs. Charles James Murray; on loan to the Scottish National Portrait Gallery, Edinburgh.

JOHN MURRAY, LORD DUNMORE

LITTLE more than three weeks after the news of the battles of Lexington and Concord arrived in Williamsburg, three violent storms swept over the town. Hailstones "as big as pigeons eggs" smashed some seven hundred windowpanes in the buildings of the College of William and Mary and in the Palace, pelted the governor's fishpond, lacerated the young leaves of his Scotch linden trees, and rattled like musket fire on the cannon he had recently placed at his gates.

The storms broke upon an uneasy capital on the eve of war. The Second Continental Congress, sitting in Philadelphia, would soon choose George Washington as chief of its armies. An association of Virginia planters and merchants was boycotting British goods. It was only a month since the governor, Lord Dunmore, had taken the colony's gunpowder from the Magazine on Market Square and set off a commotion in Virginia. Less than a month later the governor, Lady Dunmore, and their children took sudden leave of Williamsburg in the dark of night.

The governor was a lively Scot, John Murray, fourth Earl of Dunmore, Viscount Fincastle, and Baron of Blair, of Moulin and of Tillymont, descended from the royal line of Stuart. He was born in 1730, had become a peer at the age of twenty, had served as an army officer, was at home in fashionable London society, and was fond of hunting and riding. His wife was Charlotte Stuart, a daughter of the Earl of Galloway. In the House of Lords, Dunmore had sided with the Whigs and had said somewhat naïvely that the troublesome Americans "would soon be quiet, if they were only left to themselves." In 1770, as the break with the colonies drew near, he left his pleasant life in London to become governor of New York.

One admiring New Yorker described him on his arrival as looking younger than his forty years: "Short, Strong built, well shaped with a most frank and open countenance, easy and affable in his manners, very temperate, and a great lover of field Sports, indefatigable and constant in his pursuit of them." An earlier portrait by Sir Joshua Reynolds reveals Dunmore as a stubby and kilted young soldier with a plump face, hardly looking the part of a warrior.

He had ruled the colony of New York happily for less than a year when he was unexpectedly transferred to Virginia. Dunmore was angry despite the higher salary offered in the larger, more prosperous colony.

He was to be Virginia's last royal governor, and there never had been a more reluctant one. He offered to exchange places with the incoming governor of New York, William Tryon, and on the night when he gave up his post, Dunmore drank heavily, had a fist fight with an ardent Whig, insulted Tryon, and once shouted: "Damn Virginia. Did I ever seek it? Why is it forced upon me? I ask'd for New York—New York I took, & they have robbd me of it without my Consent." He tried in vain to have his appointment changed, since Virginia's climate was so bad that he would be obliged to live there without his family. That he found a tiresome prospect in a country with little or no society; without family or society he doubted that he would be able to stay any length of time.

His Lordship tactlessly wrote President William Nelson of the Virginia Council that he had asked London to leave him in New York because he was so fond of it, which did little to inspire a warm welcome for him. The New York publisher James Rivington put Dunmore's distaste for southward migration more plainly: "He is a Chearfull free liver & an Anguish Climate will ill suit his convivial Disposition."

It was fortunate that Virginians did not hear most of the New York gossip about Dunmore. Lieutenant Governor Colden found him "a capricious ignorant Lord," and one diarist noted that Dunmore was "a very weak Man in Matters of Business . . . so helpless a Mortal, utterly ignorant of the Nature of Business of all Kinds." Colonel John Bradstreet, who had distinguished himself in frontier warfare, condemned Dunmore as "a silly extravagant buck" who gave such vile toasts at a public banquet that his friends were "sunk into silent Astonishment and the Company ashamed of him."

Other opinions were more in line with Dunmore's reputation in England. One New Yorker said he was "affable, polite and good natured," and another, "a verry honest good Man & I think would have made us all very happy."

At least one Dunmore story that reached Virginia delighted gossips but did not augur well for the dignity of the new administration. It appeared that His Lordship "with a set of Drunken companions" while roistering one night had raided the stables of Chief Justice Horsmanden, destroyed a coach, and cut off the tails of some horses.

But at first, all was well in Williamsburg. Dunmore's servants, dogs and baggage arrived ahead of him, in August, 1771. An impressive shipment came ashore at Burwell's Ferry on the James, among them a huge brown and white English bulldog named Glasgow, several pointers, and probably packs of hounds. Dunmore himself arrived at Yorktown in late September, dutifully met by the four chief officers of the colony. He was sworn in at the Palace the same day, and in the evening entertained a large party at dinner. The town was illuminated, in the custom of welcoming new governors.

Following precedent, and at the Council's suggestion, Dunmore dissolved the Assembly and called for new elections. He had come without his wife and children, and frequently entertained. George Washington dined at the Palace soon after the governor's arrival. In October a Palace ball celebrated the anniversary of the coronation of George II; the Raleigh Tavern was opened to the public and "Plenty of Liquor was given to the Populace." Within five months of his coming, two new Virginia counties, Dunmore and Fincastle, were named for the governor. Still, with the benevolent Botetourt in mind, one Williamsburg man wrote of Dunmore, "The knowledge we have of him at present is negative, he bears no simlitude to his Predecessor."

The only public criticism of the new governor came from a distance, in a South Carolina newspaper bearing a dispatch from London. It was said that Dunmore had begun in Virginia with "Negligence and Disregard" of his duties: "His Lordship was hardly ever visited, very difficult of Access and frequently could not be spoken with. . . . These spirited Colonists could not bear these haughty Airs, but deputed one of their Lawyers to remonstrate against this supercilious Behavior. . . . At first he stormed, but at last he agreed to name Office-Hours, when every Person concerned might attend on Business." Thereafter, the report went, things had gone on "very peaceably" in Williamsburg, and Dunmore became more tractable, "Thanks to the true *American* Spirit of Liberty."

Whether this was mere gossip, or whether resolute Virginians had reformed Dunmore, harmony prevailed. The governor began to enlarge the College of William and Mary and had Thomas Jefferson draw plans; only the foundations were complete when the onset of the war halted the project. (Jefferson may also have drawn plans for remodeling the Palace at Dunmore's request.) The governor postponed calling the Assembly into session for several months. It was said that he feared Virginians might follow restless northern colonies in their defiant course.

He may have been too busy settling into his new household for affairs of state, for the new executive had come in style, importing a vast stock of furnishings for the twenty-five rooms of the Palace and an array of goods and chattels that would have done justice to an imperial establishment. By the time he left Virginia, at any rate, his collection of paintings included "a number" by Sir Peter Lely. There was a library of thirteen hundred volumes, and there were assorted musical instruments, three organs, a pianoforte, and a harpsichord. There were blacksmith's tools, and a supply of mahogany and tools for four cabinetmakers. There was a large collection of arms, many of them antique.

The well-stocked cellar, even at his departure, held forty-two pipes and hogsheads of wine, mostly Madeira; twelve gross of bottled wines, claret, burgundy, champagne, port, hock, sherry, and others; 480 gallons of old rum and much "common rum."

In the Palace park were 154 head of cattle and 150 sheep; there were nineteen horses—and two coaches, a chariot, a phaeton, two one-horse chaises, and carts and wagons. Dunmore had a dozen indentured servants, not to mention fifty-six slaves.

The growing crisis in colonial affairs had no apparent effect on Dunmore's friendship with Washington. The two were the same age and had common interests, including an appetite for western lands. Dunmore's enthusiasm was fired by Washington's descriptions of rich frontier valleys and river bottoms, and they planned a trip of inspection beyond the Blue Ridge for the summer of 1773; Dunmore was to visit Mount Vernon on the way. The governor's illness prevented the journey, but he did manage to tour the "back country" that year with another companion, probably the land prospector, John Connolly. It was perhaps then that Dunmore acquired his western lands, 2,600 acres near Warm Springs in Berkeley

County, and 3,400 more in Hampshire County. Washington did not record his own opinion of Dunmore at this time, but Connolly wrote the master of Mount Vernon praising the governor as "a Gentleman of benevolence & universal Charity, & not unacquainted with either Man or the world." Washington must have agreed, for he dined with Dunmore occasionally when he was in Williamsburg and came to know him well. On a single day in their early acquaintance Washington noted in his diary that he "Breakfasted, Dined and Suppd at the Governor's." Washington found Dunmore an exceptionally able man and, after the Revolution had begun, wrote of him as potentially "the most formidable enemy America has."

Dunmore first clashed with the Assembly in 1773, over the issue of counterfeiting. A ring of clever criminals in Pittsylvania County, masterminded by a North Carolinian, was turning out bogus paper notes, dollars, and doubloons, and when this was discovered, and warnings were published, the colony's economy was virtually paralyzed. The governor was urged to convene the Assembly to deal with the problem. With the consent of Peyton and John Randolph and Robert Carter Nicholas, Dunmore issued a warrant for the arrest of the counterfeiters and sent Captain John Lightfoot to bring them in. Lightfoot soon paraded five prisoners into the capital. He had caught them in a shop equipped with dies for making spurious coins and equipment for making paper money of such quality that even its watermarks were almost identical to those of genuine Virginia issue. All but one of the suspects went to jail.

The burgesses stunned Dunmore with a protest over his handling of the counterfeiters. They conceded that action had been essential, but objected to his dragging the prisoners from their home county for trial, in a way reminiscent of Parliament's threat to carry rebellious Americans across the Atlantic for hearings. The tone of the protest was respectful but firm. Dunmore's proceedings had been "different from the usual mode, it being regular that an examining court on criminals should be held, either in the County where the fact was committed, or the arrest made. . . . The duty we owe our constituents obliges us, my Lord, to be as attentive to the safety of the innocent as we are desirous of punishing the guilty." Such violations of the ordinary processes, the legislators said, endangered the "safety of innocent men."

The governor replied irritably that if his conduct could be proven wrong he would not repeat it, but otherwise, "I shall continue to exercise the powers I am invested with, whensoever the exigencies of government and the good of the country requires such exertion." He wrote to London that "there was but one person who has the least knowledge of the laws of this Colony," and that though most of the burgesses had signed the insolent message to him, there was "hardly a man of sense" who did not approve of his method of handling the counterfeiters.

A few days later a more serious matter arose in the House. Jefferson's brother-in-law, Dabney Carr, proposed a Virginia Committee of Correspondence to inform the Assembly of affairs in England and in other colonies, since many were alarmed "by various rumors and reports tending to deprive them of their ancient, legal and constitutional rights." Leaders in other colonies welcomed the unanimous passage of this Virginia resolution and Samuel Adams predicted that it would gladden "the hearts of all who are friends of liberty."

Dunmore wrote to England that the burgesses "seem at least obliquely in some degree to censure my conduct." As to the resolution for a Committee of Correspondence, which was soon to be adopted as a colonial pattern, Dunmore wrote only, "There are some resolves which show a little ill humour in the House of Burgesses, but I thought them so insignificant that I took no matter of notice of them." He did not see that a long step toward uniting the colonies had been taken.

Still there was no estrangement between the governor and colonial leaders. Washington dined with Dunmore now and then, and in November, 1773, about a month before the Boston Tea Party, visited the governor at his farm, Porto Bello, on Queens Creek near Williamsburg.

Dunmore's popularity grew in the troubled spring of 1774. In February his beautiful wife arrived with her children, and was saluted at Yorktown by cannon, one of which wounded several men when it fired unexpectedly. News of Lady Dunmore's arrival reached Williamsburg swiftly, and men, women, and children flocked down the road to meet her. She entered the city in the evening of February 26 to find houses and public buildings illuminated.

There was a fireworks display in her honor a few nights later. The *Gazette* published odes in her honor, and officials gave her a more spirited welcome than they had her husband. Men saw at a glance what Gouvernour Morris had noted in New York, that she was "a very elegant woman [who] looks, speaks and moves and is a lady. Her daughters are fine sprightly sweet girls. Goodness of heart flushes from them in every look.

How it is possible . . . my Lord Dunmore could so long deprive himself of those pleasures he must enjoy in such a family?"

Dunmore had delayed because Virginia's climate was thought to be dangerous for women and children, but there were soon indications—bits of gossip—that he had other reasons. The Italian friend of Jefferson, Philip Mazzei, also much impressed by the ladies Dunmore, wrote: "At first sight, it seemed to me that she deserved a better husband, and I soon learned that I was not mistaken." A soldier who dined at the Palace about this time, Lieutenant Augustine Prevost, reported that Dunmore was "a Consumate Rake & does not pay that attention to his Lady that she seems to deserve. She is extremely jealous I am told . . . of a young Lady, whom it was reported was very Dear to him previous to her Ladyship arrival." Colonel Landon Carter of Sabine Hall, who also observed the couple, concluded: "His Lady really agreeable & more fond of her husband Perhaps than the politeness of the day allows of."

The colony's preoccupation with the ruling family was interrupted in May. An official ball of welcome for Lady Dunmore by the House of Burgesses was planned for May 27 in the Capitol. But about a week earlier the city learned of the closing of the port of Boston, in retaliation for the Boston Tea Party. On May 24 the burgesses took unexpected action. Robert Carter Nicholas offered a resolution: "This House, being deeply impressed with apprehension of the great dangers . . . to British America from the hostile invasion of the city of Boston . . . deem it highly necessary that the said first day of June be set apart . . . as a day of fasting, humiliation and prayer, devoutly to implore the divine interposition, for averting . . . the evils of civil war."

The resolution passed unanimously and was ordered published.

The next evening, May 25, Washington dined with Dunmore and spent the evening in the Palace. On the morning of May 26 the two rode out to Porto Bello for breakfast, and when they returned Dunmore read the resolution of the House in the *Gazette.* In midafternoon a messenger interrupted the session of the burgesses: "The Governor commands the House to attend his Excellency immediately, in the Council Chamber." Dunmore dismissed them with a few words: "Mr. Speaker and Gentlemen of the House of Burgesses, I have in my hand a paper published by order of your House, conceived in such terms as reflect highly upon his Majesty and the Parliament of Great Britain; which makes it necessary for me to dissolve you; and you are dissolved accordingly."

Even now the social amenities were observed, in this strangest of revolutions, and the next night, May 27, the burgesses held their ball for Lady Dunmore as planned.

On June 1 the burgesses marched solemnly down Duke of Gloucester Street, following a mace bearer and Speaker Peyton Randolph to Bruton Parish Church, where they prayed for peace. More than two weeks later Washington dined in the Palace once more; it was probably his last visit to the building.

The burgesses called for a congress of representatives from all the colonies, the first official body of a colony to do so, and also created a Virginia convention to meet in Williamsburg in August. Dunmore, reporting these moves to London, said that many families of influence in Virginia opposed this recklessness, but that even the most powerful "will avail little against the turbulence and prejudice which prevails throughout the country."

The purpose of the August session was to choose Virginia delegates to the congress in Philadelphia. It also considered a document by Thomas Jefferson that would hurry the crisis, *A Summary View of the Rights of British America.* Virginia was moving swiftly toward leadership of the revolution.

Just as matters in Williamsburg went beyond Dunmore's control, warfare broke out on the frontier. The governor was exasperated by the turn of events that opened this front in Virginia. For more than ten years colonists had blithely ignored a royal edict banning settlement beyond the crest of the Alleghenies, and cabins had been built in the forbidden Indian hunting grounds at the rate of more than ten thousand a year. The Indians had retaliated with ferocity.

Dunmore reported dejectedly to London. Government power was "insufficient to restrain the Americans," who were a wild and intractable people: "they do and will remove as their avidity and restlessness incite them. They acquire no attachment to Place; but wandering about seems engrafted in their nature; they do not conceive that Government has any right to forbid their taking possession of a vast tract of country."

The governor was forced into an effort to halt the burning and massacres on the frontier. In May he had sent his agent John Connolly to seize Fort Pitt in the name of Virginia and rechristen it Fort Dunmore, which did not endear him to Pennsylvanians. Then, while the Virginia Convention met in Williamsburg and Philadelphia prepared to welcome the Continental Congress, Dunmore rode northwestward toward his newly captured fort. He had ordered General Andrew Lewis to march from southwest Virginia with eleven hundred men while he, at the head of the second army, would push west from Fort Dunmore, accompanied by such frontier veterans as George Rogers Clark and Michael Cresap. The hardy Scottish huntsman took the march cheerfully, walking with his troops and carrying his own knapsack.

Lewis and his army were surprised by Shawnees under Chief Cornstalk in the battle of Point Pleasant, and lost forty-six dead and many wounded before the Indians withdrew. Dunmore, who was then more than one hundred miles upriver from the battle, was reported to have leaned with an ear close above the water and said that he heard distant gunfire. When the two armies joined Chief Cornstalk saw that he was outnumbered and sued for peace. Dunmore signed a treaty with the Shawnees at Scioto in the Ohio country, a ceremony made memorable by a message from an absent Mingo chief, Logan, who refused to come to the conference, but sent Dunmore his statement, complaining of the treachery of white men. It was an oration that became familiar to generations of American schoolboys:

> I appeal to any white man to say, if ever he entered Logan's cabin hungry, and he gave him not meat; if ever he came cold and naked, and he clothed him not. During the course of the last long and bloody war, Logan remained idle in his cabin, an advocate for peace. Such was my love for the whites, that my countrymen pointed out as they passed, and said, "Logan is the friend of white men." I had even thought to have lived with you, but for the injuries of one man. Col. Cresap, the last spring, in cold blood, and unprovoked, murdered all the relations of Logan, not sparing even my women and children. There runs not a drop of my blood in the veins of any living creature. This called on me for revenge. I have sought it: I have killed many: I have fully glutted my vengeance. For my country, I rejoice at the beams of peace. But do not harbour a thought that mine is the joy of fear. Logan never felt fear. He will not turn on his heel to save his life. Who is there to mourn for Logan?— Not one.

Jefferson later wrote: "I may challenge the whole orations of Demosthenes and Cicero, . . . to produce a single passage, superior to the speech of Logan, a Mingo chief, to Lord Dunmore."

Dunmore's war had not been a classic example, and His Lordship had reached the scene after its one battle had been fought, but he had left the comforts of his palace to travel the mountain wilderness and dictate a truce. Washington, who had a few weeks earlier thought a general frontier war inevitable, thought Dunmore's peace "conclusive and certain, and I dare say it will be of lasting duration." Patriots would later charge that Dunmore instigated the war to divert attention from the quarrels with London, and even that he betrayed Lewis' army into ambush at Point Pleasant, but there was none of this when Dunmore returned in triumph to Williamsburg, bringing Shawnee hostages with him.

His expedition was immortalized in rhyme:

> Our Royal Governor Dunmore, he being of high renown
> With fifteen hundred jovial men, he marched towards their town
> With a full resolution, to slay both old and young
> For all the barbarous actions, the savages had done.

The president and faculty of the College of William and Mary said: "And, may you always feel the enlivening Pleasure of reading in the Countenances around you, wherever you turn your Eyes, such Expressions of Affection as can be derived only from applauding and grateful Hearts!" The Council and officials of Norfolk sent a tribute to the governor for his "seasonable and vigorous Exertion," applauded his generous peace treaty, and exulted in the happiness of settlers on the frontier. The Virginia Council felt "unfeigned Pleasure" and said of his lenient dealing with the Indians: "You have taught them a lesson, which the savage Breast was a Stranger to, that Clemency and Mercy are not incompatible with Power."

Dunmore also returned to another pleasure. Lady Dunmore had given birth to a daughter the day before his arrival from the mountains. She was named, symbolically, Virginia and was christened on the queen's birthday, January 19, 1775. The ball at the Palace that evening marked the peak of Dunmore's popularity in Virginia.

There was one note of bitterness for Dunmore in the aftermath of his victory. Lord Dartmouth, the secretary of state, wrote from London, critical of the handling of affairs in Williamsburg and on the frontier; he urged firm control of Virginians. On Christmas Eve, 1774, Dunmore wrote Dartmouth to explain that Virginia was not at all what it seemed from Whitehall. He defended his frontier campaign and painted a dark picture of affairs in the colony. The associations, he said, were enforcing their boycott of British luxury goods with the "greatest rigour," haling violators before their committees and exposing them to "Outrageous and lawless" mobs. Even more ominous, Virginia was now an armed camp: "Every County, besides, is now Arming a Company of Men . . . to be employed against Government if occasion require. . . . There is not a Justice of Peace in Virginia that Acts except as a Committee Man; The abolishing the Courts of Justice was the first Step taken, in which the men of fortune and preeminence Joined equally with the lowest and meanest."

Dunmore proposed harsh remedies. Britain should cut off all trade, blockade ports in every colony, and starve Americans into submission. Unfortunately for his relations with Virginians, the letter caused a sensation in London, and not long afterwards was published in the *Virginia Gazette*. It provoked furious reactions. One reader said the letter "galls the very sole of them."

Thus, in April of 1775, when there was bloodshed in the north, and men had taken up arms in every colony, and Patrick Henry's "liberty or death" speech in Richmond still rang through the country, Dunmore's days in his Palace approached an end. Like governors of other colonies, he kept watch on the Public Magazine. As he wrote Lord Dartmouth, he thought it "prudent to remove some gunpowder . . . where it lay exposed to any attempt that might be made to seize it, & I had reason to believe the People intended to take that step."

About April 15 he took the keys of the Powder Magazine from its keeper, John Miller. When the town learned of that, local militiamen stood guard for a few nights, until they wearied of the long duty and abandoned their posts. When these volunteers left the Magazine unguarded, Dunmore moved. Fifteen British marines from a warship in the York had been hiding in the wooded park behind the Palace for several days, and at about three o'clock on the morning of April 21, Lieutenant Henry Collins led them to the Magazine, where they hauled off a cartload of powder. They were seen at their work and drums beat the alarm in the streets. The sleepy militia came back to arms, and a noisy crowd gathered at the courthouse.

The next day Mayor John Dixon, the aldermen, and common council, under militia guard, called on Dunmore to demand the powder, and were refused. Dixon protested that the powder was essential to public safety; there might be a slave uprising at any moment. In that case, Dunmore assured the mayor, he would return the powder within half an hour, though in fact the powder was already on its way to Norfolk.

The Williamsburg mob yowled at news of this refusal, but after pleas from Peyton Randolph and Robert Carter Nicholas, it disbanded quietly. Dunmore grew more defiant: he would "declare Freedom to the Slaves, and reduce the City of *Williamsburg* to ashes" if he or his men were insulted. A day later there was more exciting news. Several hundred militiamen had gathered at Fredericksburg, ready to march on the capital and seize the governor. Dunmore repeated his threat—if these men came within thirty miles of the city he would burn the place. He posted armed slaves as Palace guards.

The governor realized that he was helpless in case of attack and wrote Dartmouth: "I shall remain here until I am forced out but . . . I cannot expect to be able to make any effectual Resistance in this place." If things grew worse, he would go aboard a warship at Yorktown.

After a good deal of riding back and forth between Fredericksburg and Williamsburg, the western militia disbanded and wrote a resolution denouncing Dunmore, but advising the armed men to return to their homes, "justly dreading the horrours of a civil war, influenced by motives of the strongest affection to our fellow-subjects of *Great Britain.*"

That did not end the threat. Another band under Patrick Henry was nearer, at Hanover, and was said to be marching for the capital. On April 29 the *Gazette* published Dunmore's letter to Dartmouth urging the blockading of Virginia ports, as well as news of Lexington and Concord. A broadside published by Alexander Purdie in his *Gazette* ended on a stirring note: "The *sword is now drawn,* and God knows when it will be sheathed." Dunmore could not believe the news from Massachusetts; it was, he said, much exaggerated. Still, on the last of April, he sent Lady Dunmore and their children by coach to the frigate *Fowey* at Yorktown.

Payment for the powder (£330, about three times its actual value) was sent to Patrick Henry, but Dunmore was still unsure of himself, and sent a call for forty more marines. The reinforcements outdid themselves on the road from Yorktown, as the *Gazette* reported to the amusement of the populace: "the marines from on board the *Fowey* not being accustomed to marching, were so fatigued when they reached the confines of the Palace, that several of them tumbled into a ditch."

It was a busy day when the marines arrived. Colonel James Innes of the militia hurried through town, trying to gather men to halt the British before they reached the city. At the same time the governor's secretary, Captain Edward Foy, buttonholed men of the town, saying that the marines would merely protect the governor and would not molest the townspeople. Before Innes could muster his company the marines were in position at the Palace, ready to greet Patrick Henry's band if it came. But by now Henry had his money and was satisfied; he dismissed his men and set out for Congress in Philadelphia.

Williamsburg was by no means peaceful, but tensions relaxed. A few citizens broke into the Magazine on May 4 and took the remaining guns, swords, and equipment. The mayor, aldermen, and council announced their "abhorrence of such unlawful proceedings" and urged the culprits to return the arms. Dunmore complained of the hundreds of militiamen in town, "even in the Place where I live Drums are beating, and Men in uniform dresses with Arms are continually in the Streets, which my Authority is no longer able to prevent."

By May 12 the governor thought it safe, despite the martial clatter, for Lady Dunmore's return, and she came back from the *Fowey*, "to the great joy of the inhabitants . . . who have the most unfeigned regard for her Ladyship, and wish her long to live amongst them." The party of marines left town, but set a trap inside the Powder Magazine with loaded shotguns. Dunmore called the Assembly to meet in June; there was news of the American victory at Ticonderoga by Ethan Allen and his Green Mountain Boys, a blow which robbed Dunmore of an estate of more than fifty thousand acres on Lake Champlain.

In the first week of June a few boys, including a son of Mayor Dixon, broke into the Magazine, and three of them were wounded by a blast from the shotgun trap. The Assembly, sharing the town's outrage, sent a committee to inspect the Magazine, and at about the same time, a mob broke in once more and carried off about four hundred guns. Dunmore accused the burgesses themselves of organizing the theft. But, after a long squabble, he turned over the Magazine key to the burgesses at their request.

Dunmore had opened the Assembly session with an offer of conciliation from Lord North, to which the burgesses listened cynically. If the Americans would keep the peace, Dunmore said, they would not be taxed, but would be asked to donate their share of the costs of government voluntarily, "that your justice and liberality may be left to their full scope, and that your gift, if you should be induced to offer any, may be, in the completest manner, free." George III, he said, had "no object nearer his heart than the peace and prosperity of his subjects."

Before the Assembly could draft a reply, Dunmore slipped out of town, at about 2 A.M. of June 8, 1775. Going with him aboard the *Fowey* were his wife and children, Captain Foy, and the Reverend Thomas Gwatkin, master of the grammar school of the College of William and Mary, who was the tutor of his children and private chaplain to Lady Dunmore. Dunmore left a message for the burgesses, saying that he and his family, "in constant danger of falling sacrifices to the blind and unmeasurable fury which has so unaccountably seized upon the minds and understanding of great numbers of People," had thought it prudent to seek safety. He asked the Assembly to continue its business and send members to him from time to time to report on progress. The astonished House could not understand "this extraordinary Step," and wrote: "The City was again at rest and continued composed, till they heard of your Lordship's removal with your family in the *dead of night.*"

The Assembly begged Dunmore to return: "It is with much anxiety we consider the very disagreeable situation of your Lordship's most amiable Lady and family, and should think ourselves happy in being able to restore their perfect tranquility, by removing all their fears." Dunmore refused to budge. The legislators then sent the governor a reply to his opening address; it was written by Thomas Jefferson, and was a flat rejection of Lord North's offer, which the young burgess said, "only changes the form of oppression, without lightening its burden."

Jefferson came to the point: "We have wearied our King with supplications; he has not deigned to answer us; we have appealed to the native honour and justice of the British nation; their efforts in our favour have been hitherto ineffectual. What then remains to be done? That we commit our injuries to the evenhanded justice of that Being, who doeth no wrong; earnestly beseeching him to illuminate the councils and prosper the endeavours of those to whom America hath confided her hopes."

In short, Virginia was ready for war.

Dunmore's response shows that he read the reply accurately: "Gentlemen of the House of Burgesses—It is with real concern I can discover nothing in your address that I think manifests the smallest inclination to, or will be productive of, a reconciliation with the mother country.—Dunmore."

Correspondence continued for a few days between the Capitol and the warship. The Assembly asked Dunmore to turn over powder and muskets for public safety, and he refused shortly; the Palace was the proper place for the colony's muskets, he said, and he would send no powder. When his refusal was published in the *Gazette,* a mob broke into the Palace and took muskets from the foyer. It was on the same day, June 24, that the

General Assembly sat officially for the last time. It had asked Dunmore to sign bills already passed, but he declined to leave the ship; the bills must be brought to him. And he reminded the House that only the governor could disband its session. It disbanded without his consent, Williamsburg's last General Assembly.

Lady Dunmore sailed for home on June 29. A letter in the *Gazette* by "A Planter" bid her farewell: "Your illustrious character fills the breast of Virginia with love and admiration . . . Permit me, with real concern, to lament your departure. . . . Had your lord possessed half the engaging qualities that embellish your mind . . . he would have been the idol of a brave and free people, and not drawn upon himself their detestation."

Williamsburg had seen the last of Dunmore. Throughout the fall and winter he hung about Norfolk, aboard ship, or ashore in Gosport, raiding Kemp's Landing, where, in November, he issued his "Emancipation Proclamation," declaring all slaves and indentured servants to be free if they would join the British cause.

On December 8, 1775, with a force of fewer than three hundred men, he fought a brisk little skirmish at Great Bridge, below Norfolk, and was routed by a larger militia force under Colonel William Woodford. The British losses were seventeen dead and forty-nine wounded. Two Americans were slightly wounded. Dunmore fell back to Norfolk, but when Loyalists deserted him, he abandoned the city and went aboard ship once more. He burned Norfolk's wharves on January 1, 1776, and much of the city was destroyed. In July he fought again, at Gwynn's Island in the Mobjack Bay country, and was defeated by his old lieutenant, now General Andrew Lewis.

Dunmore returned to England, went back into the House of Lords, and, six years after Yorktown, was sent to the Bahamas as governor. He served for nine years there, retired to England, and died in 1809 at the age of seventy-seven.

Virginians did not soon forget him. His loyalty to the Crown during the Revolution, and especially his "Emancipation Proclamation," established his reputation forever in the state, and the happier early days of his administration were forgotten. A wartime letter of Richard Henry Lee stated the theme: "If the administration had searched through the world for a person the best-fitted to ruin their cause & procure union & success for these colonies they could not have found a more complete agent than Lord Dunmore."

George Washington, by Charles Willson Peale. Washington and Lee University, Lexington, Virginia.

11

GEORGE WASHINGTON

WILLIAMSBURG had often seen George Washington, but as he walked to the Capitol to sit in the House of Burgesses for the first time, the city gave him a closer look. It was his twenty-seventh birthday, February 22, 1759, and he was a celebrated man.

Only four years earlier he had buried General Edward Braddock in a wilderness road and ordered wagons of the defeated army to roll over the grave to conceal it from Indians. He had survived to win fame on the frontier, helping to drive back the French and Indians. Now he no longer wore the handsome blue and scarlet uniform of colonel of the First Virginia Regiment; he had shed his regimentals to take up life as a planter and to begin a political career.

He was also a bridegroom of seven weeks with the Williamsburg and Queens Creek properties of Martha Custis Washington to manage as well as his Potomac and western lands.

People in the crowded Capitol looked at young Washington with curiosity and admiration, none of them more carefully than his fellow burgess, George Mercer: "straight as an Indian, measuring 6 feet 2 inches in his stockings, and weighing 175 pounds . . . His frame is padded with well developed muscles, indicating great strength. His bones and joints are large as are his hands and feet. He is wide shouldered . . . is broad across the hips, and has rather long legs and arms." Mercer thought Washington's head rather small for his body, but "gracefully poised on a superb neck." He wore his dark-brown hair in a queue. His prominent nose was long and straight, his "penetrating" blue-gray eyes were wide-set in the long face, which had high cheek bones and "a good firm chin." His clear, rather colorless, skin looked as if it would burn easily in the sun.

To Mercer, Washington's expression was pleasing and benevolent, though commanding. His large mouth was usually firmly closed, but when he smiled or spoke, it revealed defective teeth. Something in the former colonel's manner suggested inner power: "His features are regular and placid with all the muscles of his face under perfect control, tho flexible and expressive of deep feeling when moved by emotions. In conversation he looks you full in the face, is deliberate, deferential and engaging. His voice is agreeable rather than strong."

The tall new burgess from Frederick County was impressive in other ways: "His movements and gestures are graceful, his walk majestic, and he is a splendid horseman." He looked the part of an active gentleman-farmer, a consecrated foxhunter, a veteran Indian fighter and surveyor.

Four days after his arrival the House embarrassed Washington. His friend, John Robinson was in the high-backed Speaker's chair, presiding over routine affairs, when a burgess (whose name did not get into the record) called for a resolution: "that the Thanks of this House be given to George Washington, Esq. . . . for his faithful Services to his Majesty, and this Colony, and for his brave and steady Behaviour, from the first Encroachments and Hostilities of the French and their Indians, to his Resignation, after the happy Reduction of Fort DuQuesne."

By tradition the burgesses roared approval, "Aye!," when Robinson asked the feelings of the House. Washington stood, his face flushing, and stammered something amid applause. Robinson is then said to have called: "Sit down, Mr. Washington. Your modesty is equal to your valor, and that surpasses the power of any language that I possess."

Washington had been placed on an important committee, propositions and grievances, where he would deal with matters in great variety. The vital work of the sessions, Governor Francis Fauquier had explained, was to help prosecute the French and Indian War to final victory, to clothe and supply ragged Virginia troops, to enlarge the First Virginia Regiment and extend its service. It was his concern for his old regiment that kept Washington in Williamsburg until April, when he had seen the bill for its support passed. In the interim he learned some political lessons.

A barrage of local issues, Washington found, was more fearsome in the Assembly than the thunder of great affairs of state, and Virginia's machinery of government seemed to deal largely with the everyday problems of people back home in the counties. Apparently trifling issues could generate emotional displays and prompt immediate action in the House. He was exposed to them quickly: the moving of Spotsylvania's courthouse from Fredericksburg, the control of stray animals in Halifax County, free passage for fish in the Rapidan River, a plea from Winchester merchants for protection against "foreign competition" in skins and furs from Pennsylvanians, changes in tobacco-inspection laws, the expansion of Winchester's city limits, an urgent call for better protection from Indian raids in exposed Augusta County. It was clear from his methodical journals and account books that Washington the planter understood that the fate of large enterprises often turned on small details. He saw now, in the presentation, debate, and passage of prosaic legislation in the Capitol's busy halls, that the principle also applied in government.

Mrs. Washington, who had never seen Mount Vernon, was with her bridegroom in Williamsburg during the first months of 1759, and her eagerness to take over her new home prompted Washington's early departure from the Assembly. This visit, one of the most important of Washington's many trips to Williamsburg, lasted about five weeks, before he returned to his plantation affairs, and Martha to the refurbishing of her new home.

He came to the capital with regularity for sixteen years as a burgess until, in 1775, the Revolution swept him into new roles, as delegate to Congress and then commander in chief of the armies. Washington made at least fifty-five trips to Williamsburg in the twenty-six years before the Revolution, and possibly many more (his diaries for several years are missing). He may have come as early as 1748, on a shopping trip to Yorktown for his mother; he probably came the next year when, as a seventeen-year-old, he was licensed as surveyor of the new Culpeper County by the College of William and Mary. He came a dozen times on military business during the French and Indian War; he came to seek his personal fortune in land speculation. He conferred with a succession of governors, dined and danced in the Palace, was entertained in many private homes, and was a familiar figure in the town.

In the seven-year period before the Revolution, for example, he listed ninety-one visits to Christiana Campbell's Tavern and twenty-three dinners in the home of Peyton Randolph, the speaker of the House of Burgesses. He noted forty-one visits to the Raleigh Tavern, where he dined, spent leisurely evenings, or took part in the political meetings which led Virginia to independence. In a three-year period he mentioned sixteen visits to the Wetherburn Tavern, and in a similar span attended twenty performances at Williamsburg's theatre. He dined less often at the King's Arms and Charlton's than in other taverns. He visited Attorney General John Randolph in his home, Tazewell Hall, Robert Carter in his house next to the Palace, and George Wythe in his house farther down the Palace Green. He saw barbers, doctors, and dentists, and attended services at Bruton Parish Church.

From his young manhood until he became a general, Williamsburg was like a second home to Washington. The 160-mile trip from Mount Vernon was not an easy one: four days by horseback; five days if his family came with him in a coach. What came to be known as "Washington's Burgess Route" led through Fredericksburg, then cross-country to West Point, and southeast to the capital, skirting marshes and streams, crossing rivers, and exposing him to the inconveniences of roadside taverns. In bad weather he took a long detour, riding down the Maryland shore and twice ferrying the broad Potomac.

Washington was just short of twenty when he made his first recorded appearance in the capital, in January, 1752. He had come by ship, thirty-six days from Barbados, where his half-brother Lawrence was dying of tuberculosis. George had been ill with smallpox during his visit to the West Indies, and bore fresh pock marks on his face. He landed at Yorktown, hired a horse, came up the sandy road to Williamsburg, and made his way to the Carter-Saunders House, where the new governor, Robert Dinwiddie, was living while the run-down Palace was being renovated.

The governor was not at home but was expected shortly. Washington waited in Williamsburg, since he had dispatches for Dinwiddie. He probably wandered through the small town which he jokingly called "the great metropolis." He may have seen workmen building an addition to the Palace, a large ballroom wing. He may have seen others at the eastern end of Duke of Gloucester Street, where a new Capitol was rising to replace the old one, destroyed by fire five years before; the legislature was meeting at the College of William and Mary. He may have seen tiny Bruton Parish Church as it had stood since 1715, still lacking a steeple, its vestrymen still planning an eastward extension of its chancel.

When the governor appeared, he gave Washington a gracious welcome, invited him to dinner, and inquired about the health of Lawrence, who had been a burgess and adjutant general of the colony's militia, responsible for the training and discipline of all troops. The first meeting of the young Washington and the experienced public servant Robert

Dinwiddie was apparently a pleasant one; together they would play an important role in the future of the continent.

Washington relaxed the next day and went to a cockfight at Yorktown, where cocks from York and Gloucester counties fought, apparently an all-day match. George placed bets, but left before the gory match was done, and was soon on his way home.

Within six months Lawrence Washington was dead. George inherited some of his property and applied to Dinwiddie for one of the four posts of adjutant when Lawrence's duties were divided. Before he became twenty-one George was named adjutant of the southern district, with the rank of major, and a salary of £100 a year. He was just in time to help launch the war between France and England for the western frontier. There was trouble in the Ohio country, where fifteen hundred Frenchmen had landed on the southern shore of Lake Erie, built forts, and opened roads. Governor Dinwiddie wrote to London, urging that he be allowed to build forts on the Ohio and enforce Virginia's claims to the vast territory.

On November 1, 1753, when the General Assembly met to consider the instructions of George II on frontier problems Washington was in Williamsburg. He had learned, probably from his friend and neighbor, Colonel William Fairfax of the Council, that the king had ordered a warning sent to the French in the Ohio country. Washington volunteered as the messenger, and Dinwiddie and the Council accepted at once. Washington was to take a letter to the French commander, demand an immediate reply, and hurry back to Williamsburg. En route he was to learn all that he could of French outposts, forts, and intentions.

Accompanied by an interpreter, Jacob van Braam, a Dutch army veteran, and by the veteran woodsman and trader Christopher Gist as his guide, plus four servants and heavily laden horses, Washington rode northwest into the wilderness, across steep ridges, along the rough country of the Youghiogheny River, past Great Meadows to the Monongahela. Washington looked closely at the wooded knoll overlooking the Ohio, formed by the junction of the Monongahela and the Allegheny rivers, and saw that a fort placed there would command these streams, whose junction was the gateway to the Northwest. The amateur soldier quickly grasped the military advantages of the site where Fort Pitt, later Pittsburgh, was to stand.

The party went on through the winter, swimming icy streams. George conferred with the important chief Half King, saw an English trader who had been driven southward by the French, and learned that three tribes had gone to war against the English. He interviewed some French desert-ers and marched north to Fort Le Boeuf, not far south of Lake Erie, to meet Legardeur de St. Pierre, the old, one-eyed French commander. Dinwiddie's letter, a demand for the "peaceful departure" of the French, was translated.

The Frenchman was courteous but firm. "He told me that the country belonged to the French," Washington wrote, that no Englishman had a right there, and that his orders were to seize those who came to trade or settle. Washington saw the strength of the French fort, the large number of canoes and other signs of a coming offensive. Throughout the talks young Washington was calm and tenacious, and a wily negotiator with both the French and the sometimes difficult Indians. The party turned back in mid-December, with Gist and Washington striking out on foot when some of the men were frost-bitten, and surviving deep snows and a musket shot from a treacherous Indian guide.

On January 16, 1754, after two and one-half months and some eleven hundred miles, Washington handed to Dinwiddie in Williamsburg the French reply, a noncommittal letter which said that St. Pierre would pass Dinwiddie's demand to his superior, the Marquis du Quesne, but that in the meantime, "As to the Summons you send me to retire, I do not think myself obliged to obey it." It was a document that was to set off a long and bloody war along the frontiers. Dinwiddie was so impressed by its importance that he ordered Washington to write a report to be given to the Council the next day.

Overnight, using notes of his journal, Washington wrote a vivid 7,000-word report, including the eloquence of the orator Half King, the macabre details of a massacre whose victims had been eaten by hogs, the visit to the Indian queen Alliquippa, to whom he gave a coat and a bottle of rum, "which latter was thought much the best Present of the two." His account gave a gripping picture of the hardships, the freezing of Gist's fingers and toes, the ice-covered streams; in all, "as fatiguing a Journey as it is possible to conceive." There was little about the conference with St. Pierre, since the exchange was chiefly in writing, but he had "an Opportu-nity of taking the Dimensions of the Fort" and of counting the men and canoes.

Dinwiddie urged that Washington's first report be published, and he agreed, apologizing for the "numberless Imperfections" of the hurriedly written account, explaining that it was meant only for the eyes of the governor, and that is was in the press before he was aware of it. The journal was published by William Hunter of the *Virginia Gazette,* and, probably the first example of pamphleteering in the French and Indian War, was reprinted in England and became widely known.

Washington had little leisure in Williamsburg. Dinwiddie badgered the House of Burgesses until it appropriated £10,000 to raise an army to protect the frontier. Washington applied for a commission as lieutenant colonel, and was accepted. He was made second in command of an expedition to seize the forks of the Ohio, where Dinwiddie had ordered a fort built. Joshua Fry, the commander, died on the march, and Washington, at twenty-two, took over Virginia's little army. He led it to disaster at Little Meadows, where he built a palisade called Fort Necessity, and was forced to surrender by a superior party of French and Indians. Washington lost one hundred men, a quarter of his force, but was allowed to return eastward to fight again. The forks of the Ohio now had a French fort: Duquesne.

There was criticism of Washington: he had been rash, exposing himself to attack before his entire army had joined him; his ally Half King said that George was good-natured but lacked experience and would not take advice from Indians, whom he treated as slaves. But men remembered longest Washington's comment on his first experience under fire: "I heard the bullets whistle, and, believe me, there is something charming in the sound." King George II, reading this remark in a London magazine, said: "He would not say so, if he had been used to hear many."

The following year, when London made its first serious effort to meet the French threat by sending General Edward Braddock and two crack British regiments to Virginia, Washington volunteered to go along, hopeful, as he wrote his brother John, of "pushing my Fortune in the Military way." Washington pushed his fortune by "frequent disputes" with Braddock, who, George said, was incapable of argument without losing his temper, was impatient, unreasonable, and over-critical of Virginians. Still the two remained on good terms, and when Braddock needed a large sum of money for the expedition, it was Washington whom he sent to Williamsburg for it.

In the disaster on the Monongahela, when Braddock's force of thirteen hundred was cut to pieces by some eight hundred French and Indians from ambush, Washington organized survivors for the long journey home. He had been wounded and had had two horses shot from under him. He wrote his mother of the bravery of Virginia troops and the "dastardly behaviour" of the British regulars who "broke and run as Sheep pursued by dogs."

Washington returned from the disaster a hero, with a reputation as an intrepid Indian fighter. Dinwiddie made him colonel of all Virginia forces, and for three years Washington was embroiled in military squabbles over rank, pay, the raising of troops, and shortages of equipment. He often threatened to resign, and once did so. In 1758, as senior Virginia officer, he marched with General John Forbes and a large army from Pennsylvania, Maryland, Delaware, and the Carolinas, to take part in the capture of Fort Duquesne, which was renamed Fort Pitt.

Near the end of the year Washington returned to Williamsburg, resigned from the army once more, ready now for his marriage to the rich widow, Martha Dandridge Custis, and for a quieter career in politics and plantation management. Martha's money enabled him to expand the Mount Vernon holdings, and he later got more than twenty thousand acres on the Ohio—as bounty for his service on the frontier or by purchase from other soldiers. There were complaints from some veterans that Washington and his friends had all the valuable bottom land, leaving other soldiers only tracts in the backcountry. Washington conceded that he had "the cream of the Country."

In the first years of his service as a burgess Washington was seldom in the public eye. He did not record a protest to London's order to Governor Fauquier of August, 1759, in which the powers of the Virginia Assembly were sharply limited. Washington may not have been present in May, 1765, when Patrick Henry aroused the country with his defiant speech against the Stamp Act, a scene which so inspired young Thomas Jefferson and dramatized the conflict with England. Washington seems to have said nothing about the Stamp Act until four months later, in a letter to a relative. He had none of Henry's zeal and wrote almost as if he were a disinterested bystander. The "Colonists," he wrote, "look upon this unconstitutional method of taxation as a direful attack upon their liberties, and loudly exclaim against the violation." He accurately predicted that the act would stimulate American manufactures and return little revenue to England, and that the British merchants would soon want it repealed. The act was repealed, and Washington wrote his London agent that he was "cordially" grateful.

But that was not the last of the troublesome new revenue measures. In 1769, when Parliament proposed strengthening the Townshend Acts by seizing American leaders and taking them to England for trial, Washington became angry. For the first time he spoke out strongly against Great Britain's policies. He was not so eloquent as some leaders of revolution in Virginia, but he was probably the first to speak of war. He wrote George Mason in April, 1769, to urge a Virginia non-importation agreement similar to those adopted in the northern colonies, binding signers to boycott British goods:

> At a time when our lordly Masters in Great Britain will be satisfied with nothing less than the deprication of American freedom, it seems highly necessary that some thing shou'd be done to avert the stroke and maintain the liberty which we have derived from our Ancestors. . . .
>
> That no man shou'd scruple, or hesitate a moment to use arms in defence of so valuable a blessing, on which all the good and evil of life depends, is clearly my opinion.

The use of arms, Washington wrote, should be the last resort, but something effective must be done: "Addresses to the Throne, and remonstrances to parliament, we have already . . . proved the inefficacy of. . . ." A non-importation policy would be the most effective weapon against England. Mason agreed and sent him a draft of a plan to carry to Williamsburg, wishing Washington "an agreeable session . . . [which] I fear you will not have." Mason was correct. When the House passed resolutions condemning the Townshend Acts and proclaiming its right to levy taxes in Virginia, the new governor, Lord Botetourt, dissolved the Assembly.

When its leaders met in nearby Raleigh Tavern to draw up a non-importation agreement, Washington was among them. After some debate and with few changes the group accepted Mason's proposal, in effect a boycott of the taxed British goods. Most of Virginia's leaders signed it, including Washington, Jefferson, Henry, Robert Carter Nicholas, Richard Henry Lee, and Peyton Randolph. The rebellious burgesses then drank about a dozen toasts, first to the king, the queen, and the royal family, and at last, "The constitutional British Liberty in America, and all true Patriots, the Supporters Thereof." The next day most of them, including Washington, helped to celebrate the Queen's Birthday at the Palace. They still thought of themselves as loyal British subjects, though one realist among them—Washington—was already thinking of the possibility of war.

Washington was otherwise busy in Williamsburg, in and out of Assembly sessions. He arrived in Williamsburg for the fall session of the

Assembly in 1769 in a new coach from London, elaborately carved, upholstered in green leather, and drawn by seven horses. As one of Virginia's leading land speculators, he was constantly planning or lobbying for land grants. He knew well every royal governor of Virginia from Dinwiddie to Lord Dunmore, the last one. His financial as well as his social interests are to be traced in his sparse journals—dinners with Dunmore or Speaker of the House Peyton Randolph, Attorney General John Randolph, or Treasurer Robert Carter Nicholas. He was to be seen at Westover, visiting Colonel William Byrd III, or at Berkeley, with Benjamin Harrison. His lands and kindred interests were scattered from the Great Dismal Swamp to the Ohio Valley, and included a projected canal along the upper Potomac. But in most instances, whether they were bought, traded for, or granted, Washington negotiated for his lands in Williamsburg.

By 1774, when the final break with England approached, Washington, though he was not one of the inner circle of political leaders of the colony, was known and respected as a firm patriot, as a planter and businessman, and was Virginia's acknowledged military expert. In response to the closing of Boston harbor after the famed Tea Party, Washington joined in signing a resolution of the Virginia House of Burgesses condemning "the hostile invasion of Boston" and calling for a day of fasting and prayer in Virginia. He went to Bruton Parish Church on the appointed day, but noted in his diary only: "Went to church and fasted all day."

By now Washington had made up his mind. Further petitions to London were futile. To him it was "as clear as the sun in its meridian brightness, that there is a regular, systematic plan formed to fix the right and practice of taxation upon us." He felt that the time had come for action: "Shall we . . . whine and cry for relief, when we have already tried it in vain? Or shall we supinely sit and see one province after another fall a prey to despotism? . . . I think the Parliament of Great Britain hath no more right to put their hands into my pocket, without my consent, than I have to put my hands into yours for money."

A few days after he wrote these words, in July, 1774, Washington was conferring with his neighbor George Mason, who was writing a firm declaration of colonial grudges against England known as the Fairfax Resolves, whose phrases were later echoed in the Virginia Declaration of Rights. In August, Washington returned to Williamsburg as a delegate to the first Virginia Convention, and in September he went as one of

Virginia's seven delegates to the First Continental Congress in Philadelphia. With him went Peyton Randolph, Richard Henry Lee, Patrick Henry, Richard Bland, Benjamin Harrison, and Edmund Pendleton. Washington was quiet, as usual, during the Philadelphia deliberations, but he attracted attention. One member circulated an allegation that Washington had made the most eloquent speech in history during the Virginia Convention: "I will raise 1000 Men, subsist them at my own Expence, and march my self at their Head for the Relief of Boston." This was news to Virginians, but it did nothing to detract from his reputation in Congress.

Washington was soon again leading Virginia militia. He was made colonel of the Fairfax Independent Company, and, while he attended the second Virginia Convention in Richmond in the spring of 1775, he was offered command of a Richmond company. He was disposed to accept, and added firmly: "it is my full intention to devote my Life and Fortune in the cause we are engaged in, if need be."

The same issue of the *Gazette* that told Virginians of the battles at Lexington and Concord carried Washington's advertisement for two runaway English servants, a joiner, and a bricklayer. Leaving such cares behind, he left almost immediately for Philadelphia and did not return to Virginia for six and one-half years. He left as a dependable but undistinguished delegate, seldom to be heard from on the floor of Congress; he returned as commander of an allied army in its moment of victory.

Washington was the only man in the Philadelphia session who wore a uniform, and he evidently wore it daily, as a reminder of the grimness of the situation. The uniform was his old one from the French and Indian wars, blue faced with scarlet, and the sight of it must have led members to think of him as the potential commander of the ragtag New England army then roosting in the hills about Boston, hemming the British in the city. Eliphalet Dyer of Connecticut, for one, was impressed, and wrote of Washington as "discreet and Virtuous, no harum Starum ranting Swearing fellow but Sober, steady and Calm."

Washington seemed to be overwhelmed by his selection as commander and his new responsibilities. With tears in his eyes he told Patrick Henry, "Remember, Mr. Henry, what I now tell you: from the day I enter upon the command of the American Armies, I date my fall, and the ruin of my reputation." He wrote his wife: "I assure you, in the most solemn manner that, so far from seeking this appointment, I have used every endeavor in my power to avoid it, not only from my unwillingness to part with you and the family, but from a consciousness of its being a trust too great for my capacity."

On July 23, 1775, the forty-three-year-old Washington was off for Boston and his new army; the years which would bring him fame did not open auspiciously. The new general looked over his troops and found the officers "the most indifferent people I ever saw," and the men, though they might fight well if properly led, were "exceedingly dirty and nasty people." By the end of the year Washington was in despair over America's future: "Such a dearth of public spirit, and want of virtue, such stock-jobbing and fertility in all the low arts to obtain advantages . . . I never saw before, and pray God I may never be witness to again . . . I tremble at the prospect. . . . Could I have foreseen what I have, and am likely to experience, no consideration upon earth should have induced me to accept this command."

Yet in the passing months the Revolution wore on, the army largely held together by Washington's dogged spirit. The British evacuated Boston, only to strike at New York, and the Continentals were defeated in terrible battles, at Long Island and Harlem Heights and White Plains, and the British seized New York City. Washington, apparently defeated, retreated to New Jersey for the winter and passed a military miracle at Trenton. In the summer and fall of 1777, while Washington was fighting for, and losing, Philadelphia, the course of the war began to turn. General John Burgoyne was defeated at Saratoga in New York, ending the threat of invasion from the north. At the news France entered the war against England. Washington and his dwindling army spent the winter at Valley Forge. Washington fought only one more major battle in the north, at Monmouth, New Jersey, in June of 1778.

At last, in 1781, after the country had survived bitter fighting and Indian warfare in the west, a British army under Lord Charles Cornwallis drove up from the south, through the Carolinas and into Virginia. Cornwallis dug in at the village of Yorktown, confident of defending himself against the tiny army of the Marquis de Lafayette, then in Tidewater Virginia, and confident of British mastery of the sea.

As recently as April of that year, even after a large French army had landed in Rhode Island, Washington had written: "We are at this hour, suspended in the Balance . . . our Troops are approaching fast to nakedness . . . our Hospitals are without medicines, and our Sick without Nutriment . . . our public works are at a stand . . . but why need I run into detail, when it may be declared in a word, that we are at the end of our tether, and that now or never our deliverance must come."

As summer passed, an incredible hope of victory began to grow; Admiral François de Grasse agreed to come to the Chesapeake with his 34-ship fleet from the West Indies. Count de Rochambeau and Washington agreed to slip away from the siege of New York, and march quickly overland to Virginia. While the army marched and big siege guns were trundled southward, de Grasse fought off a British fleet outside the Chesapeake Capes, and Cornwallis was trapped.

On the way to Yorktown, Washington, Rochambeau, and a few aides stopped at Mount Vernon. It was Washington's first visit since he had gone off to war, but they were quickly on the road again to Williamsburg. It was September 14 when they came to the old capital, so familiar to Washington for most of his life. His arrival surprised his troops.

The young Virginia officer St. George Tucker described the scene: "About four o'clock in the afternoon his approach was announced. He had passed our camp . . . before we had time to parade the militia. The French line had just time to form. . . . He approached without any pomp or parade attended only by a few horsemen and his own servants." Washington was then caught in a bear hug by the excited Lafayette, whose elation impressed Tucker: "Never was more joy painted in any countenance . . . The Marquis rode up with precipitation, clasped the General in his arms and embraced him with an ardor not easily described."

Washington reviewed the troops and then went to his headquarters at the George Wythe House. Rochambeau took over the Peyton Randolph House. For almost two weeks the small city thronged with troops—most of them French—and with preparations for the siege of Yorktown. At 5 A.M. on September 28 the army marched toward Yorktown, with the heavy guns and mortars following. After three weeks of bombardment and of building trenches ever nearer the village, of night attacks and a desperate effort by the British to escape over the York River, it was over. Cornwallis surrendered his small army and the Revolution was effectively won, though the Treaty of Paris was two years away.

Washington did not linger in Tidewater; he returned to Mount Vernon. He did not visit Williamsburg again. Thus it was on that September morning when he put his troops on the road to Yorktown and immortality that he saw for the last time the capital where he had been trained in politics, and military affairs, and the administration of government.

Peyton Randolph, by John Wollaston. Reproduced through courtesy of the Virginia Historical Society, Richmond.

PEYTON RANDOLPH

THE First Continental Congress met in Philadelphia in September, 1774, a rather hesitant band of revolutionaries torn by factions. One group pressed for independence even at the risk of war, and another urged that they patch up their quarrel with England. But they were unanimous as they took the first step in their historic task—the choice of a president.

All the Virginia delegates had drawn the attention of Congress. They were, as John Adams of Massachussets wrote, "the most spirited and consistent" men who had come to sit in Carpenter's Hall. The Virginians themselves spoke "in raptures" of Patrick Henry and Richard Henry Lee, their orators, and others took note of those large, imposing men, George Washington and Benjamin Harrison. But when the leader was chosen, Congress turned to Peyton Randolph of Williamsburg.

Thomas Lynch, a forceful South Carolinian, made the suggestion. One of the delegates, he said, had "presided with great dignity over a very respectable society, greatly to the advantage of America," and he proposed that he be made president, unanimously. Randolph was approved without dissent, and took the chair.

John Adams saw Randolph as "a large, well looking man," and Silas Deane of Connecticut wrote: "Our President seems designed by nature for the business. Of an affable, open and majestic deportment, large in size, though not out of proportion, he commands respect and esteem by his very aspect, independent of the high character he sustains."

Congress had chosen the most honored Virginia political figure of the era. Randolph had been a burgess for more than twenty-five years and speaker of the House for eight, after a long career as attorney general. He had been president of the recent Virginia Convention and had served as president or chairman of virtually every important legislative body or committee in the colony's recent history. Thomas Jefferson, who had known him intimately, admired the new president: "He was indeed a most excellent man; and none was ever more beloved and respected by his friends. Somewhat cold and coy towards strangers, but of the sweetest affability when ripened into acquaintance." Jefferson praised Randolph's pleasant manner in conversation, his good humor, tolerance, and intellect: "With a sound and logical head, he was well read in the law; and his opinions when consulted were highly regarded, presenting always a learned and sound view of the subject."

Randolph's great gift as a politician was for guiding the way to effective compromises on thorny problems, and he had played that role as a conservative among Virginia's rebels. Without loss of friends or influence he had provided balance for Assemblies that had been electrified by the oratory of the hot-headed Patrick Henry. As Jefferson said, "although sound in his principles, and going steadily with us in opposition to the British usurpations, he with the other older members, yielded the lead to the younger . . . tempering their ardor, and so far modulating their pace as to prevent their going too far in advance of the public sentiment."

Randolph was one of three men who had been models for Jefferson's own life. When faced with moral temptation during his youth, Jefferson said he asked himself how Peyton Randolph or his professors, William Small and George Wythe, would have acted.

But the first congressional president, though he guided the first two sessions into Revolution and though he was so eminent as to be a symbol of Virginia's political leadership, became a figure little known to posterity. He died suddenly, near the end of climactic events of 1775, but his relative obscurity among revolutionary leaders was perhaps also due to what Jefferson called his "listlessness," for the heavy Randolph was "rather too indolent and careless for business."

This indolence did not seem to interfere with Randolph's remarkably full career. Usually the first Virginian considered for important commissions, he was appointed to such tasks as the settlement of the New York–New Jersey boundary in 1769, was on the board of the nation's first mental hospital, and was a director of the Williamsburg Manufactory, where cloth and hemp were produced. He was on the committee to commission a suitable statue of the popular late governor, Lord Botetourt, was frequently named as executor of estates of friends, and was grand master of the Williamsburg Lodge of Masons.

Randolph left remarkably few traces in the history of his time; his personal letters are so rare as to be almost unknown, but one of them offers a good-humored explanation for their rarity. Randolph wrote his friend Landon Carter in 1773: "I must own I don't like the business of writing, not from Idleness neither, but because I had rather read the productions of any man's brain than those of my own." The same letter offers a glimpse of the spirit others found charming in Randolph, as he described the condition of affairs in Williamsburg on the eve of the Revolution: "Lawyers continue to talk as they are chanced to be feed, Judges to guess right, sometimes, Merchants to ber[ate] in England, and what is worst of all, tobacco is worth nothing."

A brief illness near the end of the Congress of 1774 removed Randolph from his chair, but he recovered to make the long journey home to his handsome house facing Williamsburg's Market Square, and to win further honors in serving Virginia and the nation.

Peyton Randolph was born, about 1721, in Williamsburg, a son of Sir John Randolph, who was the only colonial Virginian knighted by an English monarch. Peyton was educated at the College of William and Mary, was sent to study law in London's Middle Temple, and was admitted to the bar in 1743. The next year, at about the age of twenty-three, he became attorney general for Virginia and in 1748 became a member of the House of Burgesses, representing first Williamsburg and in later years the College of William and Mary. He married Elizabeth Harrison, of the James River plantation, Berkeley, in 1746, soon after he had inherited a large share of his father's estate. Mrs. Randolph was a sister of Benjamin Harrison, who was a signer of the Declaration of Independence and governor of Virginia.

Their connections with two of Virginia's most influential (and prolific) families made the Williamsburg home of the Randolphs on Market Square a social and political center, and, as Peyton became more prominent in affairs of the government, they became leaders in the dominant circle of the colony's life. When a new governor, Robert Dinwiddie, arrived in 1751 to find the Palace under repair, he lived in a temporary home, the Carter-Saunders House on Palace Green. One of his first social calls was upon his new neighbors, the Randolphs. Washington's diaries record many visits to the Peyton Randolph House, especially during Public Times, when men of influence from all parts of the colony were entertained at dinner.

Despite his distaste for writing, Randolph was evidently a cultivated man. He inherited from his scholarly father a large library that included transcripts of the colony's early laws, from 1642 to 1662. These were later used in compiling Hening's *Statutes,* a basic source of Virginia history. The library was bought after Randolph's death by Jefferson, who sold his books to the United States as part of the original collection of the Library of Congress. Jefferson's books included some of those bought from the Randolph estate.

Randolph's reputation for ability and integrity grew as the colonial crisis grew, and though he was always a leader of the wealthy and conservative group in Virginia, he never failed to speak for the rights of Americans when they clashed with those of Great Britain. When Dinwiddie provoked a crisis in Virginia affairs by attempting to collect the small fee of one pistole for signing each land grant, Randolph took a leading role in defying him in Virginia and defeating him on the issue in England. A message on this matter from the burgesses to the governor declared that Virginians "cannot be deprived of the least part of their property but by their own consent," a principle which was to become a basic argument in the revolutionary cause twenty years later.

When the governor stubbornly refused to abandon his fee, the burgesses sent Peyton Randolph to England as their agent to plead the cause, and ordered his expenses paid from the public treasury. The infuriated Dinwiddie dismissed Randolph as attorney general, complaining of this "notorious encroachment on the prerogatives of the Crown." His temper was not improved by developments while Randolph was in London. Just when it appeared that Randolph could not get a hearing on the grievances of the burgesses, anonymous newspaper notices appealed to the British public, branding Dinwiddie's scheme as a tax rather than a fee. Dinwiddie accused Randolph of writing these appeals, but Randolph denied authorship.

The burgesses were as determined as the governor, and when they were called into a new session to appropriate money for frontier warfare, they added a rider providing for Randolph's expenses. Dinwiddie said that he was sorry to find the burgesses "very much in a republican way of thinking" and gave the members a stern lecture for their rebelliousness.

He then dismissed the Assembly without a defense bill, and without paying Randolph's travel costs.

After London had ordered a compromise solution to the fee controversy, Randolph came home in triumph; the Board of Trade had directed that he be restored to his office. Although Dinwiddie had once said that Randolph had a greater share of his "favour and countenance than any other in the government," the friendship was never renewed with its old warmth.

Perhaps Dinwiddie had been attracted to Randolph because of his spirited conduct of the office of attorney general. Randolph's prosecutions were based on rigid standards. "He considered himself," Jefferson wrote, "equally charged with the rights of the colony as with those of the crown; and in criminal prosecutions exaggerating nothing . . . believing it more a duty to save an innocent than to convict a guilty man."

Attorney General Randolph was involved with most important issues of his day, some of them furious controversies at the College of William and Mary, where he served for a year as rector. One hot-tempered professor, the Reverend Jacob Rowe, was so outraged by the passage of the Two Penny Act, which in effect reduced the salaries of ministers, that he led students in a pitched battle against town boys. Rowe openly insulted Randolph, the college president, and other officials, and pointed a pistol at another teacher.

Randolph was an enormously fat man and had no military experience, but he responded to the emergency after the defeat of General Braddock and raised a company of wealthy men of the colony, called "the Associators," to march to the frontier. This band, also known as the Virginia Blues, was supported by Randolph and his friends, who pledged as many soldiers as they could enlist, providing them with muskets, pistols, swords, and ammunition. The Blues dressed in "short, plain blue Frocks . . . white Nankeen or brown Holland Waistcoats, and Breeches of the same, and plain Hats." As a newspaper said admiringly, the gentlemen had raised and equipped the company at their own expense, "to march to the Frontiers of this Colony, for relieving their distressed Fellow Subjects, and chastising the Insolence, and revenging the Cruelties of the French, and their barbarous Allies."

The company marched, 130 strong, to Fredericksburg in May of 1756, under Randolph's leadership. The company held a council of war, elected officers, heard an inspiring sermon on the text "Be of good Courage, and let us play the Men for our People," and marched on to the frontier at Winchester.

Thomas Jefferson, no military man himself, later made light of the company, whose leadership was accustomed to the life of ease and luxury, and said it was fortunate that they did not see an enemy. The Blues, at any rate, returned home, leaving defense of the west to Washington and his backwoods militiamen. They had contributed to the colony's morale by volunteering and supporting the troops.

In 1759, Randolph became a member of the committee of correspondence, by which Virginia's leaders kept in touch with their official agent in London and presented their grievances.

He continued to lead resistance of responsible Virginians to London's growing interference in colonial affairs. In 1764, when news of the projected Stamp Act reached Williamsburg, the committee of correspondence, "much alarmed," ordered its London agent to oppose the new duties. These men took a serious view of the tax, and of the future it threatened, and spoke of "the approaching Storm" and of the rights of Englishmen everywhere to be governed by laws passed by their representatives.

Resolutions of the committee of correspondence were placed before the House of Burgesses and turned over to a committee headed by Randolph. With Richard Henry Lee, Landon Carter, George Wythe, Edmund Pendleton, Benjamin Harrison, Archibald Cary, and John Fleming, he drafted messages to King George and to each house of Parliament. (Randolph himself wrote the message to the king.) Remembering Randolph's experience in London with the pistole fee cause, the committee urged their agent to have the messages printed "and dispersed over the Nation . . . that the people of England may be acquainted with the Privileges & Liberties we claim as British Subjects."

These were firm, uncompromising resolutions, one of which ended: "British Patriots will never consent to the Exercise of anticonstitutional Power, which even in this remote corner may be dangerous in its Example to the interiour Parts of the British Empire, and will certainly be detrimental to its commerce." The House leadership was still awaiting a reply from London the following spring, when it was learned that the Stamp Act had passed Parliament, and would take effect in November, 1765.

It was then that Patrick Henry made the first of his celebrated orations in the House of Burgesses and near the end of the session, when the conservatives were in the minority, pushed through his Stamp Act Resolves after his fiery Caesar-Brutus speech. Jefferson, who was then a college student, saw Randolph come angrily from the House, muttering, "By God, I would have given one hundred guineas for a single vote!"

In 1766, at the age of forty-five, Randolph was elected speaker of the House of Burgesses, after the death of the veteran John Robinson. His old post of attorney general was filled by his brother, John Randolph, and Peyton devoted the rest of his career to legislative duties. He became the unquestioned leader of Virginia resistance and the most effective force in unifying its factions.

In 1773, Virginians set up an important piece of revolutionary machinery, the intercolonial Committees of Correspondence to advance their common cause. Peyton was named chairman. A year later, when Williamsburg learned of the blockading of the port of Boston, Randolph called a meeting to take action and led a procession of dignitaries to Bruton Parish Church, for a service on the appointed day of fasting and prayer. In the summer of 1774, when he was named as the first of Virginia's delegates to the opening Continental Congress, citizens of the capital paid him a unique tribute. Reversing the usual practice of being wined and dined by the candidate, the freeholders met at the Courthouse, where one of them read an address of appreciation to Randolph; the band then escorted him to Raleigh Tavern, entertained him at "a most splendid dinner," and finally marched him to his house, and gave him three cheers. The citizens, said the *Virginia Gazette,* gave the dinner not only to show their disapproval of the old practice of plying the electorate with food and drink, but also "to show their tender regard for their speaker," because of "his many essential services towards this country."

In August of 1774 the Peyton Randolph House was the scene of a historic occasion. Thomas Jefferson, riding down from Monticello to a session of the House of Burgesses, became ill on the road and turned back. He sent to Williamsburg two copies of an important document, the first full statement of his opinions on the British-American crisis, many of which were developed in the Declaration of Independence. "A Summary View of the Rights of British America," as Jefferson's treatise was called, got its first public reading before a group gathered in Randolph's house. It was applauded by most hearers, especially the younger ones, who were willing to "tread this lofty ground" with Jefferson. The paper was later published in Williamsburg, then reprinted in Philadelphia and London.

In the same month Randolph presided over a meeting of Williamsburg townsmen at the Courthouse to subscribe cash and provisions for the relief of the people of Boston. At the end of August, Randolph left Williamsburg to go to Philadelphia, where he was chosen president of the Continental Congress.

Again in the spring of 1775, Randolph led the way toward a complete break with England. After he had presided over the historic Virginia Convention at Richmond in which Patrick Henry delivered his eloquent "liberty or death" speech, Randolph was again returned to Congress, and again presided in Philadelphia. But this time he left Williamsburg as a public enemy. Newspapers published as late news from London a "blacklist" by royal proclamation, which declared several Americans rebels. To make London's meaning clear, General Gage, the commander in Boston, had been sent blank commissions for their execution, if and when these men were captured. Several were named, including John and Sam Adams, John Hancock, John Dickenson, Henry Middleton, and Peyton Randolph.

Militiamen took no chances, and, as Randolph rolled northward with his brother-in-law, Benjamin Harrison, and Edmund Pendleton, detachments of horsemen rode guard with the delegates, passing them from one unit to another through the Virginia counties until they had crossed the Potomac. On the Maryland side two militia companies were waiting to escort them farther, and so the Virginians, "about 250 of the first Gentlemen in this part of the country . . . gave them three cheers, and returned home."

Randolph presided only briefly in Philadelphia, and in late May left for Virginia to attend the session of the General Assembly—it was to be the last full session. John Hancock succeeded him as president of Congress.

A cavalry detachment of the Williamsburg Volunteers rode out to meet Randolph at Ruffin's Ferry on the Pamunkey River, and were joined by a company of infantry about two miles from the capital. The procession came into town about sunset, the troops escorted Randolph to his house, and, as the *Gazette* reported, "The bells began to ring . . . there were illuminations in the evening, and the volunteers, with many other respectable Gentlemen, assembled at the Raleigh, spent an hour or two in harmony and cheerfulness, and drank several patriotic toasts."

The next morning the militiamen presented an address to Randolph: "We, the members of the volunteer company in Williamsburg . . . are exceedingly alarmed to hear, from report, that the same malevolent daemons, from whom have originated all the evils of America, are now exerting their utmost treachery to ensnare your life and safety. . . ." The volunteers urged the president to be careful of his safety, and offered themselves as guards. The tribute ended grandly: "MAY HEAVEN GRANT YOU LONG TO LIVE *THE FATHER OF YOUR COUNTRY,* AND THE FRIEND TO FREEDOM AND HUMANITY!"

Randolph replied gratefully and said that he hoped the reports that he was marked for death by the Crown were untrue: "Such unjust and arbitrary proceedings," he said, "would bring on the authors of them the resentment and indignation of every honest man in the British empire."

Randolph was not long known as "The Father of His Country." He had about four months to live, and an exclusive claim to national paternity would fall to his friend George Washington, who was chosen as commander in chief of the American armies in the same month that Randolph returned to Williamsburg.

The last days of his life were busy for Randolph. He presided over another Virginia Convention in Richmond in July and August and left there just in time to travel to Philadelphia once more. He and Mrs. Randolph left in a party of coaches carrying Thomas Nelson and George Wythe and their wives. Bad luck dogged them on the route; the carriage in which Randolph and Nelson rode was wrecked, and when they borrowed another the driver smashed it against a tree and demolished it. Unharmed, the delegates reached Philadelphia in another conveyance.

John Adams noted a very different Randolph in this session of Congress, with John Hancock presiding: "our former President is here and Sits very humbly in his Seat, while our new one continues in the Chair, without Seeming to feel the Impropriety."

Randolph died suddenly on Sunday, October 22, just after dining three miles outside the city, with a party which included Jefferson. As Congressman Samuel Ward of Rhode Island reported it, "soon after dinner he was taken with choaking, and one side of his face was distorted, and about eight he expired." Congress went into mourning and attended an impressive funeral service at Christ Church, joined by many soldiers and public officials of Pennsylvania and Philadelphia. The next year, in November, 1776, Peyton Randolph's body was brought home by his nephew, Edmund. Burial was in a vault of the chapel of the College of William and Mary, beside his father, Sir John Randolph.

Edmund Pendleton, attributed to Charles Willson Peale. Colonial Williamsburg.

EDMUND PENDLETON

IN the President's chair, facing the crowded House of Burgesses where the last of Virginia's revolutionary Conventions was in session, sat an urbane man of fifty-five in a gray wig and a neat black suit. He looked very much the part he had played in the colony's affairs for many years, a firm conservative among rebels who looked to him for leadership.

He was Edmund Pendleton, the only major figure among Virginia leaders of the era who had made his own way in life without the aid of inherited position or estate. (Even Patrick Henry, the spokesman of the small planter and frequent opponent of landed Tidewater aristocrats, was the son of the owner of a modest plantation who was also a vestryman, justice of the peace, and colonel of his county's militia. Patrick's uncle was also a man of influence, the rector of St. Paul's Parish.) Pendleton had been prominent in politics and law for a full generation, and now directed the 128-man body which would transform Virginia from colony to commonwealth.

Hugh Blair Grigsby, biographer of this Convention, described him:

As a parliamentarian, he had no equal in the House; a superior nowhere. . . . He was fully six feet in height, and was in the vigor of life . . . [he had] the reputation of being the handsomest man in the Colony . . . lithe and graceful in all his movements . . . his manners polished . . . his voice clear and ringing, so that its lowest note was heard distinctly throughout the hall; and a self-possession so supreme as to sustain him in the fiercest collisions of debate as if in a state of repose.

It was May, 1776. On the sixth of the month the House of Burgesses, America's oldest representative assembly, had died quietly in Williamsburg's Capitol, closing its journal laconically: "Several Members met, but did neither proceed to Business, nor adjourn, as a House of Burgesses." It was supplanted by the Convention, and Pendleton was chosen president.

Patrick Henry's faction had fought bitterly for the chair, since Henry and Pendleton, though allies in principle, had often clashed. Pendleton thought Henry was a demagogue, and had opposed his methods since the orator's Stamp Act speech of eleven years before. Recently, as president of the Virginia Committee of Safety, he had outraged Henry by denying him the field command of Virginia militia in favor of a more experienced officer.

Yet, in this Convention, Henry had hesitated to move for independence until America had found foreign allies, and it was Pendleton who proposed the bold step. The president would lead this Convention throughout, as it instructed congressional delegates to propose independence from Great Britain, passed the Declaration of Rights, wrote a constitution, and elected a governor. Pendleton recognized the great crisis in Virginia history as he accepted the chair: "We are now met at a time truly critical, when subjects of the most important and interesting nature require our serious attention. . . . In the discussion of these, and all other subjects . . . permit me to recommend calmness, unanimity, and diligence, as the most likely means of bringing them to a happy and prosperous issue."

The delegates were not idle under Pendleton. Committees met at seven o'clock each morning, the Convention heard reports at ten, and many men worked far into the nights, for there was much to be done and history provided no guide for their tasks. As Pendleton wrote Thomas Jefferson: "We build a Government slowly, I hope it will be founded upon a rock."

On May 15, after long debate, a compromise resolution was passed, a blueprint for the creation of a commonwealth. Pendleton was its author. It included instructions to the congressional delegates "to declare the United Colonies free and independent states," and ended: "Resolved unanimously, That a committee be appointed to prepare a DECLARATION OF RIGHTS, and such a plan of government as will be most likely to maintain peace and order in this colony, and secure substantial and equal liberty to the people."

It was the most important document of Pendleton's career, and, though it was hastily drawn and combined several conflicting views, it was also to endure as an important document of American history. Pendleton sent copies to Philadelphia and to each of the colonies almost as soon as it had been approved.

A collection was taken up to entertain the soldiers who thronged in Williamsburg, and the next day the Committee of Safety inspected troops in Waller's grove near the Capitol, many toasts were drunk, and the new "Union Flag of the American States" went up on the cupola. Pendleton's resolution was appropriately celebrated.

Pendleton was kept busy while the new state was being born in the Convention, raising troops, trying to supply salt, lead, and food for the army, turning the Palace into a hospital for troops, guarding against expected raids by the hostile Governor Dunmore, and raising money for mounting expenses. He named a committee to write the Declaration of Rights, adding George Mason when he came late to the session, and wrote Jefferson: "I find our session will be a long one, and indeed the importance of our business requires it & we must sweat it out with fortitude."

Once the Declaration of Rights had been passed after fierce debate, the constitution was approved in three days, as if the architects of the new government had exhausted themselves. Patrick Henry was then elected governor; Pendleton stayed out of the race, though many had expected him to enter. Years afterward he told a friend "he did not think it became those who pushed on the revolution to get into the first offices."

The Convention met for the last time on July 5 to attend the final details of statehood, eliminating references to the king from the services of the church, and adopting a seal for the commonwealth. Virginia's revolution had been accomplished and its fate was now with the armies. Pendleton rose to announce adjournment. The historian Hugh Blair Grigsby wrote rather emotionally of the handsome president at that moment: "when the clear tones of that silver voice fell on the ears of the members now for the last time, feelings too deep for utterance were excited in every bosom. Yet his self-command was such, no emotion save in the tremulous fullness of his voice appeared in his manner."

At the end of the session Pendleton went home to his isolated plantation near Bowling Green, in the country between the Rappahannock and the Mattaponi rivers, where, as he said, "my old woman and I continue happy." For thirty years, almost as long as he had been married, Pendleton had been a dominant figure in the public life of Virginia, as lawyer, prosecutor, burgess, justice, delegate to Congress, friend and confidant to most of the great men of the colony. He had advised and aided George Washington at more than one important moment in his life.

When he went home in July of 1776, when the greatest work of his career was done, Pendleton still had before him almost twenty-five years of public service to Virginia.

Edmund Pendleton was born in 1721 in what is now Caroline County, the youngest of seven children of a struggling planter, Henry Pendleton, who died in the year of Edmund's birth. He was descended from Philip Pendleton, an English schoolteacher who had come to the valley of the Rappahannock River in 1674 as an indentured servant.

Edmund's mother, Mary Taylor Pendleton, remarried when he was two years old and the boy grew up at hard farm work, ploughing by day and studying at night. He spent only two years in a neighborhood school before he was bound as a fourteen-year-old apprentice to Colonel Benjamin Robinson, the county clerk of court, and went to live in Robinson's house, Moon's Mount. Situated on a tall bluff above the Rappahannock near Port Royal, the house offered long views of hills to the west and of the rolling valley eastward toward Chesapeake Bay. Pendleton had limited time to enjoy the plantation or the company of Robinson's numerous children. Caroline was "a Quarrelsome County," and the clerk and his apprentice were kept busy with affairs of court.

Colonel William Byrd II, who had stopped at Moon's Mount not long before Edmund arrived, wrote of his visit: "The Major receiv'd us with his usual good Humour. He has a very Industrious wife, who has kept him from Sinking by the Weight of Gaming & Idleness." Byrd noted that Robinson had reformed and that his clerkship might save him from ruin. Pendleton played a role in that salvation.

Robinson was a jolly, cultivated man, educated in England, whose faults as a public official were blessings in disguise to Pendleton. As Edmund recalled him, Robinson was "very negligent and inaccurate in his accounts," and the new apprentice, a meticulous workman, was soon handling Robinson's personal affairs, as well as routine office chores, and became invaluable to his master. The boy passed through a practical school of law, processing wills, bonds, accounts, inventories, deeds, and every other kind of pleading in the active court. He wrote the forms, noted the tactics of lawyers filing their cases, and heard hundreds of arguments in the courtroom.

It was a hard but effective training ground for young Pendleton, and an appropriate one for a boy whose ancestors had come from the English county of Norfolk, where a farmer would "sue another for trespass if a cow so much as looked over a hedge." Edmund did not resent his lowly role, and wrote with pride years later that he had grown up "without any classical education, without patrimony, without what is called the influence of family connection." (As one Virginia historian described the handicap Edmund had to overcome: "He was not in a legal sense nobody's son, but in the estimation of a haughty generation he was something worse—he was the son of nobody.") He took advantage of all opportunities. At sixteen his reputation for reliability made him clerk of the vestry of St. Mary's Parish, keeping records of ministers' salaries (paid in tobacco), the boundaries of all property in the parish, taxes on members, vital statistics, and lists of indigents. With his first small income he "purchased a few books, and read them diligently."

Pendleton also became clerk to the county court-martial, keeping accounts of the large militia force and recording trials of miscreants. Thus at nineteen Pendleton had intimate knowledge of every official process of his county and a basic understanding of the mechanics of government of Virginia, invaluable to a man who was to become prominent in each of the three branches of state government.

Pendleton had long since determined to become a lawyer, but when he tried to read the few volumes of old cases to be found near Caroline Courthouse, he was lost among their Latin phrases. He went to a Latin school nearby and within three months had such a working knowledge of the language that he could continue studies at home. He was so industrious that by the time he was admitted to the bar "few were able to translate Latin more correctly." All of his general education came in this way, from reading books in his spare time: his later writings reveal a familiarity with Shakespeare and the Bible. More important, as a friend said, "He soon acquired a profound knowledge of the character of mankind, and of human affairs. And . . . extracted his opinions from realities, rather than from the speculations of philosophers."

In April, 1741, at the age of twenty, Pendleton made his first visit to Williamsburg, where he was examined by the skilled English-trained attorney general, Edward Barradall, and was licensed to practice in Virginia's lower courts. Back home he began as all young lawyers began, with difficult and trifling cases, many from clients who could not pay him. He faced serious competition from older lawyers in Caroline and surrounding counties where he rode the circuit: John Mercer of Stafford, in whose fine library George Mason had educated himself; Zachary Lewis of Spotsylvania, who was king's attorney for both Orange and Caroline counties; and William Waller, Lewis' brother-in-law.

Despite his youth, his competitors, and small fees from a beginner's practice, the methodical Pendleton made his way. He was so effective in his home county that Mercer gave up his circuit trips there within six months after Edmund began to appear in court.

While he was still twenty, and described as "of the first order of manly beauty," Edmund married Betty Roy, a county belle, who died within less than a year in the delivery of a stillborn child. Soon after his first wife's death, Pendleton married Sarah Pollard, with whom he lived happily though childlessly, for sixty years.

Pendleton built a house in eastern Caroline County, a sturdy, rambling and unpretentious farmhouse that was to be expanded informally over the years. He called the place Edmundsbury. As his practice grew he bought surrounding land, until at last he owned about six square miles of land which had once belonged to his maternal grandfather, James Taylor.

In his twenties Edmund was already a leading lawyer of his territory and was eager to try himself against the best legal minds of the colony; he went back to Williamsburg and was licensed to practice there, in the General Court, Virginia's highest. He took lodgings in town during court sessions, attracting clients with advertisements in the *Virginia Gazette,* but returning afterward to his practice in Caroline. He was named deputy attorney, or prosecutor, for Essex County, and from that point his civil practice grew more rapidly. On one day of court in Essex he was listed as attorney in more than fifty cases.

In 1751, when he was made county justice in Caroline, he began a career of more than fifty years on the bench. The next year, at the age of thirty-one, he was elected to the House of Burgesses, where he remained until that body expired. He never lost an election for public office.

Pendleton's opening House session was the first called by the new governor, Robert Dinwiddie, a member of the Ohio Company, which had a great stake in western Virginia lands. The House speaker was John Robinson, a nephew of the master of Moon's Mount, who took such an interest in his uncle's protégé as to place him on three important standing committees.

He also handled troublesome matters for his constituents: Port Royal was divided between men who favored the free roaming of hogs and sheep in the town and those who demanded that they be penned; there

was a brisk quarrel between owners of private ferries across the Rappahannock and those who wanted free public ferries. Though he was a
freshman Pendleton was frequently asked to help other burgesses draw
their bills; he wrote these wholesale, "without classical decorations," but
in concise and vigorous language. As Edmund Randolph wrote of him:
"Labour was his delight."

At the end of the session, with burgesses safely out of Williamsburg,
Governor Dinwiddie announced that all land grants processed in Virginia
would bear a fee of one pistole, a small Spanish coin of modest value. The
matter affected almost every burgess, since they speculated in lands on the
rapidly expanding frontier. The controversy over the fee plunged Pendleton into the power struggle for the west which was to outlast the French
and Indian War.

Speaker Robinson took him into the Loyal Company, a rival to the
Ohio Company dominated by the Lees and Washingtons; Pendleton soon
patented claims himself, the largest for three thousand acres near the
present city of Bristol. Throughout his career he continued to acquire and
trade in land.

The "pistole fee" controversy became so heated in Pendleton's second
term as burgess that the House sent Peyton Randolph to London as its
representative to plead for removal of the fee. In the months before
London eased the tension by ruling that the pistole fee should not apply
to land grants beyond the mountains, the House and the governor fought
over the financing of the French and Indian War. One burgess saw in
Dinwiddie's treatment of the burgesses "all the Venom and all the
Falsehood of an Angry Passionate man." It was only when Braddock's
defeat shocked the colony that the legislators and the governor were
united. The House, finally stirred to action, said it was ready to raise the
astronomical sum of £100,000 to save the frontier. Pendleton was named
to the committee chosen to oversee spending for war. The appointment
was a recognition of his growing stature as a leader of the House.

In their effort to support the war with France, at a time when declining
tobacco revenues were crippling the plantation system, the burgesses
wrestled with overwhelming financial problems. Their solution was the
issuance of paper money, which merchants in London protested, demanding to be paid in English specie, "hard money." Pendleton was named,
with Charles Carter, George Wythe, and Richard Henry Lee, to write a
resolution condemning the merchants, who sought favored position as
creditors. The committee produced one of the early documents of protest

which led to revolution. It acknowledged dependence upon England, but added spiritedly: "this is not the Dependence of a People subjugated by the Arms of a Conqueror, but of Sons sent out to explore and settle a new World, for the mutual Benefit of themselves and their common Parent."

Throughout these struggles with finance Pendleton had made himself one of the most popular burgesses by aiding others in their work and offering practical suggestions for improvement of their relations with voters back home. Washington once learned of Pendleton's effectiveness when he tried, and failed, to pass a bill "to prevent Hogs from running at large in the Town of Winchester." Pendleton took him aside and gave him a quick lesson in politics and public relations, and got Washington's bill passed without dissent under a new title of such appeal that no one could oppose it: "a Bill to Preserve the Water for the Use of the Inhabitants of the Town of Winchester . . . by preventing Hogs from running at large."

News of the proposed Stamp Act, with its new taxes, came to Virginia in 1763, when the colony was £500,000 in debt and literally bankrupt. The burgesses immediately protested the heavy new burden to Parliament, and Pendleton was one of eight men assigned to write the message. It was another historic document, setting forth principles that Patrick Henry would dramatize in the Capitol the following year when the Stamp Act crisis was played out in Virginia: "Your memorialists conceive it to be a fundamental Principle of the British Constitution, without which Freedom can no Where exist, that the People are not subject to any Taxes but such as are laid on them by their own Consent. . . ."

When he learned that Parliament had passed the Stamp Act, Pendleton wrote, "Poor America!" Still he did not approve of Henry's Caesar-Brutus speech or his resolves against the Act, since he thought the House should wait for a response to its earlier protest before acting. He was absent from the House, and back home in Caroline County, when Henry delivered his heady oration in May, 1765, but he always felt that it was rash and twenty-five years later still defended the "Manly but decent language" of the messages he had helped to write to Parliament. Pendleton declared that the Stamp Act was unconstitutional from the first, before Henry made a public comment on the question, but he refused to "enter into noisy and riotous companys" in its debate. He condemned the mob spirit in which the Sons of Liberty demonstrated in Virginia for some months before the act was repealed.

Pendleton was next plunged into the most onerous and perplexing experience of his life: he was persuaded to become administrator of the involved estate of Treasurer John Robinson, whose death revealed a skein of scandal and debt touching almost every man of influence in Virginia. For years, as the colony's financial crisis deepened, Treasurer Robinson had been the only major source of credit in Virginia. As wartime issues of currency matured, Robinson was required by law to burn them; but money was scarce, and when his wealthy friends pleaded that destruction of these issues would ruin them, Robinson yielded. His actions were not prompted by a desire to defraud but by concern for his friends, "to whom he could never give a denial [because of] his too Benevolent heart." At his death prominent Virginians owed his estate almost £140,000 of which £100,000 had come from the public treasury.

The estate could not be settled quickly. If Pendleton pressed for payment of these debts, the market would be swamped by the sale of hundreds of thousands of acres of land, fine houses, and thousands of slaves. He spent years unraveling the tangle, slowly collecting the debts, until, in 1781, the year of victory at Yorktown, the state was repaid in full. The task drained Pendleton's energies for many of the best years of his life.

Throughout his legislative career, his years on the county bench, and all other public service before the Revolution, Pendleton's chief occupation was his practice before the General Court, which he had begun at twenty-four. Over the years he competed with the great lawyers of Virginia, Sir John Randolph and Edward Barradall, John Mercer and Richard Bland, Peyton Randolph, George Wythe, and Robert Carter Nicholas. His rivalry with Wythe became legendary. The two were very different in style and outlook, as historian Grigsby wrote:

> Pendleton was a man of the world, and transacted business as a thing to be done; Wythe was sometimes beguiled by the mode of doing it. Pendleton, who inherited nothing, brought his mind to bear on the game of life, and amassed a large fortune; Wythe, who inherited a handsome patrimony, died poor. Pendleton was strictly a man of talents . . . Wythe was a man of genius.

Pendleton's strength lay in his intimate knowledge of cases; he had not studied law as a system nor dealt with its great philosophers of the past. He was more "a great advocate than . . . a great lawyer."

Wythe praised Pendleton's ingenuity and agility in attack: "His conceptions were quick, acute and full of resource. He possessed a dexterity of address which never lost an advantage and never gave one." As Patrick

Henry's biographer, William Wirt, put it: "Though [Wythe was] a full match for Mr. Pendleton in the powers of fair and solid reasoning, Mr. Pendleton could whenever he pleased . . . tease him with quibbles, and vex him with sophistries, until he destroyed the composure of his mind and robbed him of his strength." Jefferson remembered Pendleton at the bar as "cool, smooth and persuasive; his language flowing, chaste and embellished," and praised him highly, "taken all in all . . . the ablest man in debate I have ever met with."

The lessons of youth in the county courts had made Pendleton an all but invincible courtroom lawyer, and his success in the highest court earned him an enormous practice. Jefferson was fascinated by the techniques of this self-taught man who was "never vanquished," and wrote of him: "if he lost the main battle, he returned upon you, and regained so much of it as to make it a drawn one, by dexterous manoeuvres, skirmishes in detail, and the recovery of small advantages which, little singly, were important all together. You never knew when you were clear of him, but were harassed by his perserverance, until the patience was worn down of all who had less of it than himself. Add to this, that he was one of the most virtuous and benevolent of men, the kindest friend, the most amiable and pleasant of companions, which ensured a favorable reception to whatever came from him."

Pendleton had practiced in General Court more than twenty years before Jefferson and Henry appeared there. Though Henry was to become one of his chief antagonists, Pendleton generously helped him in his first days in the court. Jefferson said that Henry's judgment in matters of law "was not worth a copper," and the orator realized that he needed formal training. He took his problem to Pendleton, who mapped out a course of study and lent him law books to help prepare himself.

As the Revolution approached, Pendleton played an effective role. He organized an association in Caroline County to help boycott British goods, he was colonel of his county militia, he continued in the House of Burgesses and the General Court. In 1774, when Governor Dunmore dissolved the Assembly and Virginia leaders called for a day of fasting and prayer out of sympathy with the people of blockaded Boston, Pendleton went with eighty-eight other burgesses to the Raleigh Tavern and helped to draw up a second, and more effective, association. Pendleton was the fourth man to sign. He also helped to call the first Virginia Convention, which met in Williamsburg in August, 1774, and when seven Virginia delegates were chosen for the opening Continental Congress the next month, Pendleton was among them.

Pendleton and Patrick Henry rode together to Mount Vernon to join Washington for the trip to Philadelphia; George Mason came over to discuss the coming session with them, and on September 1 the three delegates rode toward the north, Washington, Henry, and Pendleton, all destined to play major roles in the Congress.

John Adams of Massachusetts was pleased with the Virginians: "All the 7 delegates . . . are here and more sensible, fine fellows you would never wish to see." Silas Deane of Connecticut compared Pendleton and Henry: "Mr. Pendleton is a lawyer of eminence, of easy and cheerful countenance, polite in address, and elegant if not eloquent in style and elocution. Mr. Henry is . . . the completest speaker I ever heard . . . I can give you no idea of the music of his voice."

Pendleton's role in this Congress was minor, though he was one of two Virginians appointed to the important committee to define the rights of the colonies and set forth how these had been violated. He worked with the group through weeks of wrangling over theories of government and means of organization, but he had left Philadelphia by the time the Congress finally adopted a plea to King George, and Washington signed his name for him.

Pendleton opposed Patrick Henry the following spring, in the Virginia Convention at Richmond, when the Hanover orator proposed that Virginia should organize two militia regiments. Pendleton expressed the view of conservatives: why antagonize London needlessly, when war was not yet inevitable and, as everyone knew, men in every county were already arming themselves, unofficially, in a way that might not bring retaliation. Henry swayed the Convention with his "liberty or death" speech, and Virginia moved a step nearer war. Long afterward Pendleton explained his own position:

> Under the Regal Government I was a Whig in principle. . . . When the dispute with Britain began, a redress of grievances, and not a revolution of Government was my wish: in this I was firm, but temperate; and whilst I was endeavouring to raise the spirits of the timid to a general united opposition . . . I opposed and endeavoured to moderate the violent and fiery, who were plunging us into rash measures, and had the happiness to find a majority of all the public bodies confirming my sentiments; which, I believe, was the corner stone of our success.

The moderates continued to dominate the Convention in Virginia, as well as its delegation to Congress, and Pendleton, Robert Carter Nicholas and Benjamin Harrison, the conservative leaders, were named to a defense committee for Virginia. When delegates were elected for the Second Continental Congress, Pendleton was in fifth place, behind Peyton Randolph, Washington, Henry, and Richard Henry Lee, and only seven votes behind the leader.

The Congress of 1775 was eager to see the Virginians. When they arrived in Philadelphia some five hundred officers and civilians rode six miles into the country to meet them: bands played as they were conducted through the city. Now, since fighting had begun in Massachusetts, militiamen were drilling everywhere. Congressmen no longer dealt with abstractions and protests; they had to prepare for war.

Washington quickly became the popular choice as commander in chief of the armies, and Pendleton played a strange role in opposition. He reasoned that since Boston was the occupied city, the New England army then besieging it should have a New England commander, the veteran Artemus Ward; but privately Pendleton may have resisted because he did not wish to commit Virginia to defense of Boston, and to a war from which there would be no turning back. He apparently convinced the rest of the Virginia delegation (Washington himself was most reluctant to accept the command), and it was only after long discussion that the Virginians joined the unanimous vote for Washington.

There was no personal animosity between the old friends. Pendleton had drawn Washington's will only a few days before. Most revealing of all, when Washington stood before Congress to read his speech of acceptance, he read lines written for him by Pendleton. Washington added only nine words to the draft in Pendleton's hand.

When he returned to Virginia after the session, Pendleton declined to serve again as a delegate to Congress, pleading poor health, but he was given no leisure. He became president of the Committee of Safety, directing Virginia's war effort, and was soon involved in distressing details of trying to arm a state with few resources. In 1775 and again in 1776, he was president of Virginia's wartime Conventions, carrying out, as one historian said, "the details of a policy which he had strenuously opposed in debate." Pendleton's management of the Convention of 1776 was decisive in Virginia's course toward independence.

Afterward he resisted Jefferson's attempts to pass a bill for religious freedom; he helped to revise Virginia's laws, opposing Jefferson at many points in that work. He served as speaker of the House of Delegates, and was involved in every phase of the state's war effort until the spring of 1777, when he was crippled by a fall from a horse. He was still on crutches when he became presiding judge of the High Court of Chancery, Virginia's new court, over which he presided until the court system was revised and he became president of the Supreme Court of Appeals, a post he held until death.

Invasion of Virginia once chased Pendleton to the hills, where he was a refugee for two months, hiding from the raiders of Cornwallis. He was back at home in Edmundsbury when the surrender came at Yorktown and by then had a clear-eyed view of the conflict, which seemed likely to continue. He wrote James Madison: "even if we had a much better prospect of peace than we have . . . it is best to treat with arms in our hands."

In June, 1788, white-haired, infirm, and still hobbling on crutches, Pendleton went to Richmond to preside over the month-long struggle in which Virginia's Convention finally ratified the federal Constitution; he played a major role in overcoming the forces of Henry and George Mason, who championed states' rights. More than once, when some section of the Constitution seemed in danger of being rejected, Pendleton left the chair and took the floor himself to speak in its defense. As the Convention adjourned, Pendleton spoke quietly, urging unity after the partisan battle: "We are brothers; we are Virginians. Our common object is the good of our country. Let our rivalry be who can serve his country with the greatest zeal; and the future will be fortunate and glorious." Many delegates remembered until they were old men the scene that followed, when Pendleton's most caustic opponents wept, remembering the young Pendleton of the early days of the revolutionary movement. The old man left the rostrum quietly and sat for a few minutes while friends crowded about to shake his hand.

When Washington became President he offered a federal judgeship, but Pendleton declined. He and Washington remained friends despite his opposition to foreign and financial policies of the first presidential administration. Near the end of his life he joined the Republicans and wrote a campaign document for Jefferson, but this did not represent a change in the conservative beliefs he had held all his life. Pendleton died in October, 1803, in a tavern in Richmond, where, despite his feeble condition, he had gone to attend a session of the Supreme Court. He was buried on his plantation, Edmundsbury, in Caroline County.

Detail of George Wythe (on the left), from *The Declaration of Independence*, by John Trumbull. Yale University Art Gallery, New Haven, Connecticut.

GEORGE WYTHE

ONE morning at sunrise, in the years before the American Revolution, a cheerful middle-aged man welcomed a young student into the library of his brick house on Palace Green. Taking a leather-bound book from a shelf, he opened it at random and sat as the boy repeated his Greek lesson. The recitation in the ancient tongue went on until breakfast was announced.

This kindly teacher was one of the most influential Americans of his day. After scanty education in youth he became an accomplished classical scholar and, though largely self-taught, the acknowledged leader of the Virginia bar. He taught law to John Marshall and Henry Clay; numbered George Washington among his law clients; was either a member of the House of Burgesses or its clerk for more than a generation; signed the Declaration of Independence as a member of the Continental Congress; was author of most of the laws of Virginia's early statehood; and probably designed the state seal.

In 1762, George Wythe accepted his best-known student, Thomas Jefferson, nineteen, who spent most of the next five winters in Williamsburg under Wythe's direction and studied at his own Albemarle County home in the summers. Wythe drove Jefferson, as he had driven himself, to probe the origins of Roman and Saxon law, including such formidable works as Braxton's on early English law, which offered a contemporaneous interpretation of the Magna Charta. As Wythe had done, Jefferson began keeping a voluminous commonplace book with detailed notes of his studies and observations.

When the College of William and Mary was reorganized because of Jefferson's urging in 1779, Wythe became professor of law and police, the nation's first. He taught at the college for ten years—interrupted only when the army of Cornwallis passed through Williamsburg on its way to Yorktown. (Before the battle of Yorktown the Wythe House was headquarters for Washington and after the battle, for Count Rochambeau, the French commander.) His unique methods of teaching law impressed his contemporaries and set a pattern for the teaching of jurisprudence long afterward. Jefferson described Wythe's practical methods of training young lawyer-politicians: "He gives lectures regularly, and holds moot courts and parliaments wherein he presides, and the young men debate . . . learn the rules of parliamentary proceeding, and acquire the habit of public speaking."

A student who was subjected to this process wrote of the day of his "political birth": "I delivered an oration for the first time in your grand and august Assembly . . . Mr. Wythe has had a lofty presidential Seat erected, which adds very much to its dignity. . . . This throne has a greater effect in throwing a damp upon the spirits of the speaker, than you can imagine." This young man, Thomas Lee Shippen, debated the merits of a recent congressional tax measure "which I attacked in all its parts with warmth and violence . . . I had the satisfaction to find that I had made many proselytes to my opinion among those who had been warmly attached to the Bill." The mock action was taken through committees to final passage or death.

Many students remembered the "divine virtues" of Wythe and wrote of his kindnesses and of their love for him. One noted that he was going to the extreme of teaching a house servant to write. Nathaniel Beverley Tucker, son of Wythe's successor as law professor at the college, St. George Tucker, recalled that as a young lad he had met Wythe when the old man was "silent and grave, his whole manner betokening a gentle sadness." Wythe had a lesson even for the little boy, who always remembered being led by the hand "into his house, and up stairs, and into his bedchamber," where Wythe lifted him to a window, so that he could see a hive of bees at work storing honey against a windowpane.

After his wife's death in 1787 young students boarded in Wythe's home and submitted to the demanding routine he set for them; at least some of them had free schooling and board. He advertised in the *Virginia Gazette* that he would accept boys reading higher Latin and Greek poets, "approved English poets," and mathematics. Wythe installed in his house a microscope, a telescope, an electrical machine, terrestrial and celestial globes, an air pump, and other early scientific apparatus. He continued to rise before the sun and to teach his college law students as well.

Jefferson had once written a friend, in a letter recommending the College of William and Mary: "Williamsburg is a remarkably healthy situation, reasonably cheap, and affords very genteel society. I know no place *in the world,* while *present professors remain,* where I would so soon place a son." But in 1791, Wythe left Williamsburg for Richmond and Jefferson wrote: "Mr. Wythe has abandoned the college of William & Mary, disgusted with some conduct of the professors. . . . The visitors will try to condemn what gave him offence & press him to return: otherwise it is over with the college."

Whatever the faculty squabble, Wythe left it behind. He lived out his remaining years in Richmond.

George Wythe was born in 1726 on a Back River farm called Chesterville settled by his great-grandfather, near the present Langley Air Force Base. For three generations men of his family were justices of Elizabeth City courts, and his father, Thomas, was sheriff and member of the House of Burgesses. Through his grandmother, Ann Keith Walker, George was heir to a tradition of religious dissent. In a day when neither women nor churchmen had conspicuous rights, she astonished the House of Burgesses by appearing to complain that her Quaker husband refused to allow her and their children to worship as they pleased. She was a granddaughter of the Reverend George Keith, a controversial Quaker missionary who, after influencing George Fox and William Penn, left their church to form "the Keithians" and finally became an Anglican. Mr. Keith was also author of the first Quaker tract against slavery, published in Philadelphia in 1693.

George was three years old at the death of his father, and the boy's early education came chiefly from his mother, Margaret Walker Wythe. He attended a neighboring school briefly, but learned "nothing more than reading and writing English and the first five rules of Arithmetic." Apparently it was his mother who taught him the rudiments of Latin and had him translate the New Testament from the Greek, though "she knew of Greek only the alphabet and how to hold the dictionary." Wythe attended the College of William and Mary for a time between 1735 and 1740, but apparently only its grammar school.

Since his older brother inherited the family property, George was forced to make his own way. He began at fifteen by reading law for two

years with an uncle by marriage, Stephen Dewey, who lived near Petersburg. He was apparently neglected and treated as a drudge, but he learned
well enough to win his law license in 1746, before he was twenty-one.

He moved northward and for about two years practiced in Spotsylvania
County and rode the circuit into adjoining counties. He became the most
active lawyer in the area's courts, but moved to Williamsburg after the
early death of his first wife, Ann Lewis of Spotsylvania. Wythe immediately took a minor political post which taught him much about Virginia
politics; he was clerk to the committees of privileges and elections and of
propositions and grievances. When he was twenty-two years old he began
practicing law in York and Elizabeth City counties and in Williamsburg.
He prospered as a courtroom attorney and, while he was in his mid-twen-
ties, had such affluent clients as John Blair and the Custis family.

While he studied the origins of English law "from doomsday down," as
one admirer said, Wythe took up, unaided, a serious study of the classics;
the combination stunned lawyers with whom he vied in court. (He never
lost his desire to learn. When, past seventy, he injured his right hand, he
learned to write with his left. He was even older when he felt the need to
learn Hebrew, which he studied daily with the aid of a rabbi.) He fired
barrages of authorities; Jefferson made brief notes of one case in which
Wythe cited as precedents four Virginia acts, two British statutes, the
decision of a British court, sections of Justinian's Roman code, and the
orations of Cicero.

In twenty years of practice in the General Court of Virginia, though he
was frequently defeated by the rapier-like wit of his arch adversary,
Edmund Pendleton, Wythe was known as the leading law scholar. The
Reverend Lee Massey of Fairfax County, who had abandoned the bar, said
Wythe was also "the only honest lawyer he ever knew"; from his youth
Wythe declined to accept cases unless he thought his clients in the right.

He was not a great orator. Jefferson remembered his courtroom manner: "He was of easy elocution, his language chaste, methodical . . .
learned and logical . . . and of great urbanity in debate; not quick of
apprehension, but with a little time, profound in penetration. . . ."

In his late twenties and early thirties Wythe was handsome, with round
head and high forehead, an aquiline nose, and blue eyes, his figure slender
and erect. He had a habit of walking with hands held behind him, which
gave him a look of thoughtfulness. His small mouth was drawn by deep
lines.

At twenty-eight he became a burgess, representing Williamsburg (he later held seats for the college and for Elizabeth City County), and because of his experience was assigned to major committees. He helped to supervise spending large funds for the French and Indian War, and was involved in an early constitutional struggle with London in the "pistole fee" case, in which Governor Dinwiddie sought to enforce payment of a fee for processing land titles. The Assembly became so incensed as to defy Dinwiddie by sending Attorney General Peyton Randolph to England to plead the colony's case. Dinwiddie declared the office of attorney general vacant and appointed Wythe, who held the post for about a year until Randolph's return and then resigned in his favor.

Wythe's prosperous years had begun. His brother Thomas died about 1755, leaving George heir to the family estate. In the same year, when he was thirty, George married sixteen-year-old Elizabeth Taliaferro, daughter of Richard Taliaferro, master of the James City County plantation Powhatan and a leading Virginia architect. The couple moved into the house on Palace Green which still bears Wythe's name, and they soon lived in style. At one time they owned eighteen slaves. Wythe ordered a handsome English chariot bearing his coat of arms, and the house was furnished with fine china and silver; Washington was an occasional guest at meals. Wythe enjoyed playing cards, especially while Francis Fauquier was in the Governor's Palace, and in the course of two years he bought thirty-six packs of cards.

He continued to build his law practice, trying cases against opponents in the small but formidable bar of the General Court, John and Peyton Randolph, Robert Carter Nicholas, and Edmund Pendleton. He served on the committee that examined applicants for the practice of law and in 1760, with reluctance, signed the license of the poorly prepared Patrick Henry.

Back in the House of Burgesses, without loss of seniority, Wythe added to his burdensome labors; he was the only member to serve on as many as three standing committees. He was chairman of a committee to determine the accuracy of Virginia acts and to publish them, a work known as the Code of 1769. Wythe was a leader in the intricate negotiations with Governor Fauquier over Virginia currency and the colony's share of financing the recent war with France.

One of his most important posts was on the committee of correspondence, which presented, through an agent in London, the Virginia position on every controversial issue. Thus he was in the midst of early struggles which grew into the revolutionary cause and saw them develop step by step. He had joined this committee after only three full years in the House. Wythe was on this committee in 1764 when first word of the proposed stamp tax reached Virginia. The committee was "much alarmed," and Wythe was named head of a group to write a protest.

His arguments accurately forecast all that would come later in impassioned public debate. Wythe and his colleagues held that the act was unconstitutional and established a precedent, giving Parliament a hand in local American affairs. The protest spoke of "liberties and privileges as free born British subjects" and sought to "avert a storm so very replete with the most dangerous consequences." This resulted in the first resolutions of the burgesses against the Stamp Act, their language considerably weakened from the original submitted by Wythe. The House was still waiting to hear from London on these protests months later.

In the following spring of 1765, when Patrick Henry swept the House with his cry of "Caesar had his Brutus . . . ," Wythe voted against him and opposed his efforts at hasty passage of defiant resolutions, since Parliament had not yet replied to the earlier ones. Wythe differed with Henry on method and not principle, but Governor Fauquier, writing to London, included Wythe as one of three of the "most strenuous opposers of this rash heat"; the other two were Speaker John Robinson and Peyton Randolph.

Still Wythe's popularity did not suffer: he led the ticket in an election in Elizabeth City County and held his seat as a burgess. He lost in his effort to become attorney general, however, when Peyton Randolph became speaker of the House and left open the legal post in a shuffle of officeholders. Fauquier urged the selection of Wythe, who, the governor said, was "void of guile and steady in the support of government." Wythe wrote to Benjamin Franklin asking his support, but it was in vain. Peyton Randolph's younger brother John won the office. Wythe was elected mayor of Williamsburg and later alderman, but he was near the end of his career as a burgess.

In 1769 he became clerk of the House, officiating in a small adjoining office, and immediately tried to improve the rather casual system of record-keeping. He ordered balloting glasses from England for the House and often sought duplicate copies of all acts of the Virginia Assembly from its origin, to add to his collection. Wythe also intended to dress the part. He ordered at least two robes like those worn by clerks in the House of Commons, once urging his agent to send one "better than that I had before . . . which indeed was scandalous."

He also cut an impressive figure in drawing rooms and on the streets of Williamsburg, Philadelphia, and Richmond. Henry Clay remembered him as he was in later years as "plain, simple, and unostentatious. His countenance was full of blandness and benevolence and I think he made, in the salutation of others, the most graceful bow I have ever witnessed." Another described Wythe in those years as wearing a single-breasted black broadcloth coat with a stiff collar, a long vest with large pocket flaps, and a white cravat that covered the bosom. He wore short breeches and silver knee and shoe buckles and was "particularly neat in his appearance, and had a ruddy, healthy hue." His accounts showed that he was regularly shaved by a local barber and that he frequently bought "a pair of curls" for Mrs. Wythe.

The approach of revolution seldom found Wythe in the midst of the increasingly tumultuous scenes in Williamsburg, since he was not a burgess. Despite his reputation for loyalty to the Crown, Virginia patriots knew that they could count on him, and his sentiments about independence were not in doubt as the crisis grew. As dean of Williamsburg's political leaders, a powerful figure before the General Court, and constitutional oracle of sorts, Wythe found that his influence did not diminish when he left the House floor.

In May of 1769, when the Townshend Acts imposed new taxes and the governor, Lord Botetourt, learned that burgesses were secretly drafting a message to the king—a set of defiant resolutions—he is said to have sent to clerk Wythe in the night, trying to get a copy of the document, but Wythe evaded his messenger. The next day the burgesses completed their action before Botetourt could stop them, and the resolutions went into the record; Botetourt dissolved the Assembly, and a rump session drew up a nonimportation agreement. It was a milestone on the road to revolution in Virginia.

Wythe's role in the incident is not otherwise known; he was not an eligible burgess, but as clerk he published the names of eleven burgesses absent from the rump session at the Raleigh who had later joined the Association boycotting British goods.

In 1774, the year of the last full session of the House of Burgesses, Wythe became a member of the local Committee of Safety, an all-powerful group that helped in the union of the colonies and literally ran Virginia in the interim between colony and commonwealth. Wythe was not among the six Virginians sent to the First Continental Congress that year, but the next year, 1775, he was elected to Congress, and in August went off by carriage with Mrs. Wythe on the rough cross-country journey to Philadelphia, to the cheers of townspeople and volleys from the militia.

In Philadelphia, Wythe became the first of the Virginia signers of the Declaration of Independence. He violated his lifelong habit of signing himself "G. Wythe" to write fully "George Wythe."

It was during this absence of the Wythes that Jefferson and his wife spent about two months in the Wythe House, evidently without paying rent. Wythe wrote his former pupil: "Make use of the house and furniture. I shall be happy if any thing of mine can contribute to make your and Mrs. Jefferson's residence in Williamsburg comfortable. . . . The conveniency of my house servants and furniture to you and Mrs. Jefferson adds not a little to their value in my estimation."

At the end of the year or early in 1777, Wythe returned to Virginia for another of the demanding roles of his career, one for which he was qualified as was no other Virginian. The House of Delegates named Jefferson, Wythe, George Mason, Edmund Pendleton, and Thomas Ludwell Lee to a committee to provide Virginia with a revised code of law. Lee resigned; Mason declined to serve on the ground that he was not a lawyer; and Wythe, Jefferson, and Pendleton divided the work among them. Pendleton, whose field was the laws previously passed in Virginia, apparently did very little of the work, and in 1779, Wythe and Jefferson completed the task of making Pendleton's portion "what we thought it ought to be." Jefferson had written the sections dealing with common law and with English laws to the time of James I, and Wythe, the more modern period. The committee reported a total of 126 bills.

Wythe also became speaker of the House of Delegates and in 1778 one of three state judges on the High Court of Chancery. (He later became the only judge of that court.)

Although George Wythe's contributions to the success of the American Revolution were mainly those of a statesman and lawyer, he did try to take an "active" part. In 1775, when militia volunteers mustered on a Williamsburg green, the forty-nine-year-old Wythe, ignoring the pleas of his wife, put on a hunting shirt, took a musket, and attempted to volunteer. Six years later, when a party of British soldiers appeared in boats near Jamestown, Wythe and a couple of hunting companions blazed away at the invaders with shotguns; one of Jefferson's correspondents thought that the old man had helped prevent the force under Benedict Arnold from landing there.

Mrs. Wythe's health began to fail soon after the Revolution, and in

1787, as Wythe wrote a friend, her state of health was "so low and she is so emaciated, that my apprehensions are not a little afflicted." She died in August of that year, at forty-eight, with few details of her life known to history beyond an occasional mention of purchases of clothing for her or new curls for her hair-do, or of her sending garden peas to a fellow gardener, Jefferson. Almost immediately Wythe disposed of all his slaves in Williamsburg except two adults and no longer kept horses or vehicles. Several of his freed slaves survived him and some were beneficiaries of his will. Through his wife he inherited a life interest in the Wythe House, which he relinquished when he moved to Richmond a few years later.

His appearance had changed greatly. His cheeks were sunken and wrinkled by the loss of his teeth, and he was almost entirely bald; the remaining hair was worn long at the back of his skull and rolled. It is this image of Wythe that has come down to posterity, largely because of the painter of the Revolution, Jonathan Trumbull, Jr., who depicted Wythe in his painting "The Signing of the Declaration of Independence."

Wythe's political career flourished into his old age. He represented Virginia in the federal convention at Philadelphia in 1787 and was vice-president of the Virginia Convention the next year (he offered the resolution for ratification of the United States Constitution). In 1791, at last, he abandoned Williamsburg to move to Richmond, where he remained chancellor of the state until his death.

Wythe died June 8, 1806, poisoned by his grandnephew, George Wythe Sweeney, who lived with him and had been made one of his heirs. A house servant, also poisoned, died before Wythe, and the old man, convinced of Sweeney's treachery, amended his will to leave the bulk of his estate to another servant. Sweeney was tried for murder but was freed because the testimony of the sole damaging witness, a Negro cook, was not then admissible under Virginia law.

Among items left to Thomas Jefferson by Wythe were two silver cups, a "gold-headed cane," some scientific apparatus, and "about 500 pounds' worth" of books. A handsome Chippendale dining table and some Hepplewhite chairs now at Monticello, though not mentioned in Wythe's will, were passed down through the Jefferson family and are said to have been a gift from Jefferson's old law professor.

Wythe is buried in the yard of St. John's Church in Richmond near the spot where Patrick Henry made his most famous speech. A bronze marker which briefly proclaims his fame was placed over the grave in 1922, 116 years after his last rites.

George Mason, by D. W. Boudet after John Hesselius. Virginia Museum of Fine Arts, Richmond; on loan to Gunston Hall.

GEORGE MASON

IN February, 1759, Virginia's House of Burgesses opened a session notable for its promising new members, most of them young. George Washington was there as a bridegroom of twenty-seven. Richard Henry Lee was the same age, and his brother, Francis Lightfoot Lee, was twenty-five. There was also a new man from Fairfax County, Washington's friend and neighbor, thirty-four-year-old George Mason, a courtly but not striking man of below average height, with "a grand head" and grey eyes.

Mason was probably pale, since he was chronically ill with what he described as "convulsive colic" and "gout of the stomach." He was reluctant to come to Williamsburg for other reasons. He felt that service in public office was, as he said many years later, "an oppressive and unjust invasion of my personal liberty." And Mason was a planter, not a lawyer. This session was to be his only public service outside his county until the coming of revolution drew him back to the capital, where he was to write one of the key documents of American history.

The House in which Mason took his seat with other newcomers devoted itself largely to problems of the French and Indian War—finance, scandals, manpower and supply, and a resolution of appreciation to Colonel Washington. The House speaker was the veteran John Robinson, fifty-five, and one of its most influential members was the thirty-three-year-old burgess from the College of William and Mary, George Wythe, who usually spoke the sentiments of the executive, Lieutenant Governor Francis Fauquier.

The session quickly confirmed Mason's suspicions that he would find practical politics distasteful. After a squabble over a fraud in supplying food to Virginia troops in the field, a member complained that the House itself was a constant display of corruption: "one holds the lamb while another skins," shouted Thomas Johnson of Louisa County, "the country's money is squandered away." He cited an example: When the salary of the clerk, John Randolph, was to be voted on, Randolph "got up, and walking through the Burgesses, gave a nod to his creatures on each side, who all followed him out of the House, and promised to be for the largest sum proposed." The agitated House ordered a committee to investigate and finally, by a vote of thirty-seven to thirty-two, reprimanded Johnson for the "false scandalous and malicious" charge. Since there was no roll call, Mason's vote was not recorded, but he must have been appalled by this glimpse into the creaking machinery of the colony's government.

Mason operated a 5,000-acre plantation on the Potomac, just below Mount Vernon, and only the year before had moved into an elegant small mansion, Gunston Hall. His relationship with Washington was intimate. They exchanged cuttings and trees for their gardens, hunted and surveyed together, and collaborated on a scheme to improve Potomac navigation. They shared important holdings in the Ohio Company, which held a 500,000-acre grant near the present site of Pittsburgh; Mason had been chosen treasurer of the company. The two were linked in another matter: they were presented to a grand jury for failure to list their fine carriages for tax purposes.

Washington and Mason had one recorded dispute. When a new church was to be built at Pohick, Mason favored the old site, nearer Gunston Hall, and Washington a new one nearer Mount Vernon. Washington won, but it was Mason who completed the building, as executor for a contractor who died during construction of the church.

George Mason, the fourth of his name to hold a great Potomac estate, was born to rebellion. The first George, his great-grandfather, had helped to set off Bacon's Rebellion by leading an attack on two Indian forts in revenge for the murder of an overseer; the Indians retaliated by pillaging settlements from the Potomac to the James, and in the ensuing crisis Bacon made his mark on history.

George's grandfather and great-grandfather, who had been trained in law in London's Middle Temple, were county militia commanders and prosperous tobacco planters. His father had ridden with Governor Spotswood to the Blue Ridge as a Knight of the Golden Horseshoe. George's mother, widowed when her husband drowned in the Potomac, was left with ten-year-old George and two younger children. Since George would inherit the family estate as the eldest son, she sensibly bought ten thousand acres of cheap wilderness lands in Loudoun County for her younger children, so that when they came of age, they owned estates of almost equal value.

George's brother Thomson was schooled in London, but George had only home tutoring, though some of it was of unusual value. His cousin, John Mercer of Marlborough, owned one of Virginia's finest libraries, and as a boy George read and worked there for several years. Mercer was disbarred from legal practice for his colorful and unbridled insults in court, and spent much time with George. Mason was probably often with Mercer as he compiled an abridgement of the laws of Virginia, including a review of all British law in effect in the colony. The work was of such value that it was used as a reference by the House of Burgesses for many years.

When he came of age Mason left his mother and moved to Dogue's Neck, where he was to build Gunston Hall. He married Anne Eilbeck of Maryland four years later and took her to the new plantation house he had named for one of his mother's family homes in Staffordshire. He described his wife as "taller than the middle size, and elegantly shaped," with black eyes, "tender and lively . . . her complexion remarkably fair and fresh." The house, which Mason planned in some detail, was built by a gifted Englishman, William Buckland, and is still noted for its fine finish, especially its Chippendale carvings.

Mason had nine children, and his wife reared them with firmness and the aid of a slender green riding whip known as "the green doctor." Mason was his own steward and kept the plantation records. In addition to tobacco and other field crops he had a large orchard and, like many of his contemporaries, produced most of his family's needs—clothing, tools, the simpler furniture, and brandy. He was paid 2,000 pounds of tobacco annually for keeping a Potomac ferry at Occoquan. There was the usual plantation school for the Mason children, as well as a dancing school in the neighborhood, one of whose pupils was Patsy Custis from Mount Vernon. Mason raced horses with other breeders on the track near Pohick and kept a well-known stallion, Vulcan, who was descended from Janus, the most famous of early Virginia thoroughbreds.

Mason devoted himself to reading after his exposure to John Mercer's library, and was often sought as a consultant on knotty legal problems. He was a trustee for the new town of Alexandria and sat as justice of the monthly county court, which ruled on most important matters of local government. Thus, despite his retired life and distaste for public office, he was a man of experience in business and politics when he was first called to serve the colony in Williamsburg.

His holdings in the Ohio Company, which he knew might become the basis of great wealth, made him a close student of the complex land laws, and even in his youth he was well known in Williamsburg for the petitions he filed to support claims to other lands which he had bought from immigrants.

Mason was not on hand in the capital as the sessions of the House grew more stormy at the close of the wars with France, but his influence was felt at every step of the difficult dealings with England. He was not involved in the Stamp Act crisis in Virginia, when his cousin, George Mercer, the London agent for the Ohio Company, was sent to Williamsburg with the despised stamps which were to be used on parchment or paper used as legal documents, bills, diplomas, newspapers, and the like, as well as dice and playing cards. Mercer, apparently unaware of the heated reactions of Virginians to the act, was beset by an angry crowd in the capital and was saved from harm only by Governor Fauquier.

As an accomplished businessman, at home in many phases of colonial law, and a realist to the core, Mason saw that British repeal of the Stamp Act was not the end of American problems. He realized that the substituted Declaratory Act only postponed trouble. His letter signed "A Virginia Planter," addressed to British merchants, was a clear warning that the colonials were not to be cowed and that they were weary of being treated as mere children. Mason sketched this parent-child relationship in a satirical way and asked: "Is not this a little ridiculous, when applied to three millions of as loyal and useful subjects as any in the British dominions, who have been only contending for their birth-right . . . ?" The letter was prophetic, forceful and direct: "Let our fellow-subjects in Great Britain reflect that we are descended from the same stock with themselves, nurtured in the same principles of freedom . . . that in crossing the Atlantic Ocean, we have only changed our climate, not our minds, our natures and dispositions . . . that we are still the same people with them in every respect; only not yet debauched by wealth, luxury, venality and corruption. . . ." He warned that it was "by invitation and indulgence, not by compulsion" that England kept her American markets. Even more plainly he said: "Such another experiment as the stamp-act would produce a general revolt in America." As if he saw into the future he asked: "Do you think that all your rival powers in Europe would sit still and see you crush your once flourishing and thriving colonies, unconcerned spectators of such a quarrel?"

Mason wrote, he said, as "a man who spends most of his time in retirement, and has seldom muddled in public affairs . . . an Englishman in principles . . . who adores the wisdom and happiness of the British Constitution."

The letter appeared in the *London Public Ledger* in 1766, and, though it lacked the stirring rhetoric of Patrick Henry's Stamp Act oration of the year before, it struck more directly at the source of trouble. Mason realized that it was the London and Scottish merchants, and not the persuasive Henry, who had dictated repeal of the Stamp Act. He also saw beyond the issue of the moment as clearly as any man of the day.

Mason never compromised his views and, in each succeeding crisis with London, was the intellectual leader of the Virginia cause. In 1769, when the Virginia burgesses responded to a circular from Massachusetts that protested the new taxation of the Townshend Acts, Governor Botetourt dissolved the session. When most of the House met in the Raleigh Tavern to take action on their own, Mason was not present, but the resulting agreement of nonimportation of British goods, an "Association" of Virginians, was his work. Washington presented the plan, a boycott which would have banned both imports and exports; the names of violators were to be published in newspapers. The rump session placed a partially successful boycott on imports. The Townshend Acts were soon repealed by Parliament, except for a tax on tea.

Mason was not satisfied. A tighter boycott would have won complete victory. He wrote an English friend that though "not five men of sense in America . . . would accept of independence if it was offered . . . we will not submit to have our own money taken out of our pockets without our consent. . . . We owe our Mother Country the duty of subjects; we will not pay her the submission of slaves."

Mason's wife died in 1773 of "a slow fever" after a long illness, a shock he described as an "irreparable loss" and wrote poignantly of her, "she never met me without a smile." He was forty-eight, and a few days after her death he made a will as if his life were done, and remained at Gunston Hall to care for his children, who ranged in age from twenty to three. Mason resisted efforts to lure him back into public service, pleading "the duty I owe to a poor little helpless family of orphans." He turned again to his work on the land claims of the Ohio Company, and was interrupted only by the alarm following the Boston Tea Party. Mason was in Williamsburg when the news of the closing of the Boston port was fresh there and the colony staged its day of fasting and prayer.

On July 18, 1774, the leaders of Fairfax County passed a set of twenty-four resolves setting forth their complaints against Great Britain, urging a more effective boycott, calling for a Continental Congress to "Plan for the defence and preservation of our common rights," and incidentally demanding "an entire stop" to the "wicked, cruel and unnatural" slave trade. Washington presided over the meeting, but Mason had spent the previous afternoon and evening at Mount Vernon and had written the resolutions himself. The document was, as the early historian Sparks said, "one of the ablest and most luminous expositions of the points at issue" in the whole course of the break with England.

Mason declined once more to return to the House of Burgesses, but he did join the Fairfax Committee of Safety and presided over the formation of the Fairfax Independent Company of volunteers, one hundred militiamen commanded by Washington, whose handsome uniform of buff and blue was so admired by the colonel that it became the uniform of the American army.

Mason's next public speech was delivered to the Fairfax company, in support of a plan for annual election of officers, and went far beyond the issue at stake: "We came equals into this world, and equals shall we go out of it. All men are by nature born equally free and independent. . . ." He spoke of how governments oppressed natural rights and said: "In all our associations; in all our agreements, let us never lose sight of this fundamental maxim—that all power was originally lodged in, and consequently is derived from, the people."

Such independent militia companies had sprung up in other colonies, but no other seems to have been addressed in so stirring a fashion. That was the year of Patrick Henry's "liberty or death" speech, of bloodshed in Massachusetts, and of Washington's election as commander of the armies. Lord Dunmore fled Williamsburg, and the Virginia Convention met in Richmond. To that Mason was a delegate, much against his will, and one of the session's most moving scenes took place on the floor as he was urged to go to Congress.

More than two thirds of the Convention, Mason said, had asked him individually to agree to go to Philadelphia, but he had refused because of his children, alone at Gunston Hall. When a vacancy occurred in the Virginia congressional delegation with the resignation of old Richard Bland, Henry and Jefferson led an effort to force Mason's acceptance. These men would not be refused, as Mason reported it to a friend: "laying it down as a rule that I would not refuse if ordered by my country . . . just before the ballot, I was publicly called upon in Convention and obliged to make a public excuse, and give my reasons for refusal, in doing which I felt myself more distressed than ever I was in my life, especially when I saw tears run down the President's cheeks."

Mason had found the Convention itself trying for other reasons. As he wrote Washington: "I never was in so disagreeable a situation, and almost despaired of a cause which I saw so ill conducted.—Mere vexation and disgust threw me into such an ill state of health, that . . . I was sometimes near fainting in the House." After his return to Gunston Hall he had an attack of the gout which crippled him.

Mason's neighbors came near to allowing him to continue in retirement, for he was barely re-elected to a Convention seat for the spring session in Williamsburg in 1776 and was late in arriving because of his gout. Edmund Pendleton was president of the Convention, Patrick Henry was on hand to push the members to a complete break with England, and there was an air of expectancy in Virginia. Richard Henry Lee had written almost a month earlier: "Ages yet unborn, and millions existing at present, may rue or bless that assembly on which their happiness or misery will so eminently depend." Many members came with petitions from their counties to speak for independence.

On May 15, while Mason was still on the road from Gunston Hall, the Convention resolved to instruct the congressional delegates from Virginia to propose independence. In a final paragraph it asked for a committee "to prepare a DECLARATION OF RIGHTS and such a plan of Government as will be most likely to maintain peace and order in this Colony, and secure substantial and equal liberty to the people."

When Mason arrived on May 17 he was an inevitable addition to the committee of thirty-four working on the declaration and Virginia's constitution. Archibald Cary was the chairman, but Mason was its leading spirit from the moment of his arrival. He wrote Richard Henry Lee that the committee was "overcharged with useless members," and predicted that he would have to combat "a thousand ridiculous and impracticable proposals." But he began with confidence, and word of his progress crept out of the committee room during the few days of work. Edmund Pendleton wrote to Jefferson in Philadelphia: "the political cooks are busy in preparing the dish, and as Col. Mason seems to have the ascendancy in the great work, I have sanguine hopes it will be framed so as to answer it's end."

Mason's work of many years had prepared him well for this task. In little more than a week the committee had a draft of a declaration. For about two weeks it was debated, sometimes bitterly, and on June 12 it was adopted by the Convention without a dissenting vote. Conservatives blocked progress for a few days by arguing that Mason's opening statement was dangerous, and would invite a slave uprising. Either all men in America were free or they were not. The Convention bogged in an unexpected wrangle over slavery.

Mason's draft of the declaration opened: "That all men are created equally free and independent, and have certain inherent natural rights, of which they cannot, by any compact, deprive or divest their posterity. . . ." The compromise finally reached included the qualification in defining free men as *"when they enter into a state of society,"* evading the issue of slavery, since slaves were not considered to belong to society. Mason opposed slavery, but he fought to prevent the issue from killing the declaration. There is no record of the debate on the document, though Mason's speeches from the floor were described as "neither flowing nor smooth, but his language was strong, his manner most impressive, and strengthened by a dash of biting cynicism when provocation made it seasonable."

In the end the Convention accepted Mason's fourteen proposed guarantees of individual liberties (many of them may be traced to Locke and other earlier philosophers), but added two more; the additions were, in Mason's opinion, "not for the better." Other attempted articles were beaten back when Henry warned that some "towering public offender" might make use of them.

The Declaration of Rights was a straightforward document, unmistakable in meaning, proclaiming that all power derived from the people and that government was their creature, to be altered or abolished as they saw fit. Offices should not be hereditary; government should be divided into three distinct branches, executive, legislative, and judicial. Elections should be free, with a broad base of suffrage for voters. Laws could be made or changed only by representatives of the people. All men in capital cases should have fair treatment and fair trial by a jury of their peers; they could not be made to testify against themselves. There should be no excessive bail or fines or cruel punishments. Freedom of the press and religion were essential. A militia must be organized for defense, but standing armies in peace time were dangerous, and the military should always be controlled by "the civil power."

This summary of American protests against British abuses and their remedies owed much to the past, but two of its sections, on the freedom of press and religion, were of special importance. The declaration was not only, as Mason said, "closely imitated by the other United States," but it served as the basic form for the first ten amendments to the United States Constitution, after a bitter battle over its ratification, and spread to other nations in very much its original form. Its principles and language are still to be detected in a document so recent as the International Covenant on Human Rights adopted by the United Nations.

Mason completed his work in the Convention by writing a major part of the Virginia Constitution to implement his guarantees of freedom. It was adopted on June 29, about a week before the Declaration of Independence was signed in Philadelphia, a pioneer work as a permanent, written Constitution.

The Convention having elected Patrick Henry the first governor, Mason headed a committee to notify him of his election and composed the oath of office. He also presented the report of the committee that designed Virginia's seal, though the actual design seems to have been George Wythe's.

Mason returned to Williamsburg in the fall, late again for the Assembly, and joined Jefferson in a vain attempt to pass a bill for religious freedom. Despite the separation from England and the Declaration of Rights, the Anglican church was still supported by taxes, and the dissenting sects of Virginia complained loudly. Mason's committee was deluged with petitions, one of which bore ten thousand names. The conservatives, led by Edmund Pendleton and Robert Carter Nicholas, defeated the effort to bring complete freedom of religion to the state, in debates so warm that Jefferson remembered them as "the severest contest in which I have ever been engaged." The battle ended in a compromise, freeing dissenters from the necessity of supporting the Anglican church and removing rectors from public payrolls. It would be ten years before James Madison guided the complete bill to passage.

A smallpox inoculation, Mason said, prevented his attending the Assembly of 1777, and he was seldom in regular attendance again. John Parke Custis, his companion from Fairfax, complained to Washington: "I have often wished my colleague had been present . . . he is most inexcusable in staying away." He was effective when he did arrive, however. John Augustine Washington once wrote: "I have not heard particularly what our Assembly are about; but it is said it will be a short session, unless Col. Mason, who is not yet got down, should carve out more business for them than they have yet thought of."

Mason returned once at Washington's plea that he help battle inflation, which was ruining the country as well as its army. Mason's plan for Virginia was to base currency on the vast lands beyond the mountains, by making those lands a sinking fund for state debts. After a long struggle with conflicting interests—which was interrupted by news of the conquest of the Northwest by George Rogers Clark—Mason's ingenious plan to bolster the currency with Virginia's most precious assets was abandoned.

He played a major role, chiefly as consultant, in the cession of Virginia's western lands to the United States, ending a problem which had stalled acceptance of the Articles of Confederation by several states. Mason did that work in a spirit of sacrifice, "anxious to do this last piece of service to the American Union, before I quit the Assembly, which I am determined to do at the end of the next session."

Mason remarried in 1780 at the age of fifty-four. The new mistress of Gunston Hall was Sarah Brent of Woodstock. The Masons fled Gunston Hall more than once during the last months of the war when Virginia was invaded, but George stubbornly refused to take part in the national government, as Washington urged, or to return to Richmond. About a year before the battle of Yorktown he wrote his son prophetically: "If our Allies had a superior Fleet here I shou'd have no Doubt of a favorable Issue to the War, but without it, I fear we are deceiving both them and ourselves."

Mason's work in Williamsburg was over. In Richmond he took part in the bitter battles over the Articles of Confederation and the new federal Constitution, and was defeated on most counts, since he strongly favored states' rights and guarantees of freedom that would have hobbled a central government. He and Henry and their allies were overwhelmed by the Federalists, but when the Constitution had been ratified and the Bill of Rights set forth as the first ten amendments, Mason confessed that, with two or three additions, "I could chearfully put my hand and heart to the new government." However, Virginia, which he put above national interests, was the last of the nine states necessary to pass the Bill of Rights and to put it into effect.

Jefferson visited Mason in the fall of 1792 at Gunston Hall, to find him suffering a bad attack of gout and on a crutch. Jefferson took notes as they talked about the Constitutional Convention and the maneuvering in which compromises had been reached. The old man's chief complaint was of the coalition of southern and New England states which had prevented the elimination of slavery: "under this coalition the great principles of the Constitution were changed in the last days of the Convention." Mason was also bitter about Alexander Hamilton's plans of finance. Jefferson wrote, "He said he considered Hamilton as having done us more injury than Gr. Britain and all her fleets and armies."

Mason's mind was as alert as ever, and his principles were the same he had taken to Williamsburg thirty-three years before, but when Jefferson saw him that day, it was for the last time. Mason died a little more than a week later, on October 7. He was buried at Gunston Hall, in a grave overlooking the Potomac.

Jefferson, who had been at Mason's side in many crucial moments of the struggle toward freedom, paid him tribute as "a man of the first order of wisdom among those who acted on the theatre of the Revolution, of expansive mind, profound judgement, cogent in argument, learned in the lore of our former constitution, and earnest for the republican change on democratic principles."

Thomas Jefferson, by Mather Brown. Reproduced by permission of the owner, Mr. Charles Francis Adams, Waltham, Massachusetts.

THOMAS JEFFERSON

THE College of William and Mary was favored by Virginia planters who could not afford to send their sons to England, or who feared that a European education would make them "inconceivably illiterate . . . corrupted and vicious." At the time of which we speak there were a faculty of only three professors (it was down to half strength in the aftermath of a political storm) and a student body of about one hundred. The Reverend Thomas Dawson lived in the President's House, and across the yard in the Brafferton School were a few Indian boys, the sons of western tribal chieftains, manfully resisting efforts at their Christianization.

On a morning in mid-March, 1760, a young rider came into Williamsburg, trailed by a body servant and a loaded pack horse. The college—after Harvard, the oldest in the colonies—was about to enroll its most illustrious student.

The newly arrived student was not quite seventeen, about six feet tall, a rawboned, awkward boy with large hands and feet, reddish hair, and a freckled, square-jawed face. There was an expression of quick intelligence in his hazel eyes. He was Thomas Jefferson, from Albemarle County, heir to a large estate in the foothills, and already trained in Latin, Greek, and geology by backcountry tutors.

The college kept young Jefferson waiting for two weeks while he was examined for his fitness to enter, since he had not attended the grammar school there. Jefferson thought this grammar school made things "disagreeable and degrading" for serious students, since it "filled the College with Children." But he must have been impressed by his first sight of a college and by the busy little capital of America's largest colony. Much later he noted the town's buildings, the "light and airy structure" that was the Capitol and the Palace that he did not find handsome on the outside, but "spacious and commodious within . . . prettily situated." The Palace, he thought, might be developed into a fine residence; within less than twenty years he was to live there as governor.

Though a stranger to the town, Jefferson had reason to feel at home. His mother's father, Isham Randolph, had sat in the House of Burgesses, and his kinsmen, Peyton and John Randolph, were leading citizens. His father, Peter Jefferson, had not only come here as a burgess, but he had become so fond of its ways that he sealed a land trade with a bowl of arrack punch from Henry Wetherburn's tavern. Peter Jefferson was also well known in the capital for his work with Joshua Fry in making the most notable map of Virginia since the time of John Smith, and the first based on an actual survey.

Great things were expected of Jefferson by his tutors, especially the strong-willed Reverend James Maury, whose protest over his salary was to launch the public career of Patrick Henry. Despite a natural reserve Jefferson was resolute, self-assured, and eager to make the most of his opportunity. At the end of two weeks he was admitted to the college.

The College of William and Mary of that day was not wholly devoted to the pursuit of learning. There were complaints of professors who "play all Night at Cards in publick Houses" and were often seen staggering in the streets. Within five months of his arrival Jefferson was to lose his professor of moral philosophy, the Reverend Jacob Rowe, who made no practical application of his specialty, and was dismissed for carousing and leading students in a battle against town boys.

Rowe's course was taken over by William Small, a Scot who was already overloaded with work ranging from physics to belles-lettres. Jefferson was immediately won by Small who, he said, "probably fixed the destinies of my life, with a happy talent of communication, correct and gentlemanly manners." Small soon saw young Jefferson's qualities and became so attached to him that they were daily companions outside the classroom. The professor gave Jefferson a fresh view of "the expansion of science and of the system of things in which we are placed."

For almost half of Jefferson's two years at the college, Small seems to have been his only teacher, but the Scot is little known to history. In 1764 he returned to England, where he became a friend of James Watt and Erasmus Darwin; he died on the eve of the Revolution.

Among Jefferson's companions in college were Dabney Carr, who later married Thomas' younger sister, Martha; two future governors of Virginia, John Page of Rosewell and John Tyler; and Francis Willis of Gloucester County, a gay blade who often came in late from an evening on the town, found Jefferson at his studies, and overturned his table or snatched his books and ran away with them. John Page recalled that Jefferson "could tear himself away from his dearest friends, and fly to his studies." By family tradition he studied fifteen hours a day at William and Mary, usually until long after midnight, only to rise at dawn. He took daily exercise, often by running through the streets of the town, and it was probably in his college years that he began his lifelong habit of washing his feet in cold water each morning, which he thought prevented colds and fevers.

He was not noted for his sense of humor, but was good-natured and optimistic. He had a habit of humming or singing to himself when he was not talking. He was unusually neat in dress, his shoe buckles always shone, and he was careful to wear overalls when he rode horseback to preserve his clothes.

Dr. Small's influence on Jefferson was not limited to experiments with an air pump, water prism or electrical machine. The teacher was an apostle of the Enlightenment, and Jefferson gained from him a broad tolerance which prepared him for the struggles for political and religious freedom in later years. Small also introduced Jefferson to an equally influential teacher, George Wythe. Thomas began reading law in Wythe's office.

Wythe was thirty-five, a leading lawyer of the colony, self taught in the classics and the law, an exacting if somewhat eccentric taskmaster who shared Jefferson's enthusiasm for a Spartan regime. Like Small, he encouraged the young man to look beyond his studies of the moment to other fields of knowledge. Jefferson spent five years reading law with Wythe and enjoying his friendship in the fine brick house on Palace Green. His numerous notebooks from this time indicate tedious study of leading law authorities and of Latin, Greek, Italian, English literature, and other subjects. In a real sense, this unusually long period of work and association with George Wythe was Jefferson's university career.

Wythe laid out a course of study, and Jefferson went home to Shadwell for nine months of study. He sometimes complained of the work, especially of the Commentaries of Sir Edward Coke: "I do wish the Devil had old Coke, for I am sure I never was so tired of an old dull scoundrel in my life." He was probably delighted to return to Williamsburg, for life at Shadwell left much to be desired. As he once wrote: "I do not like the ups and downs of country life: today you are frolicking with a fine girl and tomorrow you are moping by yourself." Some of his five years of reading law in Williamsburg were spent as a lodger with Thomas Craig in Market Square Tavern.

Thomas wrote that he revered Wythe above even William Small as "my earliest and best friend . . . to him I am indebted for first impressions which have had the most salutary influence on the course of my life." Jefferson especially admired Wythe's precision of mind; he never detected in his teacher a "useless or declamatory thought or word."

Wythe and Small also gave Jefferson a taste of a life new to him. They took him into an exclusive circle at the Palace, then occupied by Governor Francis Fauquier, whose social graces must have dazzled the nineteen-year-old from the Blue Ridge. The older men accepted Jefferson as a fourth in their quartet for intimate dinners, and the governor invited him to take part in Palace musicales, in which Fauquier joined and Jefferson probably played the second violin or cello.

Thomas, doubtless flattered to be included in such company, admired the governor's wit and liberal outlook and always thought him the ablest of governors in Williamsburg. The impressionable boy never forgot the evenings in the Palace dining rooms and supper room: "At these dinners I have heard more good sense, more rational and philosophical conversations, than in all my life besides."

He also enjoyed the musicales and said music was "the favorite passion of my soul." Other players at these concerts are unknown today, but may have included John Randolph (who once traded a violin for £100 worth of Jefferson's books) and Robert Carter, who lived next to the Palace and owned a barrel organ coveted by Jefferson. Thomas became so devoted to music that he played three hours daily and continued this habit until the time of the Revolution.

Looking back on these years, Jefferson confessed that he had been extravagant and offered to repay his father's estate for over-spending his student's budget. Some of the expense was due to small wagers made with friends; he knew virtually everyone in the town and took part in its social life. He went to plays and dances, and, though he did not seem to gamble or drink to excess, conceded that he was often among such dissolute characters as cardplayers, horse racers, and foxhunters. He visited neighboring plantations, and often, when he took a boat down Queens Creek and over the York River to John Page's great house, Rosewell, he took along fresh fiddle strings. He belonged to a small group of convivial spirits known as the Flat Hat Club, the first college fraternity in British America, apparently devoted to innocent adolescent sport.

Jefferson often wrote of the town as "Devilsburg," and once derided the college and mental hospital buildings as "crude misshapen piles" more like brick kilns than buildings. On his first trip to the North he wrote from Annapolis that the houses there were better than Williamsburg's, but that the gardens were "more indifferent." But there was a Virginian's pride in his description of the Maryland Assembly in session, behaving like a "mob," in such a hubbub as Virginia planters might raise in a private meeting. The legislators of Annapolis, at least, lacked the fine manners of the working burgesses of Williamsburg.

By then, Jefferson had suffered through the only known romance of his early years. The girl was pretty Rebecca Burwell, the sister of a classmate, Lewis Burwell. In his letters to Page, full of the groans of puppy love, Thomas wrote of Rebecca as "Belinda" and, in reverse, Adnileb, or used Latin and Greek disguises. He agonized over whether he should propose, but, when he next saw Rebecca at a ball in the Raleigh Tavern, his nerve failed him: "Last night as merry as agreeable company and dancing with Belinda in the Apollo could make me, I never could have thought the succeeding Sun would have seen me as wretched as I now am!" He confessed to Page that he had been prepared to say "a great deal," only to find himself tongue-tied: "But good God! When I had an opportunity . . . a few broken sentences, uttered in great disorder . . . with pauses of uncommon length, were the too visible marks of my strange confusion!"

After his vague and half-hearted proposal, and some months of Jefferson's inattention, Rebecca married Jaquelin Ambler, who became a member of the Council of State during the Revolution; one of Rebecca's daughters married John Marshall, the future chief justice who was to become one of Jefferson's adversaries. Jefferson reported a violent headache for two days after he had news of Belinda's loss.

This was a minor diversion. Jefferson still studied with Wythe, doubtless helping to prepare law cases. He attended some of the semi-annual sessions of General Court and listened to deliberations in the House of Burgesses. In 1765, when Virginians resisted new Stamp Act taxes levied to pay costs of the French and Indian War, Jefferson was in the Capitol at the moment of climax. His friend Governor Fauquier had hoped to distract the attention of the burgesses from this act of Parliament, but near the end of May, when only 30 of 116 burgesses were still in Williamsburg, a copy of the hated law appeared, and Patrick Henry led a spontaneous attack.

Jefferson was twenty-two as he stood in a doorway, listening to Henry in one of the great moments of the orator's life; Henry spoke for the emerging leaders of the colony's western counties as he presented his Stamp Act Resolves and shouted of the despotism of George III. Speakers on both sides of the question were well known to Jefferson, some of them intimate friends—Wythe, Peyton and John Randolph, Edmund Pendleton, and Speaker John Robinson—but it was Henry who fascinated the young law student. He complained to Daniel Webster of Henry many years later: "Although it was difficult when he had spoken to tell what he had said, yet, while he was speaking, it always seemed directly to the point. When he had spoken in opposition to my opinion, had produced a great effect, and I myself had been highly delighted and moved, I have asked myself when he ceased: 'What the devil has he said?' " But on the day of the speech itself, Jefferson had been much impressed, and remembered of Henry, "he spoke as Homer wrote."

Those who heard Henry on this day, as he pushed his Stamp Act Resolves through the House, left no clear record of the event; some remembered impassioned cries of "Treason! Treason!," and others that Henry lamely apologized for his attack. Jefferson may have recognized the moment for what it was, an early step toward independence, for its details remained vividly in his mind for life, and he later acknowledged that it was Henry who set the train of revolutionary events in motion. Thomas also heard his angry cousin Peyton Randolph swear in frustration on that day, and saw Peter Randolph seeking ways to undo Henry's work the next morning. Jefferson got a lesson in practical politics when the conservative burgesses repealed the boldest of Henry's resolutions after the orator had left Williamsburg, though it was in the end a futile gesture. Copies of all of Henry's defiant paragraphs went to newspapers throughout the colonies and sounded "an alarum bell to the disaffected."

In the years after this climactic scene of 1765, Jefferson was in and out of Williamsburg, ever busy. He made a northern tour, going as far as New York, where he met a future ally, Elbridge Gerry of Massachusetts.

Back at Shadwell he began his garden book, noting details of plant life, and his own experiments, the first of an elaborate set of journals he kept of his travels, expenses, the weather, and assorted information. His inspiration may have been Governor Fauquier's records of weather in Williamsburg.

In 1767, Wythe thought him ready for the bar at last, and Jefferson was admitted and began practice immediately, trying about one thousand cases in forty Virginia counties in the next seven years. His practice grew from sixty-seven cases in his first year to about two hundred in 1769, but like other Virginia lawyers he collected few of the fees due him. He once joined Edmund Pendleton, Patrick Henry, John Randolph, and others in a public notice, warning that fees must be paid in advance. Finally as the Revolution approached, in 1774, Jefferson sold his practice to Edmund Randolph.

Two of his important cases were tried in Williamsburg's General Court, one in which he defended a clergyman accused of drunkenness, profanity, adultery, and obscenity and one in which he lost to George Wythe on a basic cause of human freedom. Without fee, Jefferson defended a mulatto, Samuel Howell (the great-grandson of a white woman), who sought his freedom from servitude. Jefferson argued the injustice of punishing distant generations for past sins and told the court: "under the law of nature all men are born free, every one comes into the world with a right to his own person, which includes the liberty of moving and using it at his own will." These were daring words in the Capitol of a society based on slavery, spoken by a slaveholder before a court of slaveholders. Mr. Wythe had only to stand and merely begin his argument before the Court summarily dismissed Jefferson's plea; Virginia was not ready for his application of the rational views from Bacon, Locke, and Voltaire that he had drunk in from Small, Fauquier, and Wythe himself.

The Howell case may have branded Jefferson as a dangerous free-thinker in the eyes of some Virginia leaders but he was already a burgess and militia commander of his county, and his public career did not suffer. His industry, intelligence, winning manners and sound training made him an immediate favorite with other burgesses, and he managed to avoid factionalism in spite of his liberal outlook. When Lord Botetourt, the new governor, arrived in 1769, Jefferson wrote the stiffly formal official message of greeting (and smarted under the criticism when it was re-written by Robert Carter Nicholas).

Troubles with England grew. In the 1769 session, when the burgesses passed resolutions against the Townshend Acts, claiming the sole right to levy taxes in Virginia, Botetourt dissolved the Assembly. When members walked the few steps to the Raleigh Tavern, elected Peyton Randolph as speaker of the rump session, and passed a non-importation agreement written by George Mason (but presented by George Washington), Jefferson was a signer, one of eighty-nine. He signed a similar agreement of boycott the next year, hoping to force Parliament to repeal all duties.

Just after his first experience as a burgess, the ten-day session of 1769, Jefferson ordered several volumes from England which were not on sale at the *Virginia Gazette* office, where he usually bought books. These were chiefly theories of government, among them Locke's *Government* and the works of Montesquieu. In their pages, he found phrases later to become familiar to Americans, "all men are by nature equal and free" and "pursuit of happiness." Jefferson copied striking passages in his notebooks.

In 1772, Jefferson married Mrs. Martha Wayles Skelton, an attractive widow from Charles City County, and took her to the new home, Monticello, he was building in Albemarle. His honeymoon and his new home kept him from the next Assembly session, which was held under the eye of a formidable new governor, Lord Dunmore. But in 1774, when the burgesses protested the closing of the port of Boston and Dunmore dissolved the Assembly, Jefferson was among the members who adjourned to the Raleigh Tavern once more.

He may have helped to write the resolution for a day of fasting and prayer which resulted, though it was presented under the name of Robert Carter Nicholas. Elected to the Virginia Convention which was formed in that year, Jefferson became ill on the road to Williamsburg, and for guidance of delegates he sent to the capital one of the important early documents of his career. This was printed in the *Virginia Gazette,* as "A Summary View of the Rights of British America," but it was first read in public in the home of Peyton Randolph, before a group of burgesses, some of whom were shocked by Jefferson's daring.

There were stirring phrases in the *Summary View:* "The God who gave us life gave us liberty at the same time; the hand of force may destroy, but cannot disjoin them" and "kings are the servants, not the proprietors of the people. Open your breast, sire, to liberal and expanded thought. Let not the name of George the third be a blot in the page of history." Still, he said, the colonies did not wish to separate from Great Britain.

A few weeks later, with other delegates, he heard Patrick Henry cry for liberty or death in the Convention at Richmond. And the following year, 1775, as violence threatened, Jefferson went back to Williamsburg to spend ten days in the last session of the General Assembly. A few weeks earlier Lord Dunmore had seized gunpowder from the Magazine on Market Square, and during the session the governor fled to a British warship in the York River, from which he sent messages ashore to the burgesses.

Jefferson was in Philadelphia in 1776, as a delegate to the Continental Congress when Virginia's Convention passed the resolves of May 15, a decisive document in the course of the revolutionary movement which called upon Virginia delegates to move for freedom. In eventual response Jefferson wrote the Declaration of Independence and saw it signed by the Continental Congress.

Jefferson soon returned to Williamsburg, and now began the work cited by historians as the most creative of his life. He lived with Mrs. Jefferson in the Wythe House on Palace Green as the work of the Convention began and led Assemblymen in an effort to transform Virginia from an outpost of colonial aristocracy into a more democratic society. In his service of almost three years in the House of Delegates he attacked artificial privilege wherever he saw it, and though all of his bills failed to pass, he "laid the ax to the root of pseudo-aristocracy" as he put it. He pushed through repeal of the law of entail, the practice under which great estates passed down through generations in wealthy families, subject to neither sale nor debt nor indiscretions of wasteful heirs. Virginia became the first state where entail was forbidden. Jefferson also attacked the law of primogeniture, under which the oldest heir to an estate profited at the expense of others.

Though opposed by many of his conservative friends, Jefferson won so many of these causes as to bring a new social and economic climate to Virginia and more than a touch of democracy to its affairs. He helped to form a new county of the Kentucky territory and fought to prevent speculators from dividing western lands into huge tracts. His sympathies were with the squatters who tended small farms in the wild country, and eventually a law was passed which favored these men.

There were outraged protests. Landon Carter, a rich conservative, complained to Washington that Jefferson must be a "midday drunkard" to propose such schemes. Carter argued that Jefferson was depriving men of "the right to do as we please with our property" and "overturning the very principles of justice on which they built their very claim of freedom."

Jefferson dismissed such critics as Carter as a "half-dozen aristocratical gentlemen, agonizing under the loss of pre-eminence." Jefferson was proud of this work of rebuilding Virginia with such a minimum of turmoil. He wrote to Benjamin Franklin: "Not a single throe has attended this important transformation." Jefferson had sped processes which were destroying the old class structure in Virginia, and his role was one of the most important factors of all. (Washington, who was alarmed that the best men in America were not in Congress, thought that Jefferson should have been devoting more time to his country than to his state and wrote of this several times in private letters: "Where is Mason, Wythe, Jefferson, Nicholas, Pendleton . . . ?" and "Let this voice . . . call upon you, Jefferson and others." But Jefferson thought no work more important than that of these years in Williamsburg.)

The Assembly named a committee under Jefferson to revise all of its laws, but did not dream that he was looking so far into the future, or that he approached the task "with a single eye to reason and the good of those for whose government it was framed." George Wythe resigned from the Congress to join this committee; George Mason, Edmund Pendleton, and Thomas Ludwell Lee also were members. When work was divided Jefferson was assigned laws on crimes and punishments and religion—but went far afield, especially into education. In the spring of 1779 the committee met in Williamsburg to put the first sections into final form.

Jefferson's contributions were revolutionary and were not merely based on the teachings of European rationalists; he made a series of brilliant and prophetic attempts to transform his state. He proposed a system of public education by dividing Virginia into small districts, each with an elementary school teaching reading, writing, and arithmetic. Any white child could attend these schools for three years without payment and remain for as long as his parents were willing to pay. There were to be twenty grammar schools in larger districts of the state where Latin, Greek, geography, and higher mathematics would be taught. Each year every elementary school would send the poor boy "of best genius" to a grammar school on a trial scholarship that might last seven or eight years. The ten finest scholars would enter William and Mary for three years; other bright students would probably go into lower schools as teachers.

As Jefferson said: "We hope to avail the State of those talents which nature has sown as liberally among the poor as the rich, but which perish without use, if not sought for and cultivated." Of the program of scholarships he said, "twenty of the best geniuses would be raked from the rubbish annually." It was the first proposal for a complete state school system in America, but Virginia was long in accepting it, and by the end of the eighteenth century it had adopted only Jefferson's primary schools. The scheme remained one of the passions of Jefferson's life. He later wrote Wythe: "Preach, my dear Sir, a crusade against ignorance; establish and improve the law for educating the common people . . . the tax which will be paid for this purpose is not more than the thousandth part of what will be paid to kings, priests and nobles who will rise up among us if we leave the people in ignorance."

Jefferson's attack on the harsh penal code of the day was spectacular. He proposed much more humane punishments and urged an end to capital punishment except in crimes of murder and treason. As a substitute for the death penalty he urged work on public projects and later recommended a penitentiary. His tolerant view of many crimes and misdemeanors seem remarkable even two centuries later, but once more Virginia denied him, and it was a generation before a watered-down version of his reforms became law.

He had for years advocated emancipation of slaves, wrote of this often, and left some of his most eloquent commentaries on the degrading institution of slavery: "And can the liberties of a nation be thought secure when we have removed their only firm basis, a conviction in the minds of the people that these liberties are the gift of God? That they are not to be violated but with His wrath? Indeed I tremble for my country when I reflect that God is Just." Again: "Nothing is more certainly written in the book of fate than that these people are to be free." He thought that Negroes and whites could not live peaceably under one government, however, because of "deeply rooted prejudices" on the one hand and "ten thousand recollections . . . of the injuries" on the other.

Jefferson began the bitterest fight of his career with his proposal for religious freedom. Dissenters, especially the rapidly increasing Protestant sects, had already won concessions in Virginia, but that was not enough for Jefferson. He insisted upon absolute freedom of religion and held that state religion meant an absence of freedom and reduced religion to mere form. One section of his bill (which was seven years in passage) put the issue plainly:

We the General Assembly of Virginia do enact that no man shall be compelled to frequent or support any religious worship, place, or ministry whatsoever, nor shall be enforced, restrained, molested, or burthened in his body or goods, or shall otherwise suffer, on account of his religious opinions or belief; but that all men shall be free to profess, and by argument to maintain, their opinions in matters of religion, and that the same shall in no wise diminish, enlarge, or affect their civil capacities.

Jefferson ranked this bill as second only to the Declaration of Independence among the significant works of his life; he had it printed in broadside and sent it to a wide circle of friends and public officials. Years afterward, when a revised version became Virginia law, he wrote to James Madison, who had finally seen it to passage, saying proudly that it was being read in foreign courts, had been translated throughout Europe, and published in an encyclopedia: "it is comfortable to see the standard of reason at length erected, after so many ages during which the human mind has been held in vassalage by kings, priests and nobles: and it is honorable for us to have produced the first legislature who had the courage to declare that the reason of man may be trusted with the formation of his own opinions."

In June, 1779, by a close vote over his friend John Page, the Assembly named Jefferson to succeed Patrick Henry as governor of Virginia. He was thirty-six years old, an arresting presence, though not handsome, with a large high nose in his long face. He was six feet two and one-half inches tall, and, as his overseer said, "was like a fine horse: he had no surplus flesh." Even in Virginia society where courtly manners were the rule, he was notable for the gracious way in which he bowed to everyone he met; he had a habit of talking with folded arms. He was unusually erect, as "neat a built man" as Virginia ever saw, "a straight-up man," as a servant remembered him. The visiting Marquis de Chastellux, who saw him not long afterward, found Jefferson cold and reserved at first, but becoming warm and boyish in his enthusiasms. The Frenchman sketched him "as . . . a man, not yet forty, tall and with a mild and pleasing countenance, but whose mind and understanding are ample substitutes for every exterior grace . . . at once a musician, skilled in drawing, a geometrician, and astronomer, a natural philosopher, legislator, and statesman."

Jefferson did not look forward to his administration, fearing it would mean "intense labour, and great private loss." He was in office during the two darkest years of the Revolution, but he spent only a few months in the Palace. The Assembly which named him governor also provided for moving the capital to Richmond, and though Jefferson measured the Palace, planned its renovation and brought his family to Williamsburg, his days there were short. He did not lose interest in the town or its college.

He attempted the reform of William and Mary, abolished the chair of divinity and the Indian school, introduced courses in modern languages, law, medicine, and history, increased the faculty from six to eight. He installed George Wythe as the nation's first professor of law and police and made other changes, but in the end gave up his attempt to transform the college into a university. It was the dissenting sects, he thought, who defeated this attempt, out of their distrust of the old Anglican influence.

But by 1780, Jefferson's Williamsburg life had ended, and his career belonged to the nation and the world, as second-term governor, minister to France, secretary of state, Vice-President, President, and founder of the University of Virginia. But it was in Williamsburg, as he often said, that he trained himself for the work of his life.

Patrick Henry, by Lawrence Sully. Amherst College, Amherst, Massachusetts.

PATRICK HENRY

IN the spring of 1760 a young foxhunter from the Virginia backcountry came to Williamsburg for the first time. By the standards of Tidewater gentry he was roughly dressed, probably in the homespun coat and leather breeches he wore in his Hanover County home, where he sometimes served as bartender in a family tavern. The country visitor was a refugee from agriculture; he had found Hanover life trying and already, at twenty-four, had failed as a backwoods storekeeper. He had come to Williamsburg for a license to practice law, a profession for which he had diligently prepared—for all of six weeks.

The town was quiet, shrunken to its normal population of about one thousand since the end of the Assembly and the migration of the colony's leading men to their plantations for the new tobacco season. Like most such small moments of history, the arrival of Patrick Henry in the capital caused little stir. It was notable only for its small ironies.

Henry first stopped at the College of William and Mary, where a chance acquaintance, Thomas Jefferson, had recently enrolled. The two had met during the Christmas holidays, when Jefferson visited in Hanover. Jefferson had a long memory of their first meeting:

> I met him in society every day, and we became well acquainted, altho' I was much his junior, being then but in my seventeenth year, and he a married man. . . . His manners had something of the coarseness of the society he had frequented; his passion was fiddling, dancing, and pleasantry. He excelled in the last and it attached everybody to him.

Henry's wit and charm were quickly tested in Williamsburg, for as he went before the examining board for his license he had little else to offer.

He faced four of the leading American lawyers of his day: John Randolph, the attorney general of Virginia; George Wythe, who became the first professor of law in the country; Peyton Randolph, the future president of the First Continental Congress; and Robert Carter Nicholas, who became treasurer of Virginia.

Henry's common sense and his gift for argument carried him through. As Jefferson recalled it, "Peyton and John Randolph, men of great facility of temper, signed his license with as much reluctance as their dispositions would permit them to show. Mr. Wythe absolutely refused."

Attorney General John Randolph's reaction was prophetic. At first this witty and urbane man, shocked by Henry's appearance and country speech and manners, refused to examine him. When Henry explained that he had one signature and needed but one more, Randolph reluctantly examined him. He soon found that he knew little law, but that he could defend himself in an argument with rare skill.

Randolph drew Henry into a debate, and, despite the veteran's guile, was bested by the awkward Hanoverian. "You defend your operations well, sir," Randolph admitted. He led Henry into his law office and pointed to ranked book shelves. "Behold the force of natural reason," he said. "You have never seen these books, nor this principle of the law; yet you are right and I am wrong. And from the lesson which you have given me I will never trust to appearances again." Years later Randolph was remembered to have added: "Mr. Henry, if your industry be only half equal to your genius, I augur that you will do well, and become an ornament and an honor to your profession."

Henry soon returned home with his license and began the practice of law, apparently swaying juries as easily as he had won John Randolph's approval. In the next three years, before he was again noticed in Williamsburg, he had tried almost twelve hundred cases, and was a leading figure in his region. It was obvious that Henry was no mere bumpkin from the slashes of Hanover County.

For all his rough dress and manner Henry came from a respectable background. He had been reared in the comfortable, if modest, farmhouse known as Studley. His father, a Scot trained at Aberdeen University, was a vestryman, a county judge, and a militia colonel who educated his children in the classics. Henry was related to the Dabney and Winston families, long prominent in Hanover, and through them could trace kinship to Dolley Todd Madison, the future first lady of the United States.

His neighbor Colonel Nathaniel Dandridge, Patrick's future father-in-law, was a cousin of Martha Dandridge Custis, the recent bride of George Washington.

Henry first won fame in a Hanover trial known as "the parson's cause." The Reverend James Maury, who had been encouraged to sue for his overdue salary, was bested by the young orator in Hanover County. Henry shouted that the king, by vetoing the Two Penny Act, "degenerated into a tyrant, and forfeits all rights to his subjects' obedience." Some of the audience muttered that this was treason, but Henry soared eloquently to the end, accusing the clergy of robbing the public, saying that they would "snatch from the hearth of their honest parishioner his last hoecake, from the widow and her orphan children their last milch cow! the last bed, nay the last blanket from the lying-in woman!" Henry told the jury that they must award Maury damages under the law, but that they need give him only a farthing. The verdict allowed the minister one penny, and the courthouse crowd, still under the spell of Henry's oratory, carried him on their shoulders around the yard, cheering.

Still his fame was local, and, when he returned to plead his first case in Williamsburg in 1764, a burgess noted him only as "an ill-dressed young man sauntering in the lobby . . . he seemed to be a stranger to everybody." The burgess was not curious enough to ask Henry's identity until, a few hours later, he went into a committee room and found him speaking for Colonel Dandridge, who claimed that he had lost a race for the House of Burgesses because his opponent, Littlepage, had bribed voters.

The burgesses took little note of the rough-clad Henry when he began to speak, but his voice soon seized their attention, and as a biographer said: "Soon Henry changed the attitude of his hearers. He launched forth into a full and brilliant declamation on the rights of suffrage, superior to anything ever heard before within those walls. . . . There was a deep silence while he spoke." But this time Henry was not dazzling a country jury, and the burgesses seated Littlepage, declaring Dandridge's case "frivolous." Henry left the capital a loser, but a marked man. Before he left, Williamsburg was already buzzing with news from London: Parliament was considering a stamp tax, a new scheme to raise revenue in the American colonies.

On Wednesday, May 29, 1765, Patrick Henry was back in Williamsburg, this time as a burgess from Louisa County. On his twenty-ninth birthday he gave a performance that led Jefferson to say, "Mr. Henry certainly gave the first impulse to the ball of the revolution." When Henry, the new burgess, had been in the House only nine days, he introduced a set of resolves on the Stamp Act. It was a crucial moment in American history when Henry called upon Virginians to resist the new taxes, for leaders in other colonies, including Benjamin Franklin, seemed to have given up. Older and more conservative burgesses blocked final passage of his most inflammatory resolution, but they could not keep it from spreading through the colonies.

It was this day to which Henry, as an aged man, looked back as his greatest:

> I had been for the first time elected a Burgess a few days before, was young, inexperienced, unacquainted with the Forms of the House, and the members that composed it. Finding the men of Weight adverse to Opposition, and the Commencement of the Tax at Hand, and that no person was likely to step forth, I determined to venture, and alone, unadvised, and unassisted, on a blank Leaf of an old Law Book, wrote the within. [From a document found with Henry's will, now owned by Colonial Williamsburg, and on display in the Capitol with his copy of the Stamp Act Resolves.]

The House which heard his resolves was a remarkable body, including George Washington, Peyton Randolph, and six of the seven men who would sign the Declaration of Independence for Virginia; governors, judges, eminent leaders of the stormy years ahead.

On May 30, when the resolves came to debate, young Thomas Jefferson stood in a doorway. It was a scene he remembered vividly, many years afterward:

> Mr. Henry moved and seconded these resolutions. . . . They were opposed by Messrs. Randolph, Bland, Pendleton, Wythe, and all the old members, whose influence in the House had, till then, been unbroken. . . . But torrents of sublime eloquence from Henry, backed by the solid reasoning of Johnston, prevailed. . . .
>
> The debate on it was most bloody. I was then but a student, and stood at the door of the communication between the house and the lobby . . . during the whole debate and vote.

As usual when Henry spoke, no one found time to put into writing immediately just what he had said.

Many others praised Henry's gifts as an orator. George Mason wrote of him: "He is by far the most powerful speaker I ever heard. Every word he says not only engages, but commands the attention; and your passions are no longer your own when he addresses them. But his eloquence is the smallest part of his merit. He is in my opinion the first man on this continent, as well in abilities as public virtues."

Only one observer, an unknown French tourist, wrote of the Stamp Act debate at the time, and the scene has been reconstructed from his account and from the memories of Jefferson and Burgess Paul Carrington, recalled in later years.

Henry: "Tarquin and Caesar each had his Brutus, Charles the First his Cromwell, and George the Third—"

Speaker John Robinson interrupted: "Treason!"

There were other shouts in the House: "Treason! Treason!"

Henry, after a pause: "—may profit by their example. If this be treason, make the most of it."

Carrington said Henry's speech was "beyond my powers of description," and Jefferson said, "He spoke as Homer wrote."

The French traveler, whose account was less dramatic, wrote that Henry, once he had spoken, asked Speaker Robinson's pardon and said he was ready to show his loyalty to King George "at the expence of the last drop of his blood," despite the passion with which he had spoken for "his country's dying liberty." This Frenchman's journal was not discovered until 1921, in Paris archives, and by then American tradition on the Caesar-Brutus speech had been firmly fixed.

Jefferson later wrote of Henry's victory in the debate that day: "After the numbers of the division were told and declared from the chair, Peyton Randolph came out at the door where I was standing, and exclaimed, 'By God, I would have given one hundred guineas for a single vote!' For one vote would have divided the House, and Robinson was in the chair, who he knew would have negatived the resolution."

Henry left Williamsburg, hurrying back to Hanover in triumph, but behind him the conservative members of the House moved to undo the work of his eloquence. Jefferson saw Colonel Peter Randolph at the clerk's table of the House of Burgesses the next morning, thumbing through a journal in search of a precedent for expunging the resolutions from the record. The fifth, and most controversial, of Henry's resolves, failed to pass another vote in Henry's absence. But it was too late to halt its effect.

Henry's resolutions had been sent out to other colonies, in various

forms, and by July 4 the *Maryland Gazette* published the Virginia
Resolves. The inflammatory fifth one, enough to stir other colonies to
similar resolutions of defiance, read:

> Resolved therefore, That the General Assembly of this Colony, with
> the Consent of his Majesty, or his Substitute, HAVE the Sole Right and
> Authority to lay Taxes and Impositions upon It's Inhabitants: And, that
> every Attempt to vest such Authority in any other Person or Persons
> whatsoever, has a Manifest Tendency to Destroy AMERICAN FREEDOM.

In the storm that followed, the Stamp Act was repealed and conflict
postponed. But the unknown French traveler, stopping at a tavern in the
Virginia countryside less than a week later, found that men talked incessantly of the Stamp Act taxes and that one of them said, over and over,
"I'll sooner die than pay a farthing and I am sure that all my countrymen
will do the same." As to Mr. Henry: "The Whole Inhabitants say
publicly that if the least injury was offered to him they'd stand by him to
the last Drop of their blood . . . let the worst Come to the Worst we'l
Call the French to our succour."

Francis Fauquier, the royal governor of Virginia, looking beyond his
own capital, saw that Henry had done his work all too well. He wrote
prophetically: "The Flame is spread thru' all the Continent, and one
Colony supports another in their Disobedience to superior powers."

For the next ten years Henry worked quietly for the cause of independence in Virginia and America. He attended all sessions of the House of
Burgesses and served on committees; he played a leading role in exposing
a scandal of mishandled public funds, when Treasurer John Robinson's
death revealed that he had lent his friends £100,000 from the colonial
treasury. Henry served on committees with Virginia's leaders and began to
acquire property: an interest in the Ohio Company, and extensive lands in
southwestern Virginia. He was still "a radical demagogue" to conservative
leaders, but he was becoming a man of substance.

Henry appeared in Williamsburg's General Court in its semiannual
sessions and became known as the greatest of Virginia trial lawyers. He
often defended the rapidly increasing Baptists of Virginia in their struggle
for freedom. Most important he was a leader of the Virginia Committee
of Correspondence, working with other colonies to resist tax legislation
from England.

By now Henry wore no leather breeches. Young St. George Tucker of
Williamsburg left a description of him during an Assembly session before

the Revolution: "He wore a peach-blossom-coloured coat and a dark wig, which tied behind, and I believe, a bag to it, as was the fashion of the day. When pointed out to me as the great orator of the Assembly, I looked at him with no great prepossession." Tucker noted that Henry's face was long and thin, with a Roman nose, his cheeks sunken, his complexion sallow; he had "a half sort of smile, in which the want of conviction was, perhaps, more strongly expressed than that cynical or satirical emotion which probably prompted it." Satire had become one of Henry's effective weapons in debate and in the courtroom, and he was so successful as a lawyer-politician that Robert Carter Nicholas turned over to him his law practice, when he retired in 1771. Henry had come far.

In 1774, when Parliament closed the port of Boston to enforce payment for damages done by the Boston Tea Party, the Virginia Assembly acted quickly to express sympathy for Massachusetts. It ordered a day of "fasting, humiliation and prayer" in hopes of "averting the heavy calamity which threatens destruction to our civil rights, and the evils of civil war." This was strong enough even for Henry's taste, and when Governor Dunmore read the defiant act, he dissolved the House.

The more liberal leaders of the House moved a few yards down Duke of Gloucester Street to the Raleigh Tavern for a rump session, Henry among them. With Washington, Jefferson, and Richard Henry Lee he helped to issue a call for an annual congress of representatives from all the colonies, "to deliberate on those general measures which the united interests of America may from time to time require."

When, in August of the same year the First Revolutionary Virginia Convention met in Williamsburg and named representatives to the Continental Congress, Henry was one of the six delegates.

The Second Virginia Revolutionary Convention, in March, 1775, was held in Richmond so that Governor Dunmore could not break up the meeting, and it was there, in St. John's Church, that Henry made the "liberty or death" speech for which he is most famous, a ringing personal declaration of war on Great Britain. His audience responded by making him chairman of a military committee to prepare Virginia for war.

Only a month later, in April, a party of British marines came ashore from a schooner and hid in woods near the Governor's Palace. About 4 A.M. on April 21 they robbed the Powder Magazine. They were discovered, and, to the rolling of alarm drums, a crowd gathered, the militia company turned out under arms, and hotheads shouted for an attack on the Palace. Peyton Randolph and others calmed the mob, and the incident closed with a polite protest from the mayor at removal of the powder and a plea for its return.

It was hardly forty-eight hours after the battles of Lexington and Concord in Massachusetts.

Word of the gunpowder incident and the northern fighting swept Virginia, and militiamen from northern and western counties gathered at Fredericksburg to march on the capital. They were dissuaded by Washington, Richard Henry Lee, and others. But in Hanover, where Henry led, the news sent about 150 volunteers on the road to Williamsburg, determined to force Dunmore to return the powder or pay for it.

Henry's band, in camp at Doncastle's Ordinary, about sixteen miles from Williamsburg, was turned back when a peacemaker arrived with £330 in public funds to replace the powder. Henry then hurried to a session of Congress in Philadelphia, cheered by crowds en route and enjoying the new fame of having been declared an outlaw by Dunmore.

When he returned to Virginia in August, Henry was made a colonel and commander in chief of militia by the Convention and ordered to Williamsburg to make headquarters. Lord Dunmore had fled to the British fleet, but was expected to attack the capital. Henry made camp near the College of William and Mary and received hundreds of poorly equipped troops, but he never became a field commander. While he fretted in Williamsburg, Colonel William Woodford, a veteran but subordinate officer, fought Lord Dunmore at the brisk skirmish of Great Bridge, forcing the British to evacuate Norfolk.

Henry's pride was wounded, and he fell into a squabble with Virginia politicians and other officers over rank and command. In February, 1776, Henry resigned his commission and returned to civilian life. Among others, General George Washington was pleased. He had written a friend that month that Virginia had made "a capital mistake" by moving Henry from the legislature into the field; Washington had hoped that Henry would resign. The orator's outraged and loyal officers, however, gave him a farewell dinner at the Raleigh Tavern to mourn his departure—and only Henry's eloquence prevented the wholesale resignation of his troops.

Within three months Henry was back in Williamsburg, again as a member of the Virginia Convention, but now he urged caution. When the body debated the famous May 15 resolves for independence, Henry held back. He feared that the independent colonies might be divided among England, France, and Spain; he wanted first to see foreign alliances. In the end the resolves included Henry's proposal for delay—and Virginia's delegates in Philadelphia were merely instructed to move for independence. It was, however, the first move of its kind, and there is evidence that Henry would have liked even stronger words, for all that the record indicates his caution. As he wrote John Adams five days later: "I put up with it in the present form for the sake of unanimity. 'Tis not quite so pointed, as I could wish."

Henry also sat on the committee that drafted the Virginia Declaration of Rights, and the state's new constitution; he disagreed with Jefferson that the Convention had no power to write the constitution. Henry also vainly argued for veto power for the governor. Since some members thought that Henry expected to become governor himself and sought power, they refused him.

In late June, under the constitution, Henry was elected governor by the Convention, reflecting his enormous popularity with the Virginia public. He took office on July 5 and moved with his children into the Governor's Palace where Lord Dunmore had so lately lived. Henry had lost his first wife, and in 1777, a year after moving into the Palace, when he was forty-one, he married Dorothea Dandridge, a twenty-one-year-old granddaughter of Governor Spotswood. Eventually, Henry had fifteen children.

Henry was re-elected unanimously to two more terms, the maximum. He not only remained a popular figure—perhaps the most popular in all Virginia political history—but he surprised his critics by his ease and dignity at social functions of his office. He led Virginia through difficult war times. Though the state was not invaded during his administration, he had to produce lead, gunpowder, and salt for the armies, raise men for both the army and navy, and try (with scant success) to combat ruinous inflation.

In 1776, George Rogers Clark, a young Virginian who was becoming famous on the frontier, came to Henry seeking gunpowder for the settlers of Kentucky in their Indian wars. Clark was not a stranger, since Henry had been his father's lawyer, and the governor helped to send Clark westward with five hundred pounds of precious powder. A year later, with Henry's aid, Clark attacked all British outposts north of the Ohio River. It was secret orders from Henry that launched the expedition which, with victories at Kaskaskia and Vincennes, established a new frontier. Henry and the Assembly soon afterward created the county of Illinois, including all Virginia lands west of the Ohio, a territory later ceded to the United States.

In the darkest days of the Revolution, when the cause in the North seemed hopeless for the American armies, Henry received an unsigned letter asking him to help in a plot to oust Washington as commander in chief, the Conway Cabal. Henry promptly and loyally sent the letter to Washington, who identified the anonymous writer as Dr. Benjamin Rush of Philadelphia. Henry had helped to foil the conspiracy.

When the capital of Virginia was moved to Richmond (during Jefferson's governorship), Patrick Henry was no longer associated with Williamsburg. For it and for him the days of glory had passed. His later years were marred by quarrels with old companions of the Revolution; many thought the fiery radical had become a dangerous reactionary. As an anti-Federalist, he fought Virginia's ratification of the federal Constitution with all his power, and was narrowly defeated; only at the end of his career did he join the Federalist cause.

After the Revolution, Henry might have had almost any post of honor he wished, senator from Virginia, chief justice of the United States, or secretary of state. He declined them all and ended his life as he had begun, as a countryman and foxhunter. Two long generations later, Henry foxhounds were still a tradition in Virginia.

Among the most bitter enemies of his later years was Jefferson, who wrote of Henry:

> Were I to give his character in general terms, it would be of mixed aspect. I think he was the best humored man in society I almost knew, and the greatest orator that ever lived. He had a consummate knowledge of the human heart, which directed the efforts of his eloquence and enabled him to attain a degree of popularity with the people at large never perhaps equalled. His judgment in other matters was inaccurate, in matters of law it was not worth a copper. He was avaricious and rotten hearted. His two great passions were the love of money and of fame, but when they came into competition the former predominated.

No other great contemporaries saw Henry in such a harsh light, and it was perhaps Jefferson's fear of Henry's popularity and his unpredictable nature that inspired such criticism.

When Henry gathered his papers for his executors, he left a sealed envelope with his will. It contained a copy of his Stamp Act Resolves of 1765 and his own comments on their significance; he remembered that distant May 29 as the great day of his life. At the end of his brief essay, remembering his hour of triumph in Williamsburg's Capitol, he spoke to Americans who came after him:

> After a long and warm Contest the Resolutions passed by a very small Majority, perhaps of one or two only. The Alarm spread throughout America with astonishing Quickness, and the ministerial Party were overwhelmed. The great Point of Resistance to British Taxation was universally established in the Colonys. This brought on the War which finally separated the two Countrys and gave Independence to ours. Whether this will prove a Blessing or a Curse, will depend upon the Use our People make of the Blessings which a gracious God hath bestowed on us. If they are wise, they will be great and happy. If they are of a contrary Character, they will be miserable. Righteousness alone can exalt them as a Nation.
>
> Reader! whoever thou art, remember this; and in thy Sphere, practice Virtue thyself, and encourage it in others.

George Rogers Clark, by Matthew Harris Jouett. The Filson Club, Louisville, Kentucky.

GEORGE ROGERS CLARK

A PARTY of horsemen reined in at the gates of the former royal Governor's Palace, then the residence of Governor Thomas Jefferson, at sunset of a rainy June day in 1779. One of them, an American officer, went in to confer with the governor. The others, who were handcuffed, wet, and dejected, sat their horses for half an hour, amid a growing crowd. Soon most of Williamsburg knew that one of the Revolution's most notorious prisoners had arrived: Lieutenant Governor Henry Hamilton, known as "the Hair Buyer," who with his Indian allies had so lately terrified the western settlements from his post in Detroit.

Despite his wrist irons, Hamilton flung himself angrily from his mount, disgusted at the lack of the "civilities" he had expected of Jefferson and "mortifyed" to find himself a spectacle before the gaping Virginians. His legs were covered with sores and his wrists were swollen, and like his companion he bore the signs of a march of more than twelve hundred miles. They had been driven, often on foot, through some of the country's most forbidding wilderness.

Mr. Jefferson did not appear, but the officer returned and led the prisoners "a small mile" to the capital's jail, where they were to remain for more than a year, prisoners of the commonwealth of Virginia.

Henry Hamilton, the chief prisoner, was a symbol of the most dramatic campaign yet won by the Americans, the conquest of the Northwest frontier. There was still fighting ahead, but most of the vast domain east of the Mississippi from the Great Lakes to the Gulf of Mexico was lost to the British. In a real sense, Hamilton was also a trophy offered by a red-haired Virginia soldier, Major George Rogers Clark, to his former neighbor, Thomas Jefferson.

It was not yet clear, in Williamsburg's Palace or in its jail, but the presence of the British officer meant that a crucial phase of the Revolution was over, and that in the peace to follow, the United States would begin its emergence as a continental power. The foundation had been laid for Jefferson's future Louisiana Purchase and for the expansion to the Pacific. Behind the dismal little scene marking the end of this phase of a campaign was a story—already thrilling the people of every colony—of the resolution and skill of Major Clark. With fewer than two hundred men he had won an empire, adding five future states to the Union.

From the start the campaign had been directed, supplied,.and financed from Williamsburg and led by Virginia-born officers who pressed the state's claims as they conquered. Clark himself had often come down the long trail from the mountains, pleading with Virginia officials for aid.

George Rogers Clark was born in Albemarle County, November 19, 1752, one of ten children of John and Ann Rogers Clark. The 400-acre farm on which George was born adjoined a hilly tract owned by Peter Jefferson, part of the estate where Monticello would one day stand. Five of the six Clark sons became officers in the Revolution, and the youngest, William, later won fame as a leader of the Lewis and Clark expedition in another westward venture.

Indian raids during George's early years drove the family eastward, to Caroline County on the Rappahannock, where George and his older brother Jonathan were schooled by a kinsman, Donald Robertson; James Madison was also a student there. George seems to have been an inept pupil, but he was interested in geography and history and quick to learn surveying.

Little is known of George's boyhood, but the diary of his brother Jonathan left a record of visits to other plantations, dances, barbecues, funerals, cockfights, church meetings, and hunts. There were several visits to Gunston Hall, the home of Colonel George Mason, who was a friend of John Clark. (Jonathan Clark's diary is a model of terseness. As a member of the Virginia Convention of 1775, he was on hand to hear Patrick Henry's "liberty or death" speech, but his entry for the day was: "Clear: at Richmond; the Convention continued: lay [at] Capt. Gunn's.") Before he was twenty, George was off to the wilderness, carrying little more than a rifle and a few provisions—plus surveying instruments and a book, Euclid's *Elements*. He cleared a farm on the Ohio River below Wheeling, West Virginia, surveying for neighbors and prospecting for land. In

1774, when Indian raids drove thousands of settlers eastward, Clark remained on the frontier, already so well known as an Indian fighter that Lord Dunmore made him "Captain of the Militia of Pittsburg and its Dependencies." At the opening of the Revolution the British organized the Indians as allies, supplied them with powder and lead (and more than eight thousand scalping knives) and incited them to ravage the rebel frontier, including Kentucky, where Clark had settled.

The lush landscapes of his new home enchanted him: "A richer and more beautiful country than this, I believe has never been seen in America yet." The region was troubled by conflicting claims of ownership. Virginia regarded it as Virginia soil; on the basis of a private treaty with the Cherokees, the Henderson Company, in North Carolina, included Kentucky in its own domain, called Transylvania; Colonel Arthur Campbell of the western Virginia county of Fincastle insisted that the new lands were an extension of his county; Spain, which had posts along the Mississippi, also claimed the rich country.

As a surveyor for the Ohio Company, which gave him rights to lands of his own choosing, Clark soon knew Kentucky as well as any white man. He emerged as a leader of settlers who were anxious to validate their claims while they built cabins and forts in the wilderness. He helped to write a Kentucky petition to the Virginia Convention, asking protection and revealing uncertainty about the status of the land: "If your honors apprehend that our case comes more properly before the Honorable the General Congress . . . in your goodness, recommend the same to your worthy delegates to espouse it as the cause of the Colony."

When the Convention failed to reply, Clark went to Williamsburg and sought opinions about the value of Kentucky's claims. He probably saw Governor Patrick Henry and George Mason and Jefferson who were, like his brother Jonathan, members of the Convention. He got no clear answer. Some, he found, "doubted whether Virginia would with propriety have any pretentions" to the land beyond the mountains, despite the terms of the colonial charter. He went back to Kentucky determined to force Virginia's hand, staged an election at Harrodsburg in the spring of 1776 and hastily formed a "government." He and John Gabriel Jones, a Virginia lawyer, were chosen to go to Williamsburg, where they were to petition for acceptance of the territory as a new county.

The return to Virginia was strenuous; one of the horses gave out and the two men were crippled from sore feet after long marches in wet moccasins. Jones turned back when they reached Botetourt County and discovered that the Assembly had adjourned. Clark did not give up. He went to Governor Henry, who was ill at his home in Hanover. Henry had known Clark since his boyhood, for he had been John Clark's lawyer, and he did his best for George. Only the Assembly could act on the petition, but the governor sent Clark to Williamsburg to seek gunpowder.

Clark was then little known in Tidewater Virginia, and his work had been noted only by an occasional diarist from the east (men like the Reverend Hugh Jones, a future chaplain in Washington's army, and the adventurous Briton Nicholas Cresswell, each of whom had glimpses of him in the wilderness). Clark was a striking figure in Williamsburg streets, over six feet tall, "very straight," and so bronzed that he might be mistaken for an Indian, but with blue eyes and with "hair inclined to be red." This buckskin-clad figure appeared before Virginia's Executive Council to ask for five hundred pounds of gunpowder which might mean the salvation of Kentucky. Lieutenant Governor John Page and the Council listened, but said they could do no more than lend the powder since, as Clark put it, the Kentuckians "ware a detached people not yet united to the state of Virginia." Further, if the Assembly did not later accept Kentucky as a county, Clark would be responsible for payment.

Clark refused the powder under those conditions; he had no way to carry it over the mountains and could not pay its transportation. His argument to the Council included a threat that Kentucky might turn elsewhere—to England or Spain or the rival state Pennsylvania. Much later a kinsman told the story, apparently heard from Clark, of how the Indian fighter made the Capitol ring with his shouts: "He exclaimed warmly, slapping his sword upon the table, 'By God, if the country is not worth protecting, it is not worth having!'—& hinted that some other country might think it worth attention."

Clark rode out of town, but an express rider from the Council caught him several miles from Williamsburg, with good news. The powder would be sent to Fort Pitt at Virginia's expense. For the public record, the Council's journal dismissed the matter in a paragraph, saying merely that "Mr. George Rogers Clark having represented to this Board the defence-less state of the Inhabitants of Kentucky . . . ," it had resolved to ship five hundred pounds of powder to the west. It was a beginning. Virginia had tentatively committed herself.

Clark and Jones returned in October to besiege the Assembly for the inclusion of Kentucky, but were refused seats as members until the territory's status had been settled. The battle over the ownership of

Kentucky's lands thus officially began in Williamsburg; it was to crackle for many years. Skilled lobbyists fought Clark and Jones—Colonel Richard Henderson of the Transylvania Company, Colonel Campbell of Fincastle County, and agents of the Indiana Company. The Kentuckians were once so discouraged by their apparent defeat in the parliamentary infighting that they prepared to go home. Under Jefferson's guidance as committee chairman, the House passed their bill making Kentucky a county on its first two readings, but it was killed on a third reading and had to be laboriously revived.

Campbell, Henderson and other opponents were beaten only after two months of debate and maneuver, during which Clark and Jones waited impatiently. At last, when George Mason was added to the committee, the bill passed the House and after a brief fight in the Senate, Kentucky was declared a Virginia county on December 7, 1776. It was on its way to statehood, its final boundaries to be exactly those laid out by Clark.

After he had fought his way through the Virginia Assembly, Clark had to beat off Indian attacks from Fort Pitt to Kentucky, and reached the settlers with his barrels of powder just as new warfare broke against them. He was made president of the new county's court martial, which was in effect a temporary local government. (Daniel Boone, James Harrod and John Todd were other officers.) He immediately declared martial law, calling all men into service. His diary for the last days of 1776 and spring of 1777 is sprinkled with accounts of sieges, murders, and scalpings. Boonesborough was attacked and Daniel Boone was wounded.

In the midst of such scenes Clark calmly planned one of the most audacious schemes of American military history. He sent two spies, Benjamin Linn and Samuel Moore, hundreds of miles to the north, into the Illinois country, where British posts were supplying the invading bands of Indians. It seemed that Boonesborough and Harrodsburg might fall at any moment, but Clark proposed to take the war into enemy country. Linn was a young Virginian, skilled in several Indian dialects and a veteran of wilderness fighting. When he returned to report that the distant post at Kaskaskia could be taken, Clark needed to hear no more. Again he traveled the weary way to Williamsburg.

By the time he put his scheme before Governor Henry, it was December. Washington's army was at Valley Forge; Virginia's own troops were widely dispersed, guarding the borders, and she was near exhaustion, after years of supplying the armies. Clark proposed that he raise a little force, strike north to Kaskaskia through a country held by thousands of hostile Indians, and seize the fort. It was a land most Kentuckians had never seen and of which most Virginians had heard but vaguely. In a new jacket and shirt, Clark went before Henry and the Council: "I communicated my views to Governor Henry. At first he seemed to be fond of it; but to detach a part at so great a distance . . . appeared daring and hazardous, as nothing but secrecy could give success to the enterprise. . . ."

Henry had private talks with others, "select gentlemen," as Clark said, Jefferson, Mason, and George Wythe. They questioned Clark on every phase of his plan of invasion, including a route of retreat in case of failure, and then agreed. The need for secrecy prevented Henry from asking the legislature to act. As Jefferson explained it, he, Mason, Richard Henry Lee, and others "not only advised it, but pledged ourselves to Clarke to use our best endeavors in the legislature, if he succeeded, to induce them to remunerate himself and his followers in lands." The governor issued a proclamation saying only that Clark would raise a force to defend Kentucky, and gave him his actual orders in secret. He was to raise and command, as lieutenant colonel, an army of no more than 350 men to invade Illinois; he was given £1,200 in inflated Virginia currency and orders on Fort Pitt for boats and ammunition.

Clark left Williamsburg for the west, "happy with the thoughts of fair prospects of undeceiving the public respecting their formidable enemies on our frontiers." Since his orders were secret, he could explain nothing to the frontiersmen of their mission and some opposed his recruiting efforts; at Fort Pitt, a squabble between Virginians and Pennsylvanians ensued, since the post was claimed by both states. Disgusted with quarrels and public apathy, Clark put his tiny force into boats and left Fort Pitt, heading downstream toward the rapids of the Ohio. He had expected to meet another band on the way, but less than half a company appeared. Of the 350 men he had expected, he now had only 178. The reduction, he said, "alarmed me, as I was afraid the disappointment would prove fatal to our scheme," but he added, "it made me as desparate as I was before determined." He knew that the scheme would seem foolhardly to most men, "to be taken near a thousand miles from the body of their country to attack a people five times their number, and merciless tribes of Indians . . . the more I reflected on my weakness, the more I was pleased with the enterprise."

With something of the spirit of Gideon's army the little band moved farther down the Ohio in May, and for a few days Clark isolated his men on an island near the present city of Louisville, where he told them their objective. A handful deserted, but he caught most of them. Clark did not disguise the dangers they faced, but even he did not know of the odds against them. The British had six armed vessels on the Great Lakes, some with big guns. In Detroit, Henry Hamilton was planning his own offensive against Fort Pitt, and had called a council of 1,600 Indian warriors to prepare for war. In January, by Hamilton's records, Indians had brought in 73 prisoners and 129 scalps from the American frontier.

Hamilton had a force of over 900 at Detroit including British regulars and militia; at Vincennes, on the Wabash in Indiana, were 250 more. The outpost at Kaskaskia had a population of 800; a nearby post, Cahokia, had 400. Kaskaskia's commander was a former French officer, Philippe Rastel, Sieur de Rocheblave, who had joined the British after the French and Indian War. Like Hamilton, he was known among the Americans as a "hair buyer" who paid bounties for scalps of men, women, or children.

On June 24, 1778, Clark and his men shot the rapids of the Ohio, and just as they entered the white water an eclipse darkened the sun. There was some uneasiness among the superstitious, but they hurried on, two men to an oar, and within four days passed the mouth of the Tennessee River. Clark met a party of hunters who had just come from Kaskaskia, where all was quiet, as his spies had reported. The hunters joined the expedition. As they neared the place where they must leave the river, the invaders were overtaken by a canoeman, William Linn, who had been left behind at the island camp. He brought news: the French had signed an alliance with the United States. This was the kind of news that Clark could use well among the Frenchmen in the Illinois outposts.

The troops marched 120 miles through wild country to Kaskaskia; they hid the boats and proceeded single file, carrying only four days' provisions. Clark's guide lost his way, and only when threatened with death did he find it again. For two days the men lived on berries until, on July 4, they reached the Kaskaskia River opposite the little British outpost. The army lay until darkness, watching the unsuspecting village, then ferried the river and divided into companies to take the town from all sides.

Clark and Simon Kenton led the way through the gate without a challenge and men took their posts throughout the village. Clark broke into the house of Rocheblave and took him from his bed. At a signal the men shouted to arouse the sleeping people. Soldiers who could speak French called orders: Everyone must stay indoors or be shot. Kaskaskia was in American hands. After a few shrieks, all was still. Clark wrote: "I don't suppose greater silence ever Reagned among the Inhabitants of a place." His men moved about noisily all night, deliberately terrifying the inhabitants. Each house was searched for arms. Roads and trails were guarded. The next morning Clark withdrew the troops to the edge of town and forbade the men to speak to the villagers, increasing the fears of the Kaskaskians, who were already in dread of the Big Knives.

Clark put some militia leaders in irons. His plan, he said, was first to frighten the French and then to overwhelm them with kind treatment, "to attach them to me"; he needed allies for his small band deep in hostile country. A few men soon came to Clark, led by a priest, Father Pierre Gibault. Clark noted that they were shocked by the "dirty savage appearance" of the Virginia officers, who had left their clothes at the river and were almost naked, bearded and long-haired, their bodies torn by briars. Gibault and his men were at first fearful to sit, but when he could speak, the priest asked if the people could hold a meeting in the church.

"I carelessly told him I had nothing to say to his church," Clark wrote, "that he might go there if he would. . . . The whole town seemed to have collected to the church." Clark cleverly led on the priest and other leaders until they begged that they be spared some of their clothing, and that men not be separated from their families. Clark roared at the frightened Frenchmen: Did he think the Americans were savages, that they meant to strip women and children? His object, he said, was to prevent bloodshed, and bring peace to the Illinois. And, since the French had joined the Americans in the war on Britain ("this information very apparently affected them"), they were free to join either side they wished.

Within two days he had made friends of the French, and, keeping careful watch on the town, he sent spies to Vincennes and a company under Captain Joseph Bowman to take Cahokia. Some of the French volunteered to join Bowman and to persuade their friends and relatives at Cahokia to give up. Bowman occupied the post without resistance, and won the confidence of the people at once. They had been living under military rule, and were astonished when they were offered American citizenship and a free election for a magistrate was ordered.

Clark's next conquest was the Indian chiefs of the region, who were alarmed at this raid by their old enemies into the Illinois country and puzzled by reports that their friends the French and Spanish were at peace with the Kentuckians. Late in August the Indians came to make peace with Clark, hundreds of them from a dozen or more tribes and some from as far as five hundred miles away. Clark confessed that he was "under some apprehension among such a lot of devils," but he handled them with skill.

The chiefs had never heard speeches like Clark's at a peace parley; he offered no gifts and did not flatter or cajole. He told them to stop warring on the settlements and that if they continued fighting under Henry Hamilton "they would see their great father as they called him given to the Dogs to eat." He gave the chiefs an ingenious and imaginative version of the American Revolution in terms the Indians understood:

The Big Knives are very much like the Red People; they don't know well how to make blankets, powder and cloth. . . . They buy from the English . . . and live chiefly by making corn, hunting and trade. . . . But the Big Knives daily are getting more numerous, like the trees in the woods, so that the land got poor and hunting scarce . . . the women began to cry, to see their children naked, and tried to learn to make clothes for themselves, and soon gave the husbands blankets of their own making; and the men learned to make guns and powder, so that they did not have to buy so much from the English. They, the English, got mad and put a strong garrison through all the country . . . and would not let our women spin, nor the men make powder, nor let us trade with anybody else. . . . The women and children were cold and hungry and continued to cry. The young men were lost and had no councillor to put them in the right path. The whole land was dark . . . and thus there was mourning for many years.

At last the Great Spirit took pity on us and kindled a great council fire that never gave out, at a place called Philadelphia, stuck down a post, and left a tomahawk by it, and went away . . . . The old men . . . took up the hatchet, sharpened it and put it into [the] hands of the young men and told [them] to strike the English as long as they could find one on this side of the Great Water. . . . Thus the war began, and the English were driven from one place to another until they got weak and hired you Red People to fight for them. . . . The Great Spirit, getting angry at this, he caused your old Father the French King and other nations to join the Big Knife and fight with them all their enemies, so that the English is become like a deer in the woods.

From this you may see that it is the Great Spirit that caused your waters to be troubled, because you fought for the people he was mad with; and if your women and children should cry, you must blame yourselves for it and not the Big Knife.

Clark held up two symbolic belts, a red one for war and a white one for peace and told them to choose one:

> If you take the bloody path, you shall go from this town in safety and join your friends the English; and we will try like warriors [to see] who can . . . keep our clothes the longest perfumed with blood. . . . As I am convinced you never before heard the truth, I would not wish you to give me an answer before you have time to counsel.

Even Clark was surprised at the effect of his speech on the Indians. He said it "did more service than a Regiment of Men cou'd have done." Though he made no formal treaty, Clark agreed on peace with ten or twelve tribes within five weeks. He did not halt all Indian raids in the region, but he gave the tribes pause and took many of them out of the war. He established friendly relations with the Spanish lieutenant governor of St. Louis, Don Fernando de Leyba.

Clark sent the Kaskaskia commander, Rocheblave, eastward to Governor Henry, and the prisoner was soon walking the streets of Williamsburg on parole. (He later escaped with the aid of a Virginia girl and made his way back to the frontier.)

Clark next took Vincennes in another bloodless coup. Father Gibault paved the way, persuading the French to yield, and Captain Leonard Helm of Clark's band was sent to hold the place with a handful of men. Henry Hamilton learned of Clark's raid and in early October retook Vincennes as easily as Helm had seized it. Winter had come, the rivers were in flood, and the flat Wabash country became a chain of vast shallow lakes. Hamilton sent home part of his militia and set some Indians to guard the Ohio River and others to raid the settlements. All would meet in the spring and descend on Clark, then take Fort Pitt, and drive the Americans east of the mountains. Hamilton holed up for the winter, convinced that the flooded prairies would protect him. The stage was set for Clark's most dramatic feat.

Clark wrote Patrick Henry of his plan: "I am resolved to . . . risk the whole on a single battle . . . on this forlorn hope. . . . I know the case is desperate, but Sr., we must either quit the country or attack Mr. Hamilton. : . . . Great things have been effected by a few men well conducted . . . in case we fail, though . . . this country as well as Kentucky, I believe, is lost."

He wrote later, "I would have bound myself for seven years a slave to have had five hundred troops." Vincennes was 240 miles away, through cold waters and half-frozen mud. He marched with only 130 men, 60 of whom were French volunteers; 40 others went by boat with some cannon, but did not reach Vincennes in time.

The march began on February 7, and the men slogged through shallow ponds and rain for most of the way. Many were mounted at first, but in the bottomlands of the Wabash the water was so deep that horses could not go farther. They marched 174 miles in the first six days, already often waist-deep in water, until they reached the two branches of the Little Wabash, usually three miles apart, but then forming a huge lake. Clark had the men build a boat and sent it to find the nearest high ground five miles ahead. With the aid of the boat, a high scaffold to hold their baggage above the water, and swimming horses, they made the crossing. A drummer boy paddled himself over on his drum.

They floundered on through one morass after another, often searching for river channels in broad lakes, sometimes ferrying the army at a painfully slow rate in two canoes. At times the water was neck-deep on the tall Clark, and shorter men clung to each other, swam, or hung on floating debris. Clark constantly bolstered their morale. On some nights, as they camped on soggy knolls above the water the men laughed and sang and Clark thought, "they really began to think themselves superior to other men."

Food gave out, and there was only an occasional deer to divide among the 130 hungry marchers. Once they found a fox in a tree above the waters, killed and ate it, roasting entrails over the fire. Still breast-deep in water on each march, they came within sound of the morning gun of the fort at Vincennes, but the way became so difficult and the men so weak from hunger that many wanted to give up. Clark posted riflemen at the rear to shoot those who lagged, and the column cheered him. At one point, when Clark saw that all were "alarmed" and "bewailing their situation," the leader saved the day by blacking his face with gunpowder and water, giving a war whoop and plunging into the water again, followed by the men: "The party gazed and fell in, one after another, without saying a word, like a flock of sheep." Soon he had them singing.

Near the end they captured a canoeful of Indian squaws who had a half of a quarter of buffalo meat, corn, tallow, and kettles, and the soup the troops made of these treasures took them over the last miles. When they came at last to a tiny island within sight of Vincennes and its fort, "Every man now feasted his eyes and forgot that he had suffered anything. . . ." Later, when he wrote the story of the terrible march, he refused to give George Mason a detailed account. He knew that Mason, as an old friend, would not doubt him, but the adventure was, he knew, "too incredible for any Person to believe except those that are as well acquainted with me as You are."

On February 23, Clark sent a message to people of the village outside the fort, most of them French, warning them to stay off the streets and giving anyone who wished to do so a chance to join the still-unsuspecting British in the fort. There was loud rejoicing in the town, but no one entered the fort. That night Clark's men surrounded the fort, firing their deadly rifles through cracks between its logs and taking a toll of gunners when they opened ports to fire their cannon. Clark moved the men about, ordering much laughter and talking, to convince Hamilton that he was outnumbered. There was fighting for a few hours the next morning in which only one American was killed. Finally, in response to a flag of truce, Hamilton asked for terms. Clark replied with a demand for immediate surrender, saying that if he were forced to storm the palisade Hamilton could "depend upon such Treatment justly due to a Murderer." Further, Hamilton was warned against destroying his papers or burning buildings, for there would be no mercy shown him if he did.

After a good deal of negotiation, interrupted by the tomahawking of some Indians who had been caught by the Americans with fresh scalps, Hamilton gave up on terms little better than unconditional surrender. Clark freed French militiamen of Hamilton's force and sent them back to Detroit; he sent his prisoners, including Hamilton and a militia lieutenant, Guillaume LaMothe, to Williamsburg. South of the Great Lakes, the western territory was permanently American.

Jefferson long held Hamilton stubbornly against all efforts to free him and spoke of him as "the butcher of Men Women and Children." His treatment, the governor said, "must be deemed Lenity"—though Hamilton at that time wore 18-pound leg irons, was held without trial, and allowed to speak only with his jailer, Peter Pelham. Even when Daniel Boone came to Williamsburg and asked that Hamilton be released (he had once helped Boone escape Indian captors), the governor of Detroit remained in his cell. Virginians feared that "the Hair Buyer" would return to the frontier if he were freed. Washington approved at first, saying that "he had no doubt of the propriety of the proceedings against Governor Hamilton," but later, when the British threatened retaliation against Americans in their hands, the commander in chief urged Virginia to be lenient.

The Council offered Hamilton a parole, but he refused it, expecting a trick. Virginia prisoners were soon transferred to the jurisdiction of Congress, but not Hamilton, who was kept under Virginia control. It was October, 1780, before Hamilton accepted parole and was exchanged.

Soon after Vincennes fell, Clark had dispatches from Williamsburg. Help was on the way, five hundred men to take Detroit, and the Assembly had just created the new county of Illinois (which existed for five years, until Virginia ceded it to the United States).

But the reinforcements did not appear and Clark never took Detroit. Jefferson, who became governor in 1779, ordered him to build a fort at the forks of the Ohio to beat off British invasion efforts. A final attempt to raise an expedition to Detroit failed for lack of men. Jefferson saw the value of Clark's heroic campaigning and wrote Washington early in 1780 of "the enterprizing and energetic genius of Clark," but as the Revolution ended, others forgot the Northwest conquest.

Clark, short of money and food and ammunition during his invasion of the Illinois, had often pledged his own credit to keep his army alive. In postwar years he was pressed for payment—and Virginia haggled over $20,000 in the back pay due him for many years of service. In 1782 he was in Richmond, penniless, begging Governor Benjamin Harrison to advance enough money so that he could buy presentable clothes: "Nothing but necessity woud Induce me to make the . . . Request. . . ." For years Clark got at most only a few dollars given him by Harrison. Virginia was near bankruptcy, and could pay only in land grants. The final blow to Clark came when creditors who had advanced supplies to the Virginia army seized his lands for the debts.

Clark spent most of his last years in a cabin across the river from Louisville, writing his memoirs, drinking heavily, and reliving old times. He was then supported by a $400 annual pension Virginia's Assembly had voted belatedly when it learned of his destitution. Clark died in 1818, many years before Congress at last paid his heirs some of the money due the conqueror of the Northwest.

Bishop James Madison, by an unknown artist. Reproduced through courtesy of the Virginia Historical Society, Richmond.

BISHOP JAMES MADISON

PASSERSBY on the quiet streets of Williamsburg near the end of the eighteenth century sometimes saw a tall, thin man in the yard of the College of William and Mary stooping to peer through a telescope. He looked eastward toward the Capitol where a tiny figure waved a flag from the cupola. An early American "telegraph" system was under test. The flagman on the Capitol was the dignified Judge St. George Tucker. The man at the college was its president, James Madison, first bishop of Virginia, scientist, map maker, surveyor, militiaman, and professor.

Like his cousin of the same name who became President of the United States, James Madison had been born in the Shenandoah Valley, near the town of Staunton. After brief training under tutors and in a private school near his home, young Madison entered the College of William and Mary, where his lively, inquiring mind won attention. He graduated with honors in 1772, and he delivered a Founder's Day oration to fellow students, a high-flown address on the role of education in a land of liberty, in which he revealed his debt to the philosophy of John Locke: "We were born to be free. Let it be our Concern to become worthy Freemen. Let us remember how much we owe our Friends, our Country, Mankind." Madison studied law under George Wythe, but though he passed the bar, never practiced.

In 1773 he became professor of moral philosophy and mathematics at the college, and though he had already begun an active career in the sciences—he became secretary and curator of the Williamsburg Society for the Advancement of Useful Knowledge—he was drawn to the church. In 1775, on the eve of the Revolution, he went to England to study and to be ordained as a minister of the Anglican church. He reacted strongly to the British as "degenerate" and anti-American, because they reviled men "Who undoubtedly are making a struggle for Liberty unparalleled in Ancient History."

He came home to find that war had begun and became a fiery apostle of revolution. He often preached at Bruton Parish Church and was the last rector of Jamestown Parish, the first parish in America. According to legend, he once scolded his parishioners for speaking of the kingdom of heaven during the struggle to free America of a monarchy and insisted that they refer instead to "that great Republic where there is no distinction or class, and . . . all men are free and equal."

Equalitarian sentiments such as his brought about many changes. When the Protestant Episcopal Church in the United States replaced the Church of England, the prayer book was revised, and the phrase "President of the United States and all others in authority" was substituted for "George III." Also deleted was a reference to the "King of Kings, Lord of Lords and only ruler of the Princes," and in the democratic spirit God was addressed only as "ruler of the Universe."

In 1777, when the country was wracked by a war that seemed almost hopeless, Madison was made president of the college, though he was so young at twenty-eight that the trustees had to waive the requirement setting the minimum age at thirty. In addition to administering the college, he taught a great variety of subjects—sometimes in the grammar school—including chemistry and international law. In 1779, during Jefferson's term as a member of the board of visitors, the college was reorganized as a university, and the schools of law, medicine, and modern languages were opened. Other changes included the first student honor system, elective courses, and moot courts in the law school. Madison himself gave the first regular lecture course on political economy in the United States.

During these early war years he lectured four to six hours a day, still appeared regularly in church pulpits, was captain of the college militia company, and, in addition, served as chaplain to the House of Delegates in the Virginia Assembly. Still his scientific studies and correspondence continued. In 1779 he represented Virginia on a commission charged with settling the boundary between Maryland and Pennsylvania. The group surveyed "with great astronomical precision" an extension of the

Mason-Dixon line and settled a controversy over western lands dating back to the French and Indian War.

Life went on within the President's House too. In 1778 he took in a lodger, his kinsman James Madison, the future President of the United States. The younger man, who had come to Williamsburg to take his seat on the Virginia Council of State, was pleasantly surprised to get a room in the President's House, "a much better accommodation than I could have promised myself." In 1779 the president of the college married Sally Tate of Williamsburg, apparently after a whirlwind romance. The year before he had told his friend St. George Tucker that he had lost his heart to Anne Blair, so that he was "like a Boat at Sea without Rudder or Pilot," but he mourned that "Laura," as he referred to her, did not "care a Groat for me."

The college all but expired during the latter months of the war. In 1781 the passing armies took over its buildings in succession, first the British and then the Americans and French. The latter accidentally burned the President's House, but it was rebuilt by the French Crown.

In his despondency Madison wrote his brother William: "I find I must at Length remove from this Place. The College is entirely broke up, all Business in my Way at an End & of course not a Farthing to be made. But where or how shall I move?" He worried about his servants, who had been prevented from running away with the British only by a lucky accident. He thought of the practice of law, though "The law is disagreeable, but Divinity, and Philosophy in the bargain, will starve a man in these times." Williamsburg was near a state of anarchy: "These are miserable Times to most of us down here. We know not that any Thing we have is safe for a week."

Even in those gloomy days Madison was involved with his broad interests. He met, and fascinated, the urbane Marquis de Chastellux, who passed through with Count Rochambeau's army on the way to Yorktown; the two often had discussions on natural history, philosophy, government, which Chastellux continued later in long, detailed letters.

In 1784, a year after the peace treaty with Great Britain, he was relieved of some of his teaching duties, which meant that he gave up classes in mathematics. He gave more of his time to outside public affairs. From the college faculty and Virginia's leading politicians, he formed a Society for the Preservation of Liberty, which was to act as a watchdog committee to guard the young republic. One of its broadsides, written in

Madison's singular style, revealed his alarm over attacks on "those pure and sacred principles of liberty." Among the signers of the handbill were Patrick Henry, Richard Henry Lee, and Edmund and Beverley Randolph.

Madison was especially vigilant against the "Adams faction," led by John Adams, which he saw as a grave threat to republicanism in the United States. He railed against the "English sympathies" of Adams and the social "poison" of aristocracy. Madison argued that America had for generations been "free from the most absurd and degrading differences among citizens . . . which ignorance and force gave birth to and which nothing but folly . . . would now introduce." To Madison the one hope for the new American government was to maintain only the distinctions between men imposed by nature. He was drawn, reluctantly, to support the Federalists in 1787, but feared the balanced system of government and the dangers of the Constitution to rights of citizens and the states. He criticized Alexander Hamilton, urged American support of the French Revolution, and by 1797, when Adams was President, Madison called a meeting of Virginia citizens to protest the government's "unconstitutional acts" and anti-French policies.

His students were exposed to his fervor and to the advanced ideas of foreign philosophers, including Adam Smith, whose works he began to teach just after the Revolution. Young men never forgot the courteous, dignified, and gentlemanly teacher who spoke such revolutionary thoughts. President John Tyler later wrote: "I recollect nothing to equal the voice of Bishop Madison. . . . His style was copious and Ciceronian and his manner strikingly impressive." Tyler also recalled him "kind and parental," with every reproof given in "the gentlest tones, nothing harsh, nothing morose. No one who attended the College while he presided over it hesitated to acknowledge him as a second father."

The affection of his students was also won by his unpretentious ways and by the endless scientific investigations he carried on. He was usually working on Williamsburg's longitude, or keeping complete weather records, or studying the stars. One student, George Blow, once wrote his father: "The night before last I did not go to bed at all, being with Mr. Madison at College viewing through the Telescope an Eclipse of the Moon, which, from the commencement of the Penumbra to the termination of the whole eclipse continued from one until Six OClk in the morning; and last night I was at a ball which kept me up untill twelve."

Madison won international recognition for his scientific work. He and

Dr. Benjamin Rush of Philadelphia were the only Americans admitted to the Royal Humane Society of England. In 1785, when Benjamin Franklin was its president, the American Philosophical Society elected Madison a member. To its proceedings he contributed papers on such topics as magnetism and the chemistry of medicinal springs. Madison corresponded frequently with Thomas Jefferson, the Philadelphia scientists Dr. Rush and David Rittenhouse, and many others on mastodons and Indian mounds, fossil shells, the courses of the planets, the philosophy of education, the dangerous "poison" of aristocratic ideas from England in the new American republic, and the role of the United States in bringing freedom to mankind.

Despite the pressure of work, he completed many surveys in the field and produced a new map of Virginia. This map, published in 1807, became the standard for many years, and several copies were immediately bought for official state use. The plates were engraved in France from Madison's surveys.

In the 1790's his scientific interest turned westward. He spent some time in the summers in Fincastle in western Virginia and made expeditions along the Kanawha, Elk, and Guyandot rivers, investigating the supposed fortifications of mound builders. Madison rejected the legends that DeSoto's band or wandering Welshmen had built the mounds, and proved to his satisfaction that the mounds were not forts at all, but burial sites. He excavated many Indian graves, tracing the remains and relics from prehistoric to modern times, the latest of them after the coming of the white man, as denoted by tomahawks and other iron objects. He also reported on ancient Indian stone carvings in the region near Burning Springs.

Madison was attracted to Sweet Springs, in Botetourt County, and went there for several seasons to experiment and make studies. The well-known Dr. James McHenry of Baltimore, who heard Madison preach in the summer resort, praised his "unpriestly" manner and "very animated sermon," but said that it was "in no ways sparing in rhetorical figures, allusions and similes . . . happily placed and some of the last perhaps new . . . I could have listened to another of the same kind without danger of falling asleep."

McHenry was even more pleased to note that Madison was "a philosopher as well as a Bishop," and the next day the two collaborated in chemical experiments on the waters of the springs. Madison reported on their temperature (seventy-three degrees when the air was sixty-nine) and used a hydrometer to measure specific gravity. In one test he added violets to the water and pronounced an acid present when they became reddish in color. He tested for iron, sulphur, and alkali—and tested even the air that bubbled up through the spring, concluding that this gave the water its taste, but lamenting the lack of a perfect vacuum in which to test it further.

In 1785, Madison began his campaign to organize the Episcopal church in Virginia, and served as president of its first convention in Richmond. Five years later he was elected the first bishop of the church in the state. He wrote his cousin James Madison, then in Congress, of his election to the post: "I have consented, whether wisely nor not I cannot say, to undertake it." He went to London that summer, where he was consecrated at Lambeth by the Archbishop of Canterbury.

The task of creating an organization for the church was too much for Madison, who could devote only two months each summer to visiting parishes, and for many years the project appeared to be hopeless, since virtually every parish was impoverished, poorly staffed, and suffering from public apathy. The public was hostile, and there were many efforts to seize the glebe lands of the church. Despite such conditions, Madison strove for his ideals. He became the first American churchman to speak openly of church unity, and urged other Protestant denominations to join with the Episcopalians in one church. He was especially insistent that the growing body of Methodists should do so. He aroused no public interest in his proposal.

Madison saw the Methodists as a threat to his new church, and once wrote his friend, the Reverend William White, rector of Christ Church, Philadelphia: "Methodism gains ground daily among our Flocks in this State. Something must be done, more than has yet been done, to avert its Progress."

By 1805, when his friend Jefferson was President, Madison's health had begun to fail. He asked in vain for an assistant to carry some of his duties as president of the college, "for want of bodily strength" to act alone. He carried on as usual, and "so gentle, and gradual was his decline" that the bishop lectured to one of his classes only two days before his death.

His mind was alert to the end, he talked occasionally during the final hours of his life and smiled often during the day. He died in the

President's House on March 6, 1812, "without a groan and without a struggle," on the eve of another war between his young country and Great Britain.

The Reverend John Bracken, rector of Bruton Parish, delivered his funeral oration, in which he spoke of Madison's "rational and firm Piety, an active affection for the well being and interest of mankind, a quick penetration, a solid judgment." The funeral procession included members of the Board of Visitors, faculty and students of the college, the mayor and officials of Williamsburg, and many prominent Virginians. He was buried in the college chapel.

A newspaper obituary said of him: "his piety was unaffected, his religion pure; equally unsullied by bigotry, and intollerance, as by atheism . . . his morality, immaculate . . . he lived, and died, in love, and charity, with all mankind."

St. George Tucker, from an engraving by St. Mémin. Reproduced by permission of the owner, Mrs. George P. Coleman, Williamsburg, Virginia.

ST. GEORGE TUCKER

THE St. George Tucker House, dominating the western end of Market Square with its long sweep of clapboard, broken roof lines, and massive chimneys, is the most picturesque of Williamsburg's remaining eighteenth-century houses. It is also a faithful reflection of its builder, who called the place "Fort St. George."

A widower with five children, St. George Tucker made plans in 1788 to move back to Williamsburg. From Edmund Randolph he bought two lots on the north side of Market Square, a short distance from the home of his old teacher, George Wythe. Tucker found several small buildings on his new property, none large enough for his family. The largest of them, a cottage once occupied by William Levingston, who had operated America's first theatre, faced on Palace Green. Tucker moved the old Levingston cottage a short distance, to face Market Square, and Humphrey Harwood, a leading Williamsburg contractor, began the work of enlarging and repairing that was to go on for a generation. St. George enlarged the Levingston cottage by adding a "shed" in the rear, an area now known as the great ballroom. He also added east and west wings, including a kitchen with an enormous chimney. The house began to assume the air of dignified comfort that was to make a notable example of native Virginia architecture for two centuries. Its rather random growth gave it the appearance of having sprung naturally from its setting.

The house was literally built around Tucker's family, for in January, 1789, he arrived with his children, a housekeeper, tutor John Coalter, and a few servants. They filled the small outbuildings and crowded the house, then freshly raised on its tall brick foundations. John Coalter wrote a friend: "As Mr. Tucker's house is small and his family large, I sleep in the house of a Mr. Wickham next door." The work went on steadily, the family expanding into new rooms as they were completed, but it was not until about 1802 that the house was at last finished.

Born in Port Royal, Bermuda, in 1752, St. George Tucker first came to Williamsburg in 1771 when he enrolled as a student at the College of William and Mary. The youngest of six children born to Colonel Henry and Anne Butterfield Tucker, he had attended a nearby private school under an Anglican rector and read law briefly and unhappily with an uncle. His well-educated father, Bermuda's representative in London, learned of the College of William and Mary, its reputation for discipline, its standing as "the best Institution of the sort in America," and, not of least importance, its offering of board and lodging and the "best Masters" for about £13 a year. St. George was soon on his way.

His father's letters are heavy with admonitions to be God-fearing and sober, to avoid taverns and brawls, and to cultivate people of means and importance. The colonel also thought St. George's antic sense of humor a liability and warned against "that wit and absurdity which had always so delighted his familiar friends." (The admonition seems to have been in vain, for there remained, even in the late years of Tucker's life as a dignified member of Virginia's high court, the charming quality of a boy who refused to grow up.) The colonel's fears may have been well founded because of conditions at the college and of the attitude of his son. A minister St. George met while traveling asked him to report any immorality or unorthodox teaching at the college. One of his fellow scholars warned him of his penchant for drinking too much; a later-day biographer noted delicately some "Rabelaisian" verses and jokes in St. George's papers of those days.

Those collegiate flings were brief (or perhaps associated with the high-spirited Flat Hat Club, to which Tucker belonged), for St. George was an able student. His father was soon complaining that he had sent him to Virginia to learn law and that he should not "lose sight of the Main Point." The colonel was irritated to learn that St. George was idling away his time on general knowledge: "I did not expect that you would have entered upon an Academical Education, a little Logick, Rhetorick and a small Notion of Mathematicks are all that ever can be necessary for one that is to study the Law."

At the end of a year St. George had so impressed George Wythe that the celebrated teacher took him as a private student or a clerk; it was only six years since Thomas Jefferson had been tutored by Wythe in much the same way. Colonel Tucker, writing from Bermuda, urged his son to "be as servicable to him as possible by giving him every Assistance in his business . . . so that you may be helpful to him in writing while you make your self Acquainted with the Method of Practice." The colonel had thought of sending the boy to London to complete his training, but decided against it when he found St. George "under so good a Tutor."

St. George had already developed the habit, likely encouraged by Wythe, of visiting Williamsburg court sessions and was so familiar with their practices and the personalities of the bar that he could write his father about them in detail. After working under Wythe little more than a year, St. George was granted a certificate to practice in the county or lower courts, and in another year, in the spring of 1775 (about the time of the battle of Lexington in Massachusetts), he was admitted to practice before the General Court. He had reached the goal in a fraction of the time taken by Jefferson.

By now Colonel Tucker's anxieties over his distant son had diminished. Among signs of St. George's maturity was a striking letter to Colonel Tucker from Thomas Nelson, president of the Council of Virginia: "You are extremely happy in having a Son, whose good sense, cheerfulness of disposition, & goodness of heart has recommended him in a strange country to the notice of some of the most respectable persons among us." The young immigrant was obviously happy; he wrote home of Virginia as *"Earth's latest Paradise."*

A visitor from Bermuda who saw him in his early years in Williamsburg left a brief glimpse of St. George as a young man, a "tall thin figure . . . joy sparkling" on his face, heedless of a hole in the sleeve of an "old green gown, through which a sharp elbow protruded."

In 1775 the approaching Revolution closed the General Court before which he was licensed, and St. George returned to Bermuda. He was there with his family when the "Gunpowder Plot" electrified the island, an incident in which about one hundred barrels of powder badly needed by the American rebels was stolen from a poorly guarded magazine in Bermuda and shipped to Philadelphia and Charleston. There are hints in Tucker's papers that he had some role in this theft. Before leaving Virginia he had told Peyton Randolph and Jefferson of the unguarded powder.

St. George's father provided him with funds to purchase a small ship, and the young man brought a cargo of the scarce commodity, salt, to Virginia. He is said to have arranged the sale with the new governor, Patrick Henry, and to have made more voyages south after salt. His friend John Page, then lieutenant governor, seems to have commissioned St. George for his most important blockade-running, carrying indigo to the West Indies in exchange for arms and ammunition. Tucker used four small, swift sailing ships for the trade. This traffic is said to have "entirely established that young man's financial independence," and also to have left him with an intermittent fever that hung on for three years.

In the autumn of 1777, St. George attended the services at Bruton Parish Church in celebration of the victory at Saratoga. It was there that he saw Fanny Bland Randolph, sister of his friend Theodorick Bland and the widow of John Randolph of Matoax, a lively and handsome woman who was just his age. He realized that he had found a wife, or so he later wrote: "At the age of eighteen I made a Vow never to marry a Widow . . . but from that moment, had I been a Roman Catholic, I should have applied to the Pope for Absolution from my Vow." He took it upon himself, he said, to "pronounce my own solemn recantation."

The Widow Randolph was not easily convinced, apparently, and her first reply to the young trader's love letters was amusingly prosaic: "Mrs. Randolph will be much obliged to Mr. Tucker if he will procure for her a pair of stays agreeable to enclosed measure she wishes them to be made of white satin, tabby or ticken if he should send for the shoes they must be 2 prs. of white sattin, 1 of blue, 1 of black and 1 of pink." If Fanny hesitated, she was urged to the marriage by her attractive Williamsburg friend Anne Blair, who wrote Fanny of Tucker's "many virtues, of which so long acquaintance has fully convinced me."

After Tucker and Frances Bland Randolph were married in September, 1778, he shared the responsibility of her three young sons, as well as that of her plantations, Matoax, near Petersburg, and Bizarre, near Farmville, though her brother Theodorick was guardian of the children and manager of the plantations. St. George continued his trading, often absent from Matoax, until Virginia was invaded and raiding parties forced the family to flee. In the years of confusion and alarm that followed the family was often separated.

St. George joined a militia company after a British party attacked Portsmouth and burned the town of Suffolk. Early in 1781, when the Tuckers' second child was one week old, the American traitor Benedict

Arnold led a British invasion of Virginia, and St. George took his family over punishing roads for more than fifty miles, toward safety at the western plantation Bizarre. St. George left them to join the major American army in the South, now under Gen. Nathanael Greene, facing Cornwallis in North Carolina.

As an officer of Chesterfield County militia, serving under General Robert Lawson, Tucker fought at the battle of Guilford Courthouse in North Carolina, a brief, savage encounter that cost the British much of their force, turned Cornwallis to the sea, and eventually influenced his movement to Yorktown. Despite the irregularities of mail delivery, Fanny learned that St. George had been wounded before he could tell her himself, and she wrote: "I did not know how tenderly I loved you till I was informed of your danger."

Of his wound he said: "In attempting to rally a small party of regular troops I received a wound in the small of my leg from a soldier who either from design or accident held his bayonet in such a direction that I could not possibly avoid it, as I ran up to stop him from running away." He said he was hobbling about the camp on a stick or having someone to lead him.

The longest letter of his correspondence with his wife sketches the battle at Guilford in detail, with a candid picture of American troops in action. After a brave beginning Virginia troops near Tucker found the British in their rear: "This threw the militia into such confusion that . . . Holcombe's regiment and ours instantly broke off without firing a single gun, and dispersed like a flock of sheep frightened by dogs. With infinite labour Beverley and myself rallied about sixty or seventy. . . ."

He praised the troops for much of the action, but wrote Fanny: "The Virginia militia had the honour to receive Gen. Greene's thanks for their conduct. Some were undoubtedly entitled to them, while others ought to blush." The army, however, was not to be disdained: "Should Cornwallis attack us again I think he would purchase a second victory full as dearly as the first. Our troops are now somewhat used to the noise of guns, of which many had no idea before."

St. George was home within a few weeks, fully recovered, but when Cornwallis and Lafayette campaigned up and down Virginia, he returned to the army, now as a lieutenant colonel. He wrote Fanny of meeting Lafayette: "We dined with him . . . But I have not had an opportunity of forming any fixed idea relative to him. He is tall, genteel, easy and affable, but his face does not appear to correspond perfectly with his person. He has a high forehead, is nearly bald—though very young. . . . His extreme popularity renders the idea of his talents indisputable. . . ." Tucker declined to give an opinion of the young Frenchman's abilities, since he knew that the observations of a few moments could not "confer an intuitive knowledge of a great man."

St. George wrote Fanny from Williamsburg, when Lafayette's troops entered the town after the enemy had spent a few days there, evidently looting, butchering cattle, and ravaging the place: "Among the plagues the British left in Williamsburg, that of Flies is inconceivable. It is impossible to eat, drink, sleep, write, sit still, or even walk about in peace."

During most of these months Fanny was alone with her children and servants on one of the plantations, still being driven back and forth by British raiders. In September, just before Washington and Rochambeau led the allied armies into Williamsburg, St. George assured her that the end was near. He reported the arrival of the French fleet in the Chesapeake and exulted, "Cornwallis is . . . effectually hemmed in." Fanny replied from her distant plantation: "We have already captured Cornwallis in imagination . . . may we not be disappointed!"

St. George wrote her of the arrival of Washington in Williamsburg: "He approach'd without any pomp or parade attended only by a few horsemen & his own Servants . . . I met him as I was endeavouring to get to Camp from town in order to parade the Brigade, but he had already passed it. To my great surprise he recognized my Features and spoke to me immediately by name." He wrote of Washington's ride through crowds of people, while cannon fired salutes: "His Quarters are at Mr. Wythe's house. Aunt Betty [Elizabeth Randolph, widow of Peyton Randolph] has the honor of Count Rochambault to lodge at her House."

St. George kept a journal of the siege of Yorktown, said by historians to be the most valuable record of that event. It was quite detailed until he reached the surrender climax; the marching out of the British troops to lay down their arms was, he said, "too pleasing to an American to admit of Description." The next day he went with General Lawson to see Cornwallis, whose men were to be taken as prisoners to Winchester, and the defeated general told them of his last attempt to escape with his army across the York River, a plan foiled by a storm.

After the surrender Tucker returned to Matoax and his family. Soon he was busy with the education of his stepsons—Richard, Theodorick, and

John Randolph—and of his own children and with plantation affairs and the practice of law.

He began writing on legal subjects and other problems facing the new nation. His pamphlet, "Reflections on the Policy and Necessity of encouraging the Commerce of the Citizens of the United States, and of granting them exclusive Privileges in Trade," led to his appointment to the Annapolis Convention of 1786, where, with James Madison and Edmund Randolph, he presented a proposal on the regulation of commerce in the United States. He opposed slavery and urged gradual abolition in another pamphlet, a work that was reprinted in Philadelphia sixty-five years later in the first year of the Civil War.

His years at Matoax after the war were few. Fanny had borne six children by St. George, one of whom died in infancy, and her health began to fail. In January, 1788, she died. Her death left Tucker free to accept a seat on the General Court of Virginia that he had declined during Fanny's illness. He moved back to Williamsburg, from which he rode out through his district to preside over courts.

Tucker emerged as Williamsburg's chief spokesman by publishing a spirited reply to the criticism of the Reverend Jedidiah Morse whose book, *American Universal Geography,* had dismissed the old capital briefly: "Everything in Williamsburg appears dull, forsaken and melancholy—no trade—no amusements, but the infamous one of gaming—no industry and very little appearance of religion. The unprosperous state of the college, but principally the removal of the seat of government, have contributed much to the decline of this city." Tucker counterattacked with patriotic fervor, saying that Morse had spent only a night or two in the town. "Would the reader suppose that Williamsburg, at the moment when the author drew this horrid picture, was the residence of three ministers of the gospel, a judge who now graces the bench of the supreme court of the United States, and of the chancellor of the state of Virginia . . . ?" Further, he said, "few villages can boast of a more pleasant situation, more respectable inhabitants, or a more agreeable and friendly society."

The college, recovering from its disorganization during the war, had fifty or sixty grammar school students and about forty young men studying law and philosophy, under six professors. Tucker soon joined the college himself, as successor to Wythe as professor of law, but he continued to ride the judicial circuit.

He endeared himself to his children by his gentle, humorous attempts at discipline. He once wrote out "Garrison Articles to be observed by the officers and privates stationed at Fort St. George in Williamsburg," specifying courtesy, clean hands and faces, neatly combed hair, and punctuality at meals. "No Captain, or subaltern officer, or private, shall presume to dance or run about the room at Breakfast or Dinner Time. . . . No officer or private is to presume to lay Hands or Feet on the furniture in the Parlour."

In 1791, Tucker married Lelia Skipwith Carter, who had lived at the well-known plantation Corotoman and was the daughter of Sir Peyton Skipwith. She brought two children of her own to the still-growing house. In 1796, St. George installed the first bathtub in town, a copper tank built into the dairy house in his yard. A son wrote him of the inaugural ceremony: "Mama has taken a bath and enjoyed it very much though at first she was quite frightened."

In 1801, Tucker's brother, Thomas Tudor Tucker, a Charleston, South Carolina, doctor, was named treasurer of the United States by President Jefferson. Two years later St. George succeeded Edmund Pendleton on the Supreme Court of Appeals in Virginia and served for eight years, during which he wrote several important opinions. He later spent ten years on the federal bench in the state, and these two terms revealed anew his independence of mind. He agreed with many leaders of his day that the pendulum had swung too far in the direction of democracy, and that the Virginia Assembly should not completely dominate the governor: "The executive department in Virginia is chosen, paid, directed and removed by the legislature. It possesses not a single feature of Independence."

Judge Tucker had a realistic, somewhat cynical view of public enthusiasm for the forms of liberty. Of voters he once made a complaint often repeated in modern times: "Except on some great occasion where a contest may happen, between influential persons, the whole body of free holders in a county rarely, perhaps never, attend." Among his well-known opinions are those of *Kamper* vs. *Hawkins* (in which he held that the state constitution of 1776 was the supreme law of the state, and that acts of the legislature in conflict with the constitution were null and void) and his dissent in *Woodson* vs. *Randolph* (holding it a violation of the United States Constitution for the federal government to change rules of evidence in state courts).

As St. George Tucker grew older his interests and activities hardly flagged. He spent much time annotating an edition of Blackstone, one of the best-known law works of his day; because of his efforts he has been called by some the American Blackstone. He continued correspondence with old friends of earlier days, including Jefferson and Monroe. An early advocate of the University of Virginia, in 1794 he urged the governor and legislature to build the institution near the Blue Ridge Mountains. He wrote Washington in 1796 proposing a national university. He wrote poetry, some of which has been attributed to Philip Freneau. Tucker worked on a model steam engine, directing one of his servants in its building, and he left careful drawings for its use to pump water. His invention of a "telegraph," which involved the use of signal flags, was announced to the town one day when Tucker climbed the Capitol cupola to send messages to the Reverend James Madison, the college president, who was posted in the yard of William and Mary at the west end of Duke of Gloucester Street.

After he left the state bench in 1810 he made annual summer pilgrimages into western Virginia, especially to the home of his stepdaughter, Polly Carter, who had married Joseph C. Cabell and lived at Warminster in Nelson County. He was fond of exploring the mountains and the Shenandoah Valley, and once made careful measurements of Natural Bridge as a scientific experiment. When his health failed after almost fifteen years on the federal bench, Tucker retired to Warminster and died there on November 10, 1827, at the age of seventy-six.

It had been fifty-five years since he had first arrived in Williamsburg, and he was mourned as a lawyer, teacher, and judge—and as an affectionate father, stepfather, neighbor, and town institution.

A NOTE ON SOURCES

SEVERAL of the eminent early Virginians sketched in this book are little known to the American public. Books about them are few, and material was drawn largely from documentary sources and contemporary newspapers. The *Virginia Gazettes* of the various eighteenth-century publishers and the manuscript collection and the other resources of the Earl Gregg Swem Library of the College of William and Mary were extremely valuable. Relied upon were the *Executive Journals of the Council of Colonial Virginia* (6 vols., Richmond, 1925–26), *Legislative Journals of the Council of the Colony of Virginia* (3 vols., Richmond, 1918–19), and the *Journals of the House of Burgesses of Virginia* (13 vols., Richmond, 1905–15). The resources of the Research Department of Colonial Williamsburg were most helpful, especially the reports on individuals and name data cards prepared over the last forty years. Other primary sources were: Edmund C. Burnett, ed., *Letters of the Members of the Continental Congress* (8 vols., Washington, 1921–36); Hugh B. Grigsby, *The Virginia Convention of 1776* (Richmond, 1885); Henry Hartwell, James Blair, and Edward Chilton, *The Present State of Virginia, and the College,* Hunter D. Farish, ed. (Williamsburg, 1940); William Stevens Perry, ed., *Historical Collections Relating to the American Colonial Church,* Vol. I (Hartford, 1870).

The *Dictionary of American Biography* offers sketches of all the twenty subjects, as well as brief bibliographies. *The Virginia Magazine of History and Biography* and *The William and Mary Quarterly* were frequently consulted. Other general sources of value were: E. L. Goodwin, *The Colonial Church in Virginia* (Milwaukee,

1927); Rutherfoord Goodwin, *A Brief and True Report Concerning Williamsburg in Virginia* (Williamsburg, 1941); Richard L. Morton, *Colonial Virginia* (2 vols., Chapel Hill, 1960); Marcus Whiffen, *The Eighteenth-Century Houses of Williamsburg* (Williamsburg, 1960); Marcus Whiffen, *The Public Buildings of Williamsburg* (Williamsburg, 1958).

For the individual biographies these additional sources were valuable and may be used for further reading:

James Blair: Lyon G. Tyler, *Williamsburg, the Old Colonial Capital* (Richmond, 1907).

Norborne Berkeley, Lord Botetourt: Lyon G. Tyler, ed., *The Encyclopedia of Virginia Biography*, Vol. I (New York, 1915).

William Byrd II: William Kenneth Boyd, ed., *William Byrd's Histories of the Dividing Line Betwixt Virginia and North Carolina* (Raleigh, 1929); Maude H. Woodfin and Marion Tinling, eds., *Another Secret Diary of William Byrd of Westover, 1739–1741* (Richmond, 1942); Louis B. Wright and Marion Tinling, eds., *The Great American Gentleman* (New York, 1963); Louis B. Wright and Marion Tinling, eds., *The London Diary, 1717–1721* (New York, 1958); Louis B. Wright and Marion Tinling, eds., *The Secret Diary of William Byrd of Westover, 1709–1712* (Richmond, 1941).

George Rogers Clark: John Bakeless, *Background to Glory* (Philadelphia, 1957); Temple Bodley, *George Rogers Clark, His Life and Public Services* (Boston and New York, 1926); William P. Palmer, ed., *Calendar of Virginia State Papers . . .* (11 volumes, Richmond, 1875–93).

Robert Dinwiddie: R. A. Brock, ed., *The Official Records of Robert Dinwiddie . . .* (2 vols., Richmond, 1883–84); Louis K. Koontz, *Robert Dinwiddie . . .* (Glendale, Calif., 1941); Lee McCardell, *Ill-Starred General: Braddock of the Coldstream Guards* (Pittsburgh, 1958).

John Murray, Lord Dunmore: D. S. Freeman, *George Washington*, Vol. III (New York, 1951); Ivor Noël Hume, *1775* (New York, 1966).

Francis Fauquier: John Burk, *The History of Virginia . . .* (4 vols., Petersburg, Va., 1804–16); W. S. Perry, ed., *Historical Collections Relating to the American Colonial Church*, Vol. I (Hartford, 1870); G. Woods Wollaston, "The Family of Fauquier," Huguenot Society of London, *Proceedings*, Vol. XIII (1930).

Joshua Fry: R. A. Brock, ed., *The Official Records of Robert Dinwid-*

die . . . (2 vols., Richmond, 1883–84); P. Slaughter, *Memoirs of Col. Joshua Fry* (Richmond, 1880).

Patrick Henry: Robert D. Meade, *Patrick Henry* (Philadelphia, 1957); Edmund and Helen Morgan, *The Stamp Act Crisis* (Chapel Hill, 1953).

Thomas Jefferson: Julian P. Boyd, ed., *The Papers of Thomas Jefferson* (15 vols. to date, Princeton, 1950———); Dumas Malone, *Jefferson and His Time* (3 vols. to date, Boston. 1948———).

Bishop Madison: Charles Crowe, "Bishop James Madison and the Republic of Virtue," *Journal of Southern History,* Vol. XXX (Feb., 1964); Bishop James Madison Papers, College of William and Mary; William Meade, *Old Churches, Ministers, and Families of Virginia* (2 vols., Philadelphia, 1857).

George Mason: Helen D. Miller, *George Mason, Constitutionalist* (Cambridge, Mass., 1938); Kate D. Rowland, *The Life of George Mason, 1725–1792* (2 vols., New York, 1892); Robert A. Rutland, *George Mason, Reluctant Statesman* (Williamsburg, 1961).

Francis Nicholson: Charles Dalton, *George the First's Army, 1714–27,* Vol. II (London, 1912); H. L. Osgood, *The American Colonies in the Seventeenth Century,* Vol. III (New York, 1908).

Edmund Pendleton: Irving Brant, *James Madison: The Virginia Revolutionist* (5 vols., Indianapolis and New York, 1941); David J. Mays, *Edmund Pendleton, 1721–1803, A Biography* (2 vols., Cambridge, Mass., 1952).

Peyton Randolph: R. A. Brock, ed., *The Official Records of Robert Dinwiddie* . . . (2 vols., Richmond, 1883–84); Jane Carson, "The Peyton Randolph House" (Colonial Williamsburg Research Report, 1968); H. J. Eckenrode, *The Revolution in Virginia* (Boston, 1916); Hugh B. Grigsby, *The Virginia Convention of 1776* (Richmond, 1885).

Alexander Spotswood: R. A. Brock, ed., *The Official Letters of Alexander Spotswood* . . . (2 vols., Richmond, 1882–85); Leonidas Dodson, *Alexander Spotswood* . . . (Philadelphia, 1932); Walter Havighurst, *Alexander Spotswood* (Williamsburg, 1967).

St. George Tucker: Mary H. Coleman, *St. George Tucker, Citizen of No Mean City* (Richmond, 1938).

George Washington: James T. Flexner, *George Washington: The Forge of Experience* (Boston, 1965); D. S. Freeman, *George Washington,* Vol. III (New York, 1951); Mary Goodwin, "Washington in

Williamsburg" (Colonial Williamsburg Research Report, 1954); Bernard Knollenberg, *George Washington, the Virginia Period, 1732–1775* (Durham, 1964).

George Wythe: W. Edwin Hemphill, "George Wythe, The Colonial Briton" (Ph.D. dissertation, University of Virginia, 1937; copy in Colonial Williamsburg library).